SOCIOLOGY LOOKS AT THE ARTS

Sociology Looks at the Arts is an innovative book for teaching which invites undergraduate students into the power and relevance of sociological thinking when applied to the visual arts. Author Julia Rothenberg asks students to consider *how* art is socially produced and *what* studying the arts as a social endeavor and social product can tell us more generally about society. This book is ideal for a wide variety of undergraduate sociology courses, including sociology of culture, and introduction to sociology. It will also be appealing to instructors teaching visual studies, media studies, and art history courses.

Julia Rothenberg is an assistant professor of sociology at Queensborough Community College.

Titles of related interest from Routledge

Surviving Dictatorship: A Work of Visual Sociology
by Jacqueline Adams

Point of Purchase: How Shopping Changed American Culture
by Sharon Zukin

Food and Culture: A Reader, Third Edition
edited by Carole Counihan and Penny van Esterik

Foodies: Democracy and Distinction in the Gourmet Foodscape
by Josee Johnston and Shyon Baumann

Branding New York
by Miriam Greenberg

The Senses in Self, Culture, and Society
by Phillip Vannini, Dennis Waskul, and Simon Gottschalk

Understanding Society Through Popular Music, Second Edition
by Joseph Kotarba, Bryce Merrill, J. Patrick Williams, and Phillip Vannini

Gender, Branding, and the Modern Music Industry
by Kristin J. Lieb

SOCIOLOGY LOOKS AT THE ARTS

Julia Rothenberg

NEW YORK AND LONDON

First published 2014
by Routledge
711 Third Avenue, New York, NY 10017

and by Routledge
2 Park Square, Milton Park, Abingdon, Oxon OX14 4RN

Routledge is an imprint of the Taylor & Francis Group, an informa business
© 2014 Taylor & Francis

The right of Julia Rothenberg to be identified as author of this work has been asserted by her in accordance with sections 77 and 78 of the Copyright, Designs and Patents Act 1988.

All rights reserved. No part of this book may be reprinted or reproduced or utilized in any form or by any electronic, mechanical, or other means, now known or hereafter invented, including photocopying and recording, or in any information storage or retrieval system, without permission in writing from the publishers.

Trademark notice: Product or corporate names may be trademarks or registered trademarks, and are used only for identification and explanation without intent to infringe.

Library of Congress Cataloging-in-Publication Data
Rothenberg, Julia.
Sociology looks at the arts/by Julia Rothenberg.
pages cm
Includes bibliographical references and index.
1. Arts and society. I. Title.
NX180.S6R68 2014
306.4'7–dc23
2013026361

ISBN: 978-0-415-88794-6 (hbk)
ISBN: 978-0-415-88795-3 (pbk)
ISBN: 978-1-315-85063-4 (ebk)

Typeset in Baskerville
by Cenveo Publisher Services

Printed and bound in the United States of America by Sheridan Books, Inc. (a Sheridan Group Company).

CONTENTS

Preface vi
Acknowledgments ix

1. The Arts and the Sociological Imagination 1
2. What Are the Arts?: A Historical Perspective 17
3. Lenses of Analysis 37
4. Social Class and the Arts 61
5. Gender and the Arts 82
6. Race and the Arts 105
7. Art, Politics, and the Economy 134
8. Technology and Globalization 164
9. Artists and Their Work 189
10. Meaning and Interpretation: What Does it Mean? 221

Bibliography 249
Glossary/Index 266

PREFACE

In the 1980s, when the sociology of the arts really began to take off as a field, sociologists needed to make the case that the arts are thoroughly social. Today, the assertion that the arts are a site of social processes is much less startling than it was three or four decades ago. As "digital natives," young people have an intuitive understanding of social networks and collaborative media. They are well aware of the collective and social nature of cultural production. Nonetheless, to understand *how* art is socially produced and *what* studying the arts as a social endeavor and social product can tell us more generally about society, students need to learn new tools, concepts, and history. The purpose of this book is to demonstrate why it is exciting and important for sociologists to study the arts and to present a series of frameworks for doing so. After being introduced to these frameworks, readers should be able to think about topics and questions concerning the arts from a variety of sociological perspectives.

While the orientation of this book is, broadly speaking, *sociological*, it is also aimed at students, instructors, and other readers in related areas like visual studies, media studies, cultural studies, and even art history. In the United States, the sociology of the arts has been guided by American sociology's more general orientation toward pragmatism, positivism, and discrete case studies. Professional sociologists of the arts and culture and graduate students, who hope to join their ranks, tend to produce studies of the arts that have a strong grounding in empirical data. They often eschew grand theoretical claims in favor of more modest, topical conclusions. Such studies stick closely in language and focus to the disciplinary terrain carved out by American sociology, rarely drawing on terms or traditions from other disciplines or even from European social theory.

Most of the time, however, instructors are not teaching courses in the Sociology of the Arts to PhD students in Sociology departments. In fact, most Sociology of the Arts courses are taught in undergraduate liberal-arts institutions and draw from a wide array of students whose primary interests lie in literature, studio arts, film studies, anthropology, or other fields. Sociologists will sometimes teach these courses, but they are also sometimes taught by academics from other disciplines. In addition, instructors in visual studies, cultural studies, media studies, art history and other disciplines outside of the social sciences want to introduce students to a variety of strategies for understanding the arts as a social process. These instructors may wish to include, but may not be exclusively committed to, the perspective which dominates professional sociology in the United States. With this in mind, I approach questions about the social dimensions of the arts with a broad enough brush to fit a variety of needs. While giving ample attention to dominant U.S. perspectives in the sociology of the arts, I have also included discussions of, for example, the more critical perspectives employed in the British cultural studies tradition as well as broader, less empirically based theoretical perspectives on the arts and society from European sociology. I also present ideas from African American Studies, gender studies, art history, philosophy, anthropology and other fields from which ideas relevant to the social study of the arts have emerged. Throughout, I present a comparison of the strengths and weaknesses of different approaches and suggest ways that students can combine different tools and strategies to think about the arts as an important site of social activity and meaning.

The challenge and the excitement in writing an introductory text for the sociology of the arts lies the fact that in what "counts" as necessary for newcomers is still up for grabs. As I mentioned, professional sociologists of art in the United States proceed, for the most part, according to a set of norms that conform to U.S. sociology more generally. Nonetheless, neither a canon nor a tidy system for presenting this area has been fully institutionalized. Several excellent examples, such as Vera Zolberg's *Constructing a Sociology of the Arts*, (1990), Janet Wolff's *Social Production of Art* (1981), and Victoria Alexander's *Exploring Fine and Popular Arts* (2003), exist, but these books are few. The authors each approach their subject in unique ways, which reflect, in part, their own biography, orientation, and training.

My approach draws on my own training and experience as a painter, my interest in critical sociology and history, and my experience teaching a variety of courses in sociology departments, art schools, and elsewhere that address the arts in terms of their relationship to society. My background as a practicing visual artist means that I am especially able to draw on examples from the visual arts to illustrate ideas. It also means that I have some "insider" knowledge about visual art worlds and am better able to understand what visual artists, rather than for example musicians or poets, are trying to do in their work. At the same time, I believe that generalizations can be made from one form of art to another within a historical period. While the means or material of various forms of art differ, they all share a connection to the belief systems, economic organization, patterns of social interaction, and institutions from which they emerge.

My experience teaching undergraduate students has shaped the approach that I develop in this book. Students from different cultural backgrounds in different kinds of colleges, universities, and departments, bring different skills, knowledge, background, and interests to courses like the ones toward which this book is aimed. Some students, like those in art schools or media departments have a strong interest in the arts, or media, from the perspective of potential producers. They might know about contemporary art and even something about art history, but may have little or no background in social theory or the social sciences. Others may have taken political science, economics, and sociology courses but know nothing about any of the arts from a practical or historical perspective. Other students may have a very limited background in both sociology and the arts. This book assumes that students will have a very uneven knowledge base, and for that reason I take an integrated and broad-based approach, beginning from the ground up in terms of the history and development of both sociology and the arts. Each section builds on the ideas presented in the preceding section, so that students can see the relationship between various strategies for thinking about the arts and society and how these strategies are related to their own historical period.

Despite my own fascination with history, I understand how impatient students often are with the past. They usually want to focus on the questions and objects that occupy their immediate present. In my mind, showing students how and why certain questions about art and society emerged *when* they did invites them to formulate interesting and provocative sociological questions about the arts in their own time. Indeed, one of the difficulties for sociologists of art is that the social meanings, definitions, and forms of the arts change so rapidly. Students often have their fingers on the pulse of the now and a refined knowledge about the technologies, styles, and concerns of the present. It is difficult for any textbook (or professor over 30) to keep up. I hope that this book will escape the vicissitudes of fashion by providing frameworks through which students can formulate questions about the cultural objects, worlds, and institutions that are relevant to their own experience. Thus, though I do spend a considerable amount of time presenting ideas and examples from the past, I have tried to conclude each section with provocative questions that these ideas raise for the present.

ACKNOWLEDGMENTS

This book, like any social product, is the result of a dense web of collective effort, the individual members of which are too numerous to name. I would like to give special acknowledgment to the many students at Queensborough Community College and elsewhere who have allowed me over the years to experiment on them with the material for this book. I thank them for their patience and for letting me know what did and did not work. I have also been fortunate to receive institutional and personal support from CUNY and from the administration at Queensborough Community College. I am especially indebted to my department chair, Joe Culkin, for doing everything within his power to facilitate my work on this manuscript. Reaching further back in my career at CUNY, I owe my guiding intellectual orientation to my dissertation advisor Stanley Aronowitz. I also owe a considerable debt to the other members of my dissertation committee, Bill Kornblum and Phil Kazinits. Both of them have been, and continue to be, strong sources of guidance and support to me.

I would not have been given the opportunity to write this book had it not been for Gary Allen Fine, who introduced me to Steve Rutter, the commissioning editor at Taylor & Francis. Gary believed that I had the background and passion to take on the job, and I hope he does not regret his faith in me.

Without Steve's patience, support, and vision, this project could not have come to fruition. His experience, wisdom and professionalism are extraordinary. I would also like to thank the others on the production team at Taylor & Francis, especially Margaret Moore, for their guidance and for fielding my interminable questions about manuscript preparation. Phyllis Goldenberg provided insightful and intelligent suggestions on chapters in the manuscript.

Completion of this project would not have been possible without my good friend Rob Sauté, who provided encouragement and invaluable editorial support in my hours of need, especially as the manuscript approached deadline. This is not the first time Rob has come to my rescue. I am also grateful for the efforts of Kyle Ives Garson, who helped me with the frustrating and laborious task of acquiring permissions and organizing the many images in this volume. I am also very grateful for many beautiful photographs that my husband Geoffrey Berliner has contributed to this book.

Finally, I would like to acknowledge the love and support that I've received from those people closest to me throughout the long journey to bring this book to completion. These include my many wonderful friends, but most especially Randy Priluck, my husband Geoffrey and our son Theo, who suffered through the irritability and preoccupation of his mother with grace and good nature, and my parents Marcia and Melvin Rothenberg, whose emotional, intellectual, and material guidance have provided an ongoing source of support and comfort. This book is dedicated to them.

1

THE ARTS AND THE SOCIOLOGICAL IMAGINATION

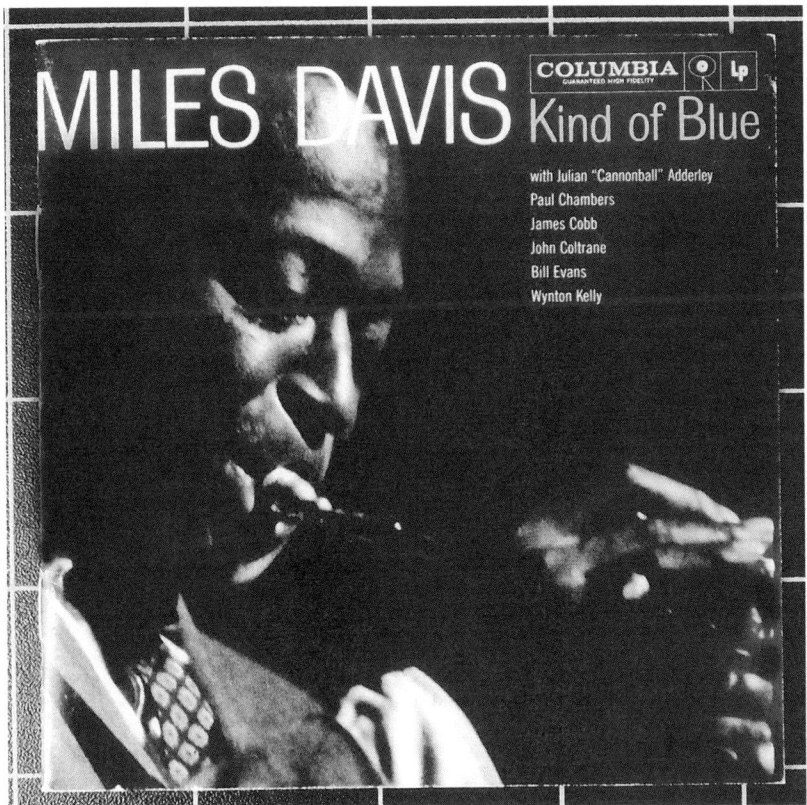

Photo 1.1 **Kind of Blue, Columbia Records.**

When I was a teenager in the 1970s, I would occasionally listen to records from my parents' LP collection (those were the plate-sized plastic disks in the colorful cardboard sleeves, sometimes accompanied by thin books of song lyrics, pictures of the musicians and other kinds of notes). While the scratchy old recordings of Spanish Civil War songs and the weighty dissonance of Igor Stravinsky's *Le Sacre du Printemps* (*The Rite of Spring*, 1913) didn't interest me much, I was continuously drawn to an album entitled *Kind of Blue* by the jazz trumpeter Miles Davis. At the time, I didn't know much about the social history of jazz and its complex relationship to slavery and racial segregation in the United States. I knew even less about the evolution of avant-garde art music and the interaction between classical and jazz forms of musical structure. I knew nothing about the recording industry or other social institutions and technologies responsible for producing this and other jazz albums. I was unaware of the demographics of the jazz audience or the sales of this sort of album (in fact, *Kind of Blue*, released by Columbia Records in 1959, achieved triple platinum status in 2008, and Columbia touts it as the best-selling jazz recording of all time). That this album could be understood as a window to history and society only occurred to me much later, after I began to study sociology. What I knew was that when I listened to *Kind of Blue*, I was transported to another kind of reality, dominated by haunting sounds, which inexplicably sparked off a range of intense and compelling emotions and sensations.

This experience is probably familiar. Most of us derive great pleasure, meaning, and satisfaction from literature, music, painting, or other forms of art. For some, the arts provide a catalyst for spiritual and transformative experiences. For others, they are a safe haven from which to retreat from the noise of everyday life. The French painter Henri Matisse captured this sentiment well when he said: "art should be something like a good armchair in which to rest from physical fatigue" (Matisse in Flam, ed. 1995). Sociology and related disciplines of cultural and social analysis, on the other hand, study just those dimensions of life—social inequality, ethnic and racial divisions, and crime to name a few— that we often want to escape from through art. It asks us to put our tendency to insist on rational consistency, and material proof that an event or phenomenon is "real," aside to experience its inconsistent, inexplicable, and fantastic reality. Conversely, the social sciences try to explain the social world by using the tools of science, systematic observation, and sustained analysis to understand how society works and identify the consistent patterns of social interaction that shape social life and social change. Sociologists explain social reality, including things that seem to defy rational explanation, such as religion, romantic feelings, and the arts, using theories and methods of the social sciences. While art asks us to suspend disbelief, the social sciences try to demystify the social world. These two modes of understanding—the social scientific and the aesthetic— may seem irreconcilable. Nonetheless, I hope to convince you that although we can explain emotional, mystical, or aesthetic experiences in terms of social patterns and structures, this does not eradicate the special qualities of these experiences or make them any less important or meaningful.

This book will provide you with strategies through which to understand and ask questions about the relationship between the arts and society while maintaining a respect for the arts as special forms of interaction through which we communicate experiences, knowledge, and feelings. We will explore art by activating what sociologist C.W. Mills (1959) called "the sociological imagination." Mills defined the sociological imagination as

> the capacity to shift from one perspective to another—from the political to the psychological; from examination of a single family to comparative assessment of the national budgets of the world; from the theological school to the military establishment; from considerations of an oil industry to studies of contemporary poetry. It is the capacity to range from the most impersonal and remote transformations to the most intimate features of the human self—and to see the relations between the two.

(Mills, 1959: 5)

I hope that this book will help you to recognize that what *feels* most personal, individual, and specific is also a product of history and collective systems of expression and interpretation and therefore shared by others. By recognizing the social nature of our experience, we may find a greater capacity to express ourselves through—and find meaning in—the arts.

Art Worlds

You will encounter repeated references to "art worlds" in this book. This term, popularized by the sociologist Howard Becker (1982), is useful because it gets to the heart of what the sociological imagination adds to our understanding of the arts. Art historians, critics, and other scholars from the humanities have traditionally focused on individual artists and works of art as well as genres, styles, and movements in their studies (Zolberg, 1990: 6). These aspects of the arts are only part of what interests sociologists and other socially minded researchers. Because sociologists regard aesthetic experience and meaning in relation to social interaction and social structures, they are interested in *all* of the social activity required to produce a work of art, not just the person who signed the painting, composed the music, or directed the film. As Becker explains, successful (and unsuccessful) works of art result from a *collective* process involving not only artists, but supporting personnel like critics, museum personnel, collectors, historians, publicists, and art consumers (Becker, 1982). The collaborative nature of art worlds may be fairly obvious in the case of music, theatre or film. After all, one person could not possibly do all the work to create a film like *Avatar* and every theatre performance requires different specialists: set designers, actors, publicists, sound technicians, and audiences.

From Becker's perspective, even works of art that appear to be intensely personal, such as paintings or novels, are only possible through collective processes. For this reason, Becker argues that to understand the arts as a *social* activity (the focus of sociologists) we need to think not only about artists but also all the other people who are necessary to produce a work of art. If we cast a wide enough net, we sometimes have to include in our studies those people who might seem peripheral to the creation of works of art, like the spouses of artists who support them emotionally or financially, the workers in a musical instrument factory, or the chemists who discover new paint formulas. The complex web of social activity required to create an artwork composes an "art world."

Defining the Arts: A Historical Perspective

It can be tricky and controversial to define what is meant by "the arts." After all, the term arts is used in conjunction with a wide range of activities, including cooking, baseball, fashion, painting, singing, and stamp collecting. In the United States, we count among our national artists Steven Spielberg, Eddie Murphy, Meryl Streep, Jackson Pollock, Walt Whitman, and Jimi Hendrix. Each engages the human capacity for expressive, imaginative, and sensual experience. At the same time, we only think of some of these figures and the works associated with them as belonging to the category of "fine arts". While the poet Walt Whitman's affirmation of the human body and erotic desire, *I Sing the Body Electric*, is taught in literature classes, the comedian Eddie Murphy's hilarious and touching performance in *Raw, Uncut* is not. The painter Jackson Pollock's work is exhibited in fine arts museums while Steven Spielberg's movies can be rented on Netflix. Art critics and other **gatekeepers** from within various art worlds often make what sound like definitive distinctions between fine arts and popular culture (i.e. the tenor Lucianno Pavarotti was a fine artist while Michael Jackson was a pop star) or try and rank the quality of individual art objects or artists against one another (i.e. Matisse was a more important painter than Picasso, or *Macbeth* a greater play than *Romeo and Juliette*). Sociologists, on the other hand, are not, at least as sociologists, interested in the "objective" validity or accuracy of such ranking systems. They are interested instead in the social processes through which ranking systems are created, accepted and reinforced, and the social processes that contribute to changes in these systems. How did the emergence of the dealer/gallery system for distributing paintings in France in the 19th century propel the commercial success of the impressionist painters? How did pop stars like Madonna, David Bowie, or Sinead O'Connor reflect changes to prevailing gender norms in the United States and Europe during the 1970s and 1980s? How do women's social networks impact how they read and evaluate romance novels? These are the kinds of questions, as opposed to normative or evaluative questions, that sociologists are likely to ask. In addition to studying the role of social processes in the formation of the arts, sociologists are also interested in what these ranking systems, and the processes and objects associated with them, can tell us about society.

Sociologists analyze the historical and social processes through which the arts came to be viewed as a special category of cultural production in society. These processes are directly linked to the development of the sorting mechanisms that are employed to distinguish the arts from other kinds of cultural products and which assign value to those distinctions. It is not enough to know that works of art are the result of collective processes of meaning making. Those processes themselves take place within a larger social and historical context, which provides the parameters within which certain kinds of ideas and cultural activities emerge (Foucault, 1970).

As you will see, the formation of a distinctive sphere of fine arts was tied to the development of other categories, like folk art, popular culture, and mass culture that we use when we talk about culture. When scholars study art worlds, they often speak of popular culture and high art to indicate which type of art world they are studying. They don't do this because one kind of art or cultural production is superior to another but rather because these are socially recognized labels. Sociologists understand that these categories emerged through a process of social construction and evaluation and they try to explain these social processes. In addition, the category of fine or high art is only meaningful in some kinds of societies and in relation to other categories of art, for example, popular and folk art or mass culture. Many of the examples I use in this book fall into the category of fine art. This is not because I prefer the avant-garde musical compositions of John Cage to the Beatles. We stick, primarily, to the fine arts of Western societies in this book because of space and time constraints and because many excellent books have been devoted to the sociological study of popular culture and non-Western and traditional arts. One author (or book) cannot adequately cover all of this ground.

Sociological Lenses

When photographers create an image, they choose a lens that is best able to capture the level of detail, the scope of coverage, and the angle or perspective that interests them. A photographer wishing to create an intimate portrait of her mother or the pattern on a butterfly's wing will choose a lens that can focus up-close. Such a lens might capture details from a single subject or small group of objects but cannot focus on a sweeping landscape seen from a mountaintop or the crowds of people at a political demonstration. For these kinds of scenes, a photographer would choose a wide-angle, landscape lens. If the photographer wants to record the interaction of a small group of children playing on a jungle gym in a playground, she will choose a medium-range lens. Each lens in the photographer's camera bag is useful for zeroing in on an aspect of reality,

Photo 1.2 **Skyline of Manhattan, Geoffrey Berliner.** (Courtesy of Geoffrey Berliner)

but no single lens can record both the fine lines on a subject's face and the patchwork of farmland in the distance with the same level of clarity.

Sociologists, including sociologists of art, are a bit like photographers in this regard. One sociological lens is useful for studying how violinists in the Chicago Symphony Orchestra manage the conflicting demands of competition with each other for seats and working together cooperatively as a section. This kind of lens can zoom in on face-to-face interaction between orchestra members. The same lens or, to put it more directly, sociological perspective, will not help a sociologist understand how or why the modern symphony orchestra developed in 18th century Europe or how the development of this institution was facilitated by the growth of other political and economic institutions of the period. For this, we

Photo 1.3 **Fourth of July, Geoffrey Berliner.** (Courtesy of Geoffrey Berliner)

Photo 1.4 **Portrait of Philip Levine.** (Courtesy of Geoffrey Berliner)

need a wide-angle lens able to capture sweeping social and historical developments. What we miss with this lens, of course, are the intricate details of small-scale social interaction. We need yet a third, medium-range lens to study the organizational structure of the Chicago Symphony Orchestra or the relationship between the Orchestra and government funding institutions. Sociologists choose from an array of tools, methods, and perspectives to illuminate different levels of social reality. Some of these "lenses" allow them to focus on up-close, small-scale social interaction but are not useful for capturing large-scale social patterns and historical change and vice-versa. Ideally, sociologists can view their object of inquiry from a variety of angles and depths of field and make connections between small-scale or "micro" interactions and larger structural dimensions of society. In reality, however, sociologists, like everyone else, face time constraints, have individual preferences, and need to keep doing the kind of work on which their reputations are based and they may (like some photographers) stick with one lens for their entire careers. Even so, sociologists should be conscious of the way in which their lenses help determine the scope of their studies.

Art in Society

Identity and Structured Inequality

When sociologists talk about **social structures**, they are referring to the range of social patterns, rules, and resources (Giddens, 1976, 1984) or "schemas" (Sewell,

1992) characteristic of any given society. Sociologists, using a variety of lenses, describe patterned types of social interaction, social roles and positions, social identities, inequality and resource distribution, social institutions and norms and values through which social activity is structured. Although sociologists argue about the degree to which social structures determine individual actions (see, Giddens, 1984, Sewell, 1992, Berger and Luckmann, 1966), most would agree that with any type of social activity (war, sex, food preparation, childrearing, dancing—to name a few) individuals choose their actions from a set of options that have already crystallized as social structure. As Karl Marx (1852) famously said "[m]en make their own history, but ... they do not make it under circumstances of their own choosing, but under circumstances existing already, given and transmitted from the past." In order to understand art worlds in relation to social life, we need to identify and understand some of the larger social structures within which art-world activity takes place.

In complex societies like our own, identity and **structured inequality** are closely related. We form our identities through group identification (i.e. we identify ourselves, and are identified by others, as male, Puerto Rican, elderly, and so forth). Through sets of conventions, schemas, and social rules, people are sorted into groups based on characteristics that a given society treats as important. Our group memberships provide us with various **roles**, tastes, behaviors, etc. out of which we compose our unique selves. Because of structured inequality, our group membership also affects access to important symbolic and material resources including wealth, social status, and access to, and knowledge of, cultural practices. Consider, for instance, that before the 1980s, women were never more than 12 percent of those invited to participate in the Venice Biennial, an important international art exhibition. A National Endowment for the Arts survey conducted in 2004 revealed that education (positively associated with income) is more highly correlated with attendance at arts events than any other demographic factor (NEA, 2008)). And, it takes only a few visits to symphony orchestra performances to realize that a miniscule number of professional classical musicians are African American. Even within musical genres dominated by African American artists, like rap, White males control the resources that are needed for recording, marketing, and distributing the music (see R&B, 2005).

In shaping identity, group membership also affects an individual's aesthetic preferences, or what we call "taste" (Bourdieu, 1984, Halle, 1993, Peterson and Simkus, 1992, DiMaggio, 1997, Lamont, 1992). We may share a common culture acquired through the educational system, mass media, etc., but in complex societies, people also have access to—and identify with—different cultural forms, including types of visual expression, music, dance, and so forth, based on group membership. Aesthetic preferences thus reinforce group identity and shared artistic forms facilitate self-expression and communication with other group members. Members of less powerful groups have restricted access to some forms of the dominant culture (e.g. less money for classical music concerts or music lessons, less leisure time to consume novels), but they may have more access to cultural forms that are not understood or valued by members of the dominant culture. Structured inequality thus provides members of social groups with shared history, social position, and experience out of which patterns of cultural production, consumption, expression, and even social opposition, emerge.

Because we possess what sociologists call "agency," however, neither group membership nor structured inequality fully determine our actions; nor are individual identities fixed or unitary and rules that determine group membership change over time. One may identify as both an Asian and a female; as homosexual in one period of life and heterosexual in another. To engage in same-sex sexual activity did not qualify a person as a "homosexual" in the early 19th century, and Jews were not considered White in the United States until the 1950s or so (Brodkin, 1998). Finally, individuals always contest, transgress, and expand on the social rules that govern identity. Because art worlds in general place such a high value on self-expression, creativity, transgression, *and* collective experience, communication, tradition and questions of identity play out in especially fascinating ways.

Institutional Structures: Governments and Economies

Social institutions are relatively stable and ongoing social arrangements through which the needs of society are managed (Turner, 1997). The distribution of material resources and power, for example, is managed through economic and political institutions, while infant care and socialization occur primarily through the institution of the family. The institutions of education and the criminal justice system enforce social rules. While charismatic individuals can rapidly shape and transform institutions (Weber, 1947), for the most part institutional patterns are maintained through positions, roles, rules, and values that, like structured inequality, are independent of any individual. Social institutions produce and reinforce characteristics of the social structure, like class inequality and gender identities. All social actors, including those in art worlds, have to work within institutional structures that both make possible and constrain their actions. Music academies, to consider one example, are social institutions through which budding musicians learn conventions like music theory, sight-reading, technical mastery of their instrument, and music history. Learning these conventions makes it possible for these students to participate in and contribute to musical life in their society. Students also make important social connections in music academies that will help them pursue their careers later on. At the same time, elite music academies accept some applicants and deny others, thereby potentially constraining the future opportunities of some young musicians. Convention determines which kinds of musical forms are given emphasis in the curriculum and which types of music and musical artists are neglected, thus placing pressure on students to favor some forms of development at the expense of others. Some students may lack the ability to promote themselves to their professors and other students, thereby constraining their future opportunities in the music industry (Jarvin and Subotnik, 2010: 3).

Political and economic institutions overlap in their coordination of the production and distribution of key material and symbolic resources and are key to understanding art worlds. Governments control access to the public space and funding that arts institutions need to support artists and arts projects. Censorship laws can restrict the distribution of certain kinds of artwork and governments can sponsor (or withhold sponsorship from) artists and arts institutions for political reasons. Sometimes artists ally themselves with political movements that oppose dominant political institutions, as with feminist artists in the 1970s and 1980s or Dada artists in the interwar period. In addition, art movements and individual artists sometimes use their work to protest against or criticize political institutions.

The structure of economic institutions shapes art worlds in important ways. Market-based distribution in capitalist societies, for example, facilitates the distribution of a variety of artistic styles but can also dilute creativity and innovation in the arts because, to stay in the market, distributors must generate a profit, which often requires promoting products that are likely to appeal to a larger or wealthier consumer base. Oftentimes, innovative or challenging works of art are less popular (at least at first) with a broad audience and may offend the sensibilities or politics of groups that have the most buying power. In capitalist societies, economic factors affect whether artists can purchase the materials they need to ensure their art, galleries, or music clubs can pay their rent, and which musicians record companies promote. Economic factors affect urban policies and indirectly the arts because artists and art worlds cluster in cities. If real-estate prices become inflated, artists are forced to move away from city centers and art communities are disrupted. Cuts in city spending on the arts cause small non-profit arts institutions to close down or flee to less expensive locations and may push larger institutions to focus on more revenue-generating activities. On the other hand, if urban economic policy is favorable to creative industries, there are more opportunities for artistic activity in cities. And, some scholars and planners have argued that the presence of a large numbers of **creative workers**, or a "creative class" (Florida, 2003; 2005) and the cultural amenities favored by the creative class like a thriving music and art scene can spur regional economic development and the **creative economy** in **post-industrial** cities (Scott, 2004; 2006). In addition, cultural amenities are central to the tourism industry and "experience economy" (Gilmore, 2011) both of which are key urban economic engines today. For contemporary cities to thrive economically, some urban planners argue, cities must adopt policies that foster the arts in order to attract and retain the kind of professional residents that build an urban economy.

Globalization and Technological Development

While scholars argue about the best way to understand contemporary society in relation to the recent past, most commentators agree that two important and interrelated phenomena—the rapid pace of globalization and the proliferation of new communications technologies—have had an especially profound effect on social life around the world. Not surprisingly, the production, distribution, consumption, content. and social meaning that people attach to the arts have been deeply affected by the increased interconnection of global regions and populations through new technologies and by technological innovation more generally.

Recent technological innovations and their corresponding impact on globalization provide grounds for optimism. Individuals today are linked in an almost constant web of communication via the Internet and cell phone technology. Images of, and information about, major events, like 9/11, the revolution in Egypt, or the tsunami in Japan, circulate around the globe within seconds. Families separated by continents and oceans can communicate daily over Skype, Facebook, and through text messaging. People connect in a potential "global village" of cosmopolitan citizenship that opens up possibilities for political participation (Beck, 2006; Held, 2004). The Internet facilitates the creation of new, borderless communities of people with shared interests in global justice, activism, and social change (for example, see Hamel et al., 2001) and has helped otherwise isolated victims of homophobia, sexual abuse, and chronic illnesses form on-line support groups. With new technology and the rise of the Internet, artists are exposed to, and can select from, a vast array of styles and influences to create new, hybrid forms of culture. Through the Internet and the global marketplace, they can form transnational arts communities and can reach global audiences. Cultural producers have greater opportunities to bypass commercial or state venues to distribute their work through image sharing sites and other software that allows people to share their creative products and cultural discoveries. Artists can use technology to interact with the viewer in new and collaborative ways and user-friendly film editing and sound recording software blurs the lines between producers and consumers of culture.

Globalization and new technologies have also had more ambiguous, if not negative effects on art and culture. The same sites and software that democratize the production and distribution of music and images also make it more difficult for artists and independent record labels to earn revenue from their work. Digital photography and computer technology have displaced artists, craftsmen, and other cultural workers. On the darker side, transnational corporations and consumer culture have infiltrated and diluted local cultures, often leading to less rather than more artistic diversity. While globalization has created a wider market for artistic products, the lion's share of wealth and status is still accorded to producers and distributors based in just a few cities located in the global north. The size and scope of the new global art market has contributed to the increased commodification of art and to a winner-takes-all rewards system, bestowing vast resources on top-selling artists and leaving the rest out in the cold. For all of these reasons, sociologists of art and culture study the impact of globalization and new technologies on social processes more generally.

The Artist

Sociologists recognize the central roles that institutions, technology, support personnel and the like play in the production of art. Most people in Western societies, however, attach a special value to individual artists. Artists' work appears unique when compared to what most adults spend most of their time doing. After all, how many Americans past pre-school spend hours at a time painting in their studios, building non-functional objects, or singing? And how many people are *paid* to engage in these activities? For better or worse, most members of our society accord a special status to artists, whom we regard as exceptionally gifted, if often unstable and neurotic individuals. Even as sociologists acknowledge the collective nature of artistic production, we should recognize the social significance of individual creativity and artistic practices. As sociologists of art, we need strategies for understanding artists that acknowledge their unique status while recognizing the social processes that produce this special status.

In order to start thinking about artists sociologically, we can look through Howard Becker's "micro" lens, focusing on the everyday activities that take place within art worlds to secure and maintain artists' reputations. In his work, Becker identifies the social construction of the common social perception of artists as "outsiders," "rebels," and "deviants." He and others also point out the **social construction** of other, less valorized statuses such as folk artist and craftsman (Fine, 2006). We also, however, need to explore longer-lens "macro" historical approaches employed by scholars who emphasize economic, political, demographic, and other social factors in the emergence and transformation of the status of the artist in Western society.

Sociologists who study work and occupational structures can provide us with some understanding of what it is artists actually do. At the same time, sociological studies of other work and occupational structures in fields, such as the law, manufacturing or science, don't tell us everything we need to know about artists' labor. Unlike other professionals, artists' work is often unpaid. And, while artists often work with their hands and bodies, they have a much higher degree of autonomy and expressive freedom in their work than other manual workers. Like scientists and other knowledge workers, artists strive for innovation. Unlike those workers, however, occupational standards regarding what counts as innovation are much more ambiguous and contested.

Works of Art, Aesthetic Experience, and Social Life

I hope I have convinced you that in order to understand any art world, we need to study the institutional structures and social interactions through which it is created and reproduced. At the same time, actual *works of art* and the unique experiences that people have when they interact with works of art are also central features of art worlds. What can art tell us about society? Do paintings, novels, poems, or symphonies actually contain information about the social worlds that produce them? Do works of art shape social interaction, identity, and social structures? These are some of the questions that sociology has not spent enough time addressing. Sociologists of art have neglected works of art in favor of studying social processes for a number of reasons. One is that artistic meaning is difficult to measure using scientific methods, so those sociologists who are committed to **positivist** modes of inquiry stick to studying things that can be measured or counted, such as the demographic composition of audiences or the economic structure of non-profit arts institutions. Another reason that sociologists of art have shied away from studying actual works of art is that they have felt they needed to distinguish their field of study from more established disciplines like art history and art criticism, aesthetics and literary theory that place works of art and aesthetic experience at the center of their investigations (see Zolberg, 1990).

While sociologists in the past have noted that more humanistic disciplines have placed emphasis on artists and works of art at the expense of studying the social interaction from which art is produced, this is no longer really the case. Other disciplines that address the arts now pay close attention to social history, institutional change, inequality, the social context of arts exhibition, and other matters of interest to sociologists. Hybrid disciplines such as visual, media, and cultural studies have actively sought to combine sociology's emphasis on society with the interpretive and analytic methods used by art historians, philosophers, literary scholars and other more humanistic disciplines. Many sociologists are, however, still reluctant to muddy disciplinary boundaries by studying actual works of art and aesthetic experience.

Aesthetics refers to the branch of philosophy that addresses questions of beauty, art, and perception. As far back as Plato (429–347 BCE.) and Aristotle

(384–322 BCE) philosophers have discussed the social value and role of art. It wasn't until the 18th century, however, that philosophy investigated aesthetic experience and judgment as discreet and independent categories of perception, grounded in the human subject. In the 18th century, aesthetic experience was associated with non-utilitarian objects like art and nature. While aesthetic philosophies of the Enlightenment and Romantic periods, which took place in Europe during the 18th century, were central to the formation of the discipline of art history, sociologists have been critical of the ahistorical, universalistic, individualistic, and elitist dimensions of such aesthetic philosophy (see Zolberg, 1990). Instead, they have focused on the historical and structural dimensions of European society from which this particular conception of aesthetic experience emerged and the class interests that these ideas served. In addition to locating the social and historical dimensions of humanistic ideas about aesthetic experience, sociologists study the collective and communicative nature of aesthetic experience and the non-universal, community-bounded nature of aesthetic judgments. A sociological perspective on aesthetic experience can address the similarities in how our collective emotions and sensory capacities are engaged when we experience works of art and when we experience more utilitarian or popular objects like food, wine, clothing, or dance music.

Structure of the Book

This book covers much ground in relatively few pages. My goal is to introduce the reader to new strategies for thinking about the arts in relation to the larger society in which they are embedded. This means thinking about how dimensions of society that we usually consider outside of the arts have helped to shape the form, content, use and meaning of the arts. It also means thinking about what works of art can tell us about the society from which they have emerged. The perspective that I develop here draws largely on sociology, but I also incorporate numerous ideas from media studies, cultural studies, art history, philosophy, aesthetics and other academic disciplines. I present ideas from each of these disciplines as clearly and with as little academic jargon as possible so that readers with a range of interests and levels of specialization can use this book. While it helps to read these chapters in sequential order, especially if the reader has little background knowledge, I've attempted to write freestanding chapters from which readers and instructors can pick and choose according to their purpose and interest. Each chapter concludes with a set of discussion questions and suggestions for further reading or viewing. Throughout the book, key terminology is bolded and a glossary is provided after the final chapter.

This chapter has provided you with a general introduction to the questions, concepts, and ideas that inform my perspective on the sociology of the arts.

In Chapter Two, I trace the historical formation and development of the categories of fine or high arts in modern, Western societies. In Chapter Three, I introduce three lenses that sociologists use to study social worlds and discuss some of the most important ideas and figures associated with these lenses. I also provide examples of how sociologists and other researchers have used each lens to understand art worlds. This chapter is intended to provide the reader with a broad range of perspectives, or lenses, from which to think and formulate questions about art worlds. In following chapters, I demonstrate how these lenses have been used together and individually to think about various aspects of art worlds and the relationships between art worlds and the larger society in which they are embedded.

In Chapters Four, Five, and Six, identity and structured inequality in relation to the arts are examined, with an emphasis on the United States and, to a lesser degree, European societies. In these chapters, I focus on social class, race, gender, and sexuality because these categories provide especially pronounced sorting mechanisms through which both identity and structured inequality are formed. In Chapter Seven I investigate how economic and political institutions affect the arts, paying particular attention to recent changes in the political and economic organization of capitalist societies. In Chapter Eight, I focus more exclusively on contemporary, "postmodern" society by examining some of the effects that globalization and new technologies have had on the arts, social interaction, and cultural production more generally. In Chapter Nine I explore a number of approaches that sociologists and other scholars have adopted to explain how and why artists have achieved their unique status in Western societies, how the social role of the artist has changed over time and what kinds of activities artists perform.

Chapter Ten spotlights what are perhaps the most defining features of art worlds: works of art and aesthetic experience. In this chapter, I explore a variety of ways to think about works of art, society, and social interaction without sacrificing the sociological imagination or the integrity of those art works. I consider a range of strategies to explain how the material, sensual, and tactile dimensions of art works as well as their form, style, content, and genre reflect, refract, or even shape society. I also explore the social dimension of aesthetic experience, aesthetic perception, and interpretation of art works.

Discussion Questions

1. What are some of the differences between the way that we usually experience art and the sociological perspective?
2. How do sociology and art history or art criticism differ?
3. Think of an example of a work of art that you enjoy. List the supporting roles necessary for the production of that work of art.

4. When sociologists use terms like high art and popular culture, do they mean that one is superior to the other? Explain.
5. What are some of the patterned rules, resources and schemas that shape your interaction with art and culture?
6. How do your tastes in visual art, music, dance, film, or other forms of culture reflect your group memberships?
7. How does your participation in culture and the arts help to reinforce your identity? Give examples.
8. How have social institutions enabled and constrained your opportunities to participate in culture and the arts? Give examples.

2

WHAT ARE THE ARTS?

A Historical Perspective

Photo 2.1 **Africa, Oceana, Americas Galleries at the Louvre.** (Photo courtesy of Kusuk Yun)

The Social Construction of Cultural Categories

In 2000, the Louvre, perhaps the most illustrious museum of fine arts in the Western world, exhibited traditional African art next to its galleries of famous European paintings and sculptures for the first time. By exhibiting traditional African art in a "fine arts" museum that had been reserved for objects created in the Western tradition, the curators suggested that social conventions regarding the categorization of cultural objects that had been in place since at least the 18th century have eroded. All societies produce paintings, sculptures, songs, dances, and other forms of cultural expression. European Imperial society, however, considered the cultural activity of peoples from outside the European tradition (for example Africans, Asians, and Native American) exotic and primitive and assigned their artistic creations to the category of "artifact" rather than "fine art" (see Chapter Six). The new installation at the Louvre demonstrated that in the 21st century museumgoers could not be sure that this distinction was still meaningful to curators, art historians, educators, and other cultural gatekeepers. The categories of "fine" and "traditional" arts aren't the only ones that have been firmly erected and then placed into doubt by museum exhibitions of the past decade or so. Objects that cultural gatekeepers have assigned in the past to the less prestigious categories of "mass" and "popular culture" have been appearing with increasing frequency at fine arts museums. The Hip-Hop exhibition at the Brooklyn Museum in 2000, the Art of the Motorcycle exhibition at the Guggenheim Museum in 1998, and the more recent Tim Burton retrospective at the Museum of Modern Art in 2010 are just a few examples of commercially produced popular culture objects at prestigious art museums. Other exhibitions, like the wildly popular 2011 retrospective at the Metropolitan Museum of Art of the fanciful clothing and accessories by the designer Alexander McQueen, further blurred the boundaries between sculpture, installation art, and fashion.

Photo 2.2 **Guggenheim Motorcycle Exhibit.** (Courtesy of Guggenheim Museum)

In the same vein, musical venues like Carnegie Hall in New York and Chicago's Symphony Center that are considered primarily classical music venues now regularly feature programing of world, pop, folk, and jazz artists alongside classical and "art music" standards.

The abovementioned examples raise a number of fascinating questions: How do rappers, motorcycles, and Hollywood films come to share a venue with artists that you learn about in art history text books? How and why did the arts of Africa, which had previously been excluded from the canon of fine arts, obtain a seal of approval from an elite circle of French fine-arts gatekeepers? Through what social processes do standards, ideas, and institutional practices change? To answer these questions, we need to explain how the creative activity that we call fine arts came to occupy the place that it does in modern society.

Since at least the Paleolithic period, which ended about 10,000 years ago, people in all societies have performed creative activities that engage human perceptions (hearing, sight, touch, and so on) through shared symbols and sign systems. These social activities take place in play, religion, and other areas of everyday life. They are a "cultural universal". The idea that they stand alone, separate from ritual or practical life, is unique to the modern world. The norms, institutions, and beliefs characteristic of the modern, Western definition of fine arts developed through historical processes that took place over several hundred years. The same processes also institutionalized social distinctions between fine and popular arts and between popular or folk art and mass culture. Even though most of us enjoy objects from all these categories (I might listen to Mozart with my morning coffee, Bob Marley when I cook

Photo 2.3 **Civil Rights March on Washington, D.C., Aug. 1963.** (National Archives and Rights Administration)

dinner, and Rihanna in an exercise class), we associate these objects with very different kinds of venues and different standards for judgment. But, as the examples that I listed demonstrate, these associations change over time. Today, we would not be surprised to learn that Joan Baez and Bob Dylan, who began their careers singing at protest rallies in the 1960s, have both performed more recently at the venerable high culture institution, New York's Carnegie Hall.

Sociologists explore why and how ideas about art—and the institutions and practices that go along with them—emerge and change. They examine written records, documents, and other historical sources. They also study the history of philosophy and ideas, noting how the most dominant intellectual currents of any period form socially accepted ideas about art and culture. Sociologists also look at how the arts have been affected by technological developments, institutions like the state, demographic patterns, and changes in class structure and the economic system. In what follows we will examine the historical emergence of the Western idea of the fine arts as a special and distinct category of cultural production and the closely related emergence of the categories of popular and, slightly later, mass culture. By the end of the chapter, you will see that the lines of distinction that people make between different artistic activities are always shifting and that social factors, which are sometimes external to actual works of art, produce systems for categorizing cultural products.

The Enlightenment

Today, Amsterdam is a small, quaint city, known by many for legalized prostitution and hash bars. In the 17th century, however, Amsterdam was a center of religious tolerance, scientific exploration, and economic activity. There, in 1632, the young painter Rembrandt van Rijn (1606–1669) unveiled *The Anatomy Lesson of Dr. Nicolaes Tulp* (see photo 2.4). Its theme, the dissection of a cadaver by a renowned physician attended by medical students, was neither religious nor mythological. Despite the sober and somewhat grim activity depicted, an otherworldly light bathes the subjects in the painting, and the faces of the medical students express the wonderment and awe of scientific awakening. Rembrandt's painting serves as a poignant representation of the new ways in which thinking about God, human beings, and nature were fast replacing the world-views of traditional society. During the late 17th and 18th centuries in Europe, new ideas about human subjectivity, autonomy, and universality accompanied the growing power of the middle or merchant class (what Karl Marx called the "**bourgeoisie**"). This class of merchants and entrepreneurs, lawyers, physicians, and other professionals was gaining economic power with the expansion of capitalism, and members of this group began to chafe under the limits to their political power and prestige imposed by the remnants of a feudal system that had insured that

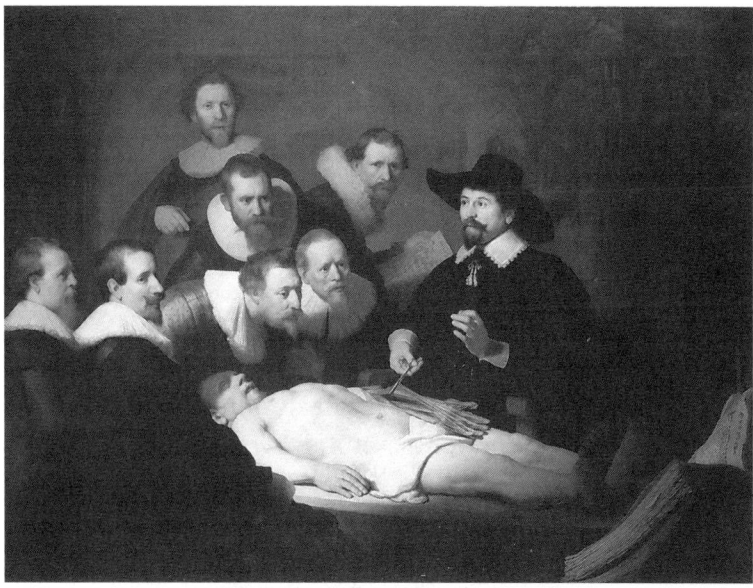

Photo 2.4 **The Anatomy Lesson of Dr. Nicolaes Tulp, Rembrant, 1632.**

the nobility and Church hierarchy controlled the reins of power. These new ideas were important in shaping the shared goals and mind-set of this new social class. They also affected the development of science, art, politics, and philosophy and ultimately gave birth to the social sciences.

Throughout the Middle Ages (CE 500–1500) in Europe the Catholic Church provided a unifying cultural and ideological framework for everyday life. It spread its religious influence and organizational power to consolidate its authority and in the process legitimated feudal authority and silenced opponents. The Church viewed God as the central organizing conscience of the world. It judged social arrangements—fair or unfair—through the lens of theologically derived natural law doctrines, and popular understanding held that disease and natural disasters represented the will of God, unresponsive to human intervention. In its quest to create a Holy Roman Empire the Church directed its vast human and material resources to produce an outpouring of cultural and artistic activity geared toward religious ritual and representation. Few people outside the Church hierarchy could read and write, and until the rise of Protestantism in the 16th century, the Old and New Testaments were only written in Latin, so worshipers had to rely on the interpretation of Church elders and visual artists who worked under Church patronage to illuminate the sacred texts.

Even during the Renaissance (CE 1350–1648) (for a short introduction see Brotton, 2006), a period of rapid artistic and scientific development and return to classical sources, philosophers and natural scientists needed to reconcile

Photo 2.5 **Scenes from the Life of St. Francis, 1320–1342.**

their investigations with sacred doctrine or else face unpleasant consequences. The astronomer Galileo, for example, was ordered to stand trial for heresy in 1632 for supporting the view, based on observation, that the planets revolve around the sun over the Church's position, based on interpretation of scripture, that the sun revolves around the earth. Rembrandt's painting signals the beginning of an important shift in the power of Church doctrine and the obedience to tradition that occurred during the Enlightenment. During this period, philosophers, scientists, and the emerging class of merchants and professionals began to confront the Church and the aristocracy with new ideas about human rationality and the capacities of scientific investigation. While Enlightenment thinkers did not question the existence of God (at least not openly), they argued that human beings possess the capacity to uncover the laws that govern social and natural life and to manipulate and shape the world around them. With the **Enlightenment** (CE 1650–1800), human understanding, rationality, cognition, and creativity replaced divine will as the object of philosophical investigation and artistic representation.

Enlightenment and Kantian Aesthetics

Along with modern ideas about science, the modern idea of art as a unique and privileged form of cultural expression has its roots in Enlightenment philosophy and in the political, economic, and social conditions of the period. In traditional societies, artistic production is explicitly tied to religious expression and ritual or to decorative but functional objects like clothing, jewelry, and pottery (objects that we tend to identify as "crafts" today). In modern, secular societies, we view art as a sort of "stand-alone" activity. It serves an aesthetic function, different and separate from the function of religion, politics, or even commerce, even though it might sometimes overlap with these other activities. The idea that aesthetic experience constitutes a discreet (separate) category of human understanding was elaborated by the German Enlightenment philosopher Immanuel Kant(1724–1804) in his efforts to understand how people gain knowledge about the world around them.

Kant explained knowledge, reason, and morality in terms of universal (we all have them) categories of the human mind, rather than as reflections of an external, divine will. Yet, his modern ideas about the unique and autonomous (independent) nature of aesthetic experience run counter to ideas about universal categories. His *Critique of Judgment* (1790) reasoned that aesthetic judgments are different from those we apply to objects of scientific or ethical knowledge. First, according to Kant, each judgment is a unique response to the aesthetic object. When we have an aesthetic experience we do not rely on or refer to prior knowledge or experience in making a judgment. In addition, beauty is not an immutable, inherent, or unchanging quality of an object. Objects cannot be beautiful in and of themselves, isolated from human perception. Instead, beauty refers to the subjective experience of a particular kind of pleasure that results from the free play between what Kant called "the understanding" and "the imagination." In accord with the Enlightenment preoccupation with the centrality of human beings and reason, Kant argued that it is the mind that creates beauty through a particular type of cognitive experience. In contrast to the kinds of knowledge claims and judgments that are made in science, or in ethics and morality, aesthetic judgments cannot be justified through the application of concepts or preformed categories. At the same time, however, when we make aesthetic judgments we are implicitly claiming that these judgments have a kind of universal validity. In other words, following Kant, something is beautiful (or ugly) because we are making a judgment that we believe others should share, even if we cannot refer to a concept or law that the object we are calling beautiful is supposed to exemplify.

The German sociologist Jürgen Habermas (1991) is interested in Kant's radical (for the time) claim that aesthetic judgments are both subjective and individual, yet, at the same time the person passing judgment is making a general case for her assessment. Habermas argues that debates and discussion about cultural topics were central to the development of the bourgeois **public sphere** in 18th and early 19th century Europe. In the coffee houses of Berlin and the salons of France, intellectuals, artists, merchants (all members of the bourgeois class that was fast gaining control of European economic, political, and cultural life), and even aristocrats gathered to discuss and debate issues of the day. Much discussion centered on music, literature, painting, and theater. Artistic performances and exhibitions helped to cement a common elite culture and served as occasions to refine strategies of communication and debate that depended on listening to and giving reasoned consideration to arguments made by peers. In these early examples of the public sphere, according to Habermas, every individual, regardless of social rank, had the opportunity to make a case for her point of view. This type of free flowing exchange of ideas among the newly emerging elite of the 18th century set the stage for a new culture of political and social participation that eventually led to the flowering of lively debates about the arts and served as a model for ideas about democracy, the rights of man, and other kinds of expressive freedom that few could publicly enjoy in traditional society. Even today, artistic freedom and the freedom to argue about the value and meaning of works of art are key features of democratic and open societies.

The Autonomy of Art

Kant pointed out that judgments fall under the category of *pure* judgments of taste when they respond to *disinterested* pleasure. In other words, the feelings of pleasure stimulated by objects that we deem beautiful are not related to the desire to possess the objects or to the object's ability to satisfy some need (e.g. hunger, vanity) that originates outside of aesthetic experience. This last point is especially relevant for later art movements such as **modernism**, **formalism**, and "**art for art's sake**." These movements, which came to dominance in the 19th and 20th centuries, connected art's distinction and quality with the degree to which it was autonomous from everyday concerns and practical values. This notion of "disinterested pleasure" was also important in the formation of bourgeois class status and identity. The ability to appreciate and discuss objects and experiences divorced from the satisfaction of material needs distinguished its possessor as a man or woman of leisure, intelligence, and education. It was these qualities (rather than the crowns worn by kings and the titles of the aristocrats) that the bourgeoisie used to identify one another and to separate themselves from the working classes, a topic that we will discuss in greater depth in Chapter Four.

> If anyone asks me whether I consider that the palace I see before me is beautiful, I may, perhaps, reply that I do not care for things of that sort that are merely made to be gaped at. Or I may reply in the same strain as that Iroquois sachem who said that nothing in Paris pleased him better than the eating-houses.... All this may be admitted and approved; only it is not the point now at issue. All one wants to know is whether the mere representation of the object is to my liking, no matter how indifferent I may be to the real existence of the object of this representation. It is quite plain that in order to say that the object is beautiful, and to show that I have taste, everything turns on the meaning which I can give to this representation, and not on any factor which makes me dependent on the real existence of the object. Everyone must allow that a judgment on the beautiful, which is tinged with the slightest interest, is very partial and not a pure judgment of taste. One must not be in the least prepossessed in favor of the real existence of the thing, but must preserve complete indifference in this respect, in order to play the part of judge in matters of taste.
>
> Immanuel Kant, from *Critique of Pure Judgment*

Today many question Kant's ideas about the special status of aesthetic judgments or the purity of art. In fact, few people (and not only sociologists) would deny that our experience of art is tied to status, desire, or social convention. That we even identify art as separate from crafts or popular culture reflects Kant's lingering influence. Rembrandt's *The Anatomy Lesson of Dr. Nicolaes Tulp* is an example of this modern idea of a work of art. Although the subject itself is not beautiful, or even elevating, we can appreciate the aesthetic values of light, composition, and painterly surface in this painting despite the unappetizing subject matter.

The Invention of Modern Art

> The irony, of course, is that art's aspirations to autonomy, its uncoupling of church and state, became possible only when literature, painting and music were first organized according to the principles of a market economy.
>
> Huyssens (1986: 17)

During the Renaissance, art was still tradition-bound by today's standards. While artists were expected to innovate, the content and even the style of visual art and music continued to be controlled by the individual patron, whether the Church,

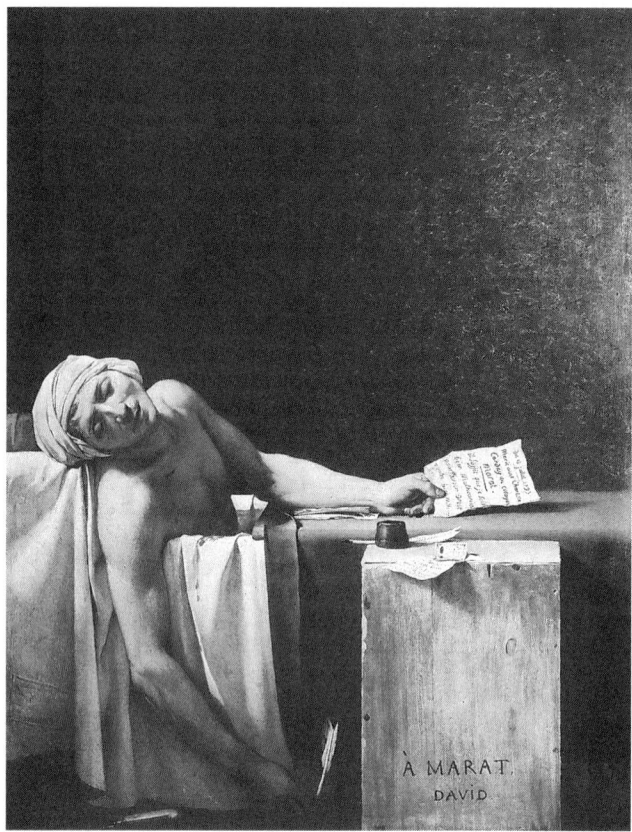

Photo 2.6 **Death of Marat, Jacques Louis David, 1793.**

royalty, or a wealthy merchant. Throughout the 17th and 18th centuries, the social status and freedom of artists grew, but painters, sculptors, composers, and writers were still bound to individual courts and patrons. In France, state-funded academies maintained rigid control over artistic training and exhibition, and they limited artists' subject matter and style. The French painter Jacques-Louis David (1748–1825) was highly successful and influential during both the radical Reign of Terror (1793–1794), France's revolutionary era when the Jacobins took often brutal steps against the monarchy and Catholic Church, and later during the more moderate rule (1804–1815) of Napoleon Bonaparte (1769–1821). He managed to maintain his status through the regime change because he politically supported successive revolutionary leaders through his paintings of historical subjects.

Artists in this period did not yet have the freedom to reject tradition or the direct control of their patrons. Nonetheless, in France and elsewhere in Europe, an active and engaged audience for and debate about the arts characterized the life of the growing bourgeoisie, and the arts had an important role to play in the development of a national identity, the state, and the self-identity of the bourgeoisie.

During the 19th century, the French state system of patronage started to crumble, and a new period of rapid change in the social status of the arts and artists began. The transition from state to private (market) patronage brought additional freedoms, and insecurities, to artists. In the late 19th century, artists and the art they made occupied a curious position between outsider and elite. **Modern** artists, composers and writers were overturning traditional modes of representation and expression and engaging in radical experimentation in their mediums at an unprecedented pace. Impressionist painters left the dingy light of the studios and set up their easels in bustling train stations and public gardens (see White and White, 1993). Symbolist poets experimented with the sound and texture of language in their poetry, intentionally substituting words associated with one kind of sensual experience (e.g. sound) with words from another (e.g. sight), and composers broke with classical conceptions of harmony and compositional development.

> There are perfumes that are fresh like children's flesh, sweet like oboes, green like meadows
>
> –And others, corrupt, rich, and triumphant
>
> From Baudelaires "Correspondences" in Baudelaire, 2006.

These artists formed communities, often in down-and-out neighborhoods, and interspersed hard work with distinctly urban pleasures like hanging out in cafes, bars, and cabarets. Many, like the artists Toulouse-Lautrec and Eduard Manet, were especially attracted to brothels and other places where the underside of Victorian propriety played out. Artists were inspired by the nightlife of the urban proletariat and under-class, and often depicted cabaret performers, prostitutes, barmaids, and alcoholics. By the end of the 19th century, modernism and the modern idea of **bohemia** as a space of creativity, rebellion, and freedom had emerged in Paris and elsewhere (see Grana, 1964 and Mizruchi, 1987). The modern values of innovation, risk, and experimentation had replaced the bonds of shared meaning and tradition.

The Invention of High Culture, Folk (Popular) Culture, and Mass culture

The special value assigned to "high culture" is historically and socially entwined with the categories of **popular culture** and **mass culture**. It is often against these other forms of culture that we value and assess "high art." Your parents, for example, may be happy to pay for violin lessons and smile proudly when you

Photo 2.7 **La Goulue, Marc Charmet, 1989.**

perform a Mozart concerto at a recital. They may be less enthusiastic (at least they would have been when I was young) about your drum-set in the basement and the music you play with your punk-revival band. And, your middle-school book report on your favorite Clone-Wars comic probably wouldn't have earned you the same grade as an essay about Charles Dickens' novel *Great Expectations*. In both of these examples, the object of lesser cultural value falls into the category of mass or popular culture. (These two categories are sometimes treated as interchangeable, but, as I hope to show here, it is useful to make a distinction between them.) If we take a historical view, as have many sociologists, we can see that all three of these categories, and the values assigned to them, depend on the other for their social meaning and significance. The origins of these distinctions illustrate their impermanence as well as why they hold such a grip on our imagination.

Culture and the Folk

In the 18th and 19th centuries, intellectuals took interest in folk culture as traditional cultures began to disappear in the wake of industrialization and urbanization (Storey, 1996). Thinkers like the German philosopher, poet, and literary scholar Johann Gottfried von Herder (1744–1803) were critical of **Enlightenment**

Photo 2.8 **Rapunzel, Otto Spekter, 1898.** (Library of Congress, Prints & Photographs Division)

rationalism and idealized the culture of traditional, agrarian communities, which they viewed as united by a common spirit and collective identity expressed through folk music, fairy tales, and myths. They thought that folk culture, as opposed to the artificial, individualistic, inauthentic and overly intellectual culture of urban elites, expressed the nature and soul of a people. During the same period, the German linguists Jacob (1785–1863) and Wilhelm Grimm (1786–1859) collected fairy and folk tales from around Germany, and, like Herder, associated these examples of folk culture, handed down through the generations, with the unique national identities of the people. It was this traditional culture of rural and village folk, not the developing culture of the new urban workers, that was used to establish a foundation for patriotism and what Benedict Anderson (1991) has called "the imagined communities" of the nation-state. In this view, a romantic and sentimental version of "*das Volk*" and traditional folk culture was "invented" by 18th and 19th century intellectuals in their desire to replace the divine rule of monarchies over multi-ethnic empires with national sovereignty based on the shared rights of citizens. The sense of a shared language and cultural forms could provide the basis for unifying various peoples of a vast territorial region. This folk culture was cast in opposition to the mannered culture of the new urban elite and the cultural forms that the growing population of urban industrial workers developed.

Culture and Civilization

The swelling urban proletariat, and its claims to equality and democracy, along with the empty materialism of industrial capitalism, engendered another view of culture among intellectuals of the 19th century. The British writer and educator Matthew Arnold (1822–1888) posed an opposition between culture and society or civilization. Civilization was technological advances and progress. It brought benefits to humankind but was at its core soulless, amoral, and cold. It engendered materialism and crass commercialism and promised the working classes a sense of equality and political inclusion for which they were, according to Arnold, unequipped. If we are not careful, Arnold warned, civilization would lead to either the triumph of petty, middle-class materialism (what Arnold called philistinism) or rioting workers and social anarchy (Griswold, 2012). Culture, on the other hand, represented for Arnold the best and highest achievement of human beings. It was, in a sense, a cure for the ravages of civilization. Through awareness of "the best that has been thought and said in the world" the middle classes (Arnold had little hope for the aristocracy, whom he called "barbarians," or for the proletarian rabble) could be brought to what he referred to as "sweetness and light." Through education and cultivation, they could learn to appreciate culture and through this appreciation they would achieve a higher sense of purpose and morality. They would then be worthy of ruling society and could serve as a good model for the working class. Their example could mitigate the negative impact of the working class' vulgar and amoral forms of amusement and lessen the possibility of revolt. The popular culture of the working class, which expressed itself in dance halls, pub songs, bawdy humor, and public spectacle, according to Arnold, was base, disorderly and dangerous. There was no role for Herder's folk cultures or non-European cultures in education and cultivation. High culture was a form of enlightenment for the upper classes and form of social control of the working class (see Storey, 2013:15). Arnold and others like him, though, fueled an interest in mass education as a remedy for poverty and a form of political socialization, which can still be felt today.

A generation later, F. R Leavis (1895–1978) and his followers, the Leavites, shared Arnold's dim view of the new mass of industrial working classes. They warned in the 1930s of a "cultural crisis" that would be brought on not only by the unruly barbarism of the working class "masses" but also by the increasing standardization and commercialization of the mass culture they consumed. The mass consumption of popular fiction, Hollywood movies and advertising posed especially dangerous threats to the minds and character of the public and threatened the future of high culture. The Leavites were unabashed elitists and believed that true culture had always been controlled by the minority. The advent of democracy, however, has brought about a collapse of authority and the culture of the elite. The best and brightest were left vulnerable to the onslaught of the lower classes who no longer respected their superiors (or the culture of their superiors). The Spanish philosopher José Ortega y Gassett (1883–1955) warned of the revolt of the masses (1930), which would result in a dangerous form of **hyperdemocracy** or the barbaric rule of the masses. Like Arnold, these thinkers thought that education would restore the culture and authority of elites.

During the past several decades there have been many challenges to the version of culture promoted by Arnold, Leavis, and others, and the role of education in promoting that culture. **Feminists**, **postcolonial theorists** and others have helped reshape the version of legitimate culture taught in schools and universities. Literature and other art forms that would have once been considered "popular" or inferior because they draw on traditions outside of European high art are now taken seriously by scholars and have become part of the standard curriculum. At the same time, defenders of tradition like the American literary scholar Harold Bloom (1994), continue to make a case for the superiority of the **Western canon**. Rather than enshrine art in a canon or wage battles between different positions within the cultural field, sociologist analyze the processes through which new cultural products exit the field of popular culture and enter the field of high art.

The Culture Industry and Art Under Siege

By the 1940s, the most serious threat to high culture, according to many intellectuals, was not social anarchy but dull conformity. The rapid development of technologies for the production and distribution of mass culture provided another set of problems for defenders of high culture. Now, cheap photographic reproductions of paintings in museums could be owned by anyone and the music of great orchestras was readily available to the distracted radio listener (Adorno, in Gephart and Arato, 1982: 270–300). Even more alarming (to some) than the degraded forms of high art that reached the uncultivated citizen through commercial reproduction and distribution were the new forms of culture churned out by organizationally complex and technologically sophisticated "entertainment" industries aimed at the masses. While some critics complained that high culture was becoming degraded through its association with unsophisticated "middle-brow" venues, like popular magazines and radio shows (see Gans, 1999), others, most notably critical theorists like Theodor Adorno (1903–1969) and Max Horkheimer (1895–1973) (1944), believed that commercially produced culture was a dangerous tool used by elites to produce conformity and neutralize any possible rebellion in the population. The **culture industry**, these critics

Photo 2.9 **Film poster for Gilda, Alfredo Capitai, 1946.** (Photo Fest)

believed, through its uniformity, conventionality and blandness, habituated consumers to the repetitive and alienating conditions they encountered in the world of work. Hollywood movies, greatest-hit songs, and glossy gossip magazines satisfied people's surface desires for distraction, escape, or titillation but weren't able to satisfy the real needs of humanity. In fact, these products stunted the capacity of audiences to form or articulate these needs. Like giving junk food to a hungry child, the culture industry created the illusion of fulfillment and satisfaction but did not provide the means for intellectual or spiritual growth. The products of consumer culture, in the words of Herbert Marcuse produce

> a pattern of one-dimensional thought and behavior in which ideas, aspirations and objectives that, by their content, transcend the established universe of discourse and action are either repelled or reduced to the terms of this universe.

Marcuse (1964:12)

Real art, according to these critics, if not an antidote to mass culture and mass society, at least protested against conformity, alienation, and consumerism. Although works of art are ultimately distributed through market mechanisms, at least—if they are authentic works of art—they are different than mass produced commercial culture because they are not created *only* to make profit. Commercial culture exists solely as a commodity and is therefore subject to the same rational calculations as any other commodity: it must be made as cheaply as possible according to a standardized process of mass production. The production and distribution of such culture obeys only the abstract force of the market. For Theodor Adorno, works of art are different from mass produced culture because they reflect the intentions of the artist and the logic of a kind of "internal" development of the art form, which, according to him, "resists" the logic of the market, mass production, and conformity (Adorno in Gephart and Arato, 1982: 300–319). Unlike mass culture, true works of art encourage an active, engaged, and focused state of mind. Adorno's view of art is compelling, especially to those who make or appreciate less commercial forms of culture. Unfortunately, however, he is burdened by some of the same elitism that plagued Arnold and Leavis. Most, if not all, of his favorite examples of legitimate art were produced by European men, and he was blind (and deaf) to the value and complexity of jazz music (see Adorno, 1953 [1981]) and other hybrid or non-European cultural forms.

Defenders of Popular Culture

For many decades, neither mass nor popular culture had many defenders among intellectuals. In *Popular Culture and High Culture*, however, American sociologist Herbert Gans (1974 [1999]) argued that popular culture's critics had exaggerated differences between high and popular culture. He pointed out that not only has mass culture borrowed (or stolen) ideas from high culture but that mass culture has always also been *part* of high culture. After all, commercial printing houses and mass markets created an audience for 19th-century novels, and classical composers like Gustav Mahler (1860–1911) incorporated dance-hall and other popular music forms into their work. The preference for so-called high culture, according to Gans, was part of a romantic and sentimental idea of a pre-industrial past. Actually, he argued, industrialization, urbanization, and mass production have brought benefits to human beings, including a greater choice of cultural products. People are better educated and have more opportunities to participate in society than ever before. Adorno, Horkheimer, and Marcuse's view of mass culture is too monolithic and doesn't get at the complexity of modern society, Gans claimed. Many different kinds of popular and high culture exist from which a variety of **taste cultures** can choose. Each taste culture is trying to fulfill, what Gans explains, are people's aesthetic urges; a receptivity to symbolic expressions of their wishes and fears; a demand for both knowledge and wish-fulfillment about their society; and a desire to spend free time ... in ways that diverge from their work routine.

(1999: 67)

Because we live in heterogeneous society, there will be diverse ways of doing this.

In a similar vein, the American sociologist Richard Peterson (1992) argues that the old association of the masses with commercial culture and elites with high culture no longer holds. Although Peterson does admit that elites have more opportunities to explore various forms of culture, he refers to today's cultural consumers as **cultural omnivores** (more on this in Chapter Three). Omnivores are not exclusive in their cultural tastes. They might seek out Hollywood films, classical music, and ethnic cuisine with equal gusto. To some degree, Peterson's arguments are convincing. Audiences for popular and high art forms do indeed overlap and mass culture is much more heterogeneous today than it was in the 1950s. There still are significant differences, however, between forms of culture that rely exclusively on a mass market and commercial distribution and those that do not. The music industry, for example, is always looking for new forms of creativity, but, as studies of world music, rap and other popular musical forms (see Connell and Gibson, 2003, Marcus and Myers, 1995) have shown, once these genres are controlled, distributed and produced by large commercial concerns, they are subject to the strictures of mass production and profit. They are likely to become standardized and homogeneous and less likely to be innovative in form or content. Cultural forms that are more independent from mass markets, like avant-garde jazz, or experimental films do not generate much profit and artists rely on grants and other forms of private funding to create their work. Because they do not have to produce profit, in the short run they are more free to experiment and innovate. On the other hand, artists of "high culture" are also subject to market demands, even if the market for their work is small. Once an artist's reputation and value have been established, collectors are reluctant to purchase work that deviates from the artist's signature style (see Rothenberg and Fine, 2008, also Velthuis, 2005). With less public funding, and the more widespread acceptance of market values in a range of social spheres, art's value seems to rest increasingly on its monetary worth (see, eg. Saltz, 2007).

Are These Distinctions Still Relevant?

People make sense of the world and communicate with each other about that world by constructing categories. These shared categories are reflections of human understandings of the social world and are neither inevitable nor universal. Different societies and cultures construct different kinds of categories and group objects and activities differently. Cows, for example, are considered a source of food in the United States and a sacred symbol in parts of India. Seizures may be interpreted as symptoms of disease in one culture and possession by spirits in another. Our categories develop in response to concrete historical phenomena like the rise of new economic and political systems, technological innovation, or migration patterns. In this chapter, you have been introduced to some of the conditions that gave rise to the categories of high art and the distinction between the categories of high and popular culture and mass culture. You have also learned about how sociologists and other social thinkers have explained the social meaning of these categories. As you have seen, they do not always agree with one another. The background provided here will help you to formulate questions about how people in our society group cultural forms and what kinds of factors influence the categories we use today. To what degree are distinctions between popular and high art still relevant? How has new technology affected the way we think about art and artists? Do we still think that artists are special geniuses? Why or why not? We will explore these topics in more depth in later chapters. With some knowledge about how the categories that we take for granted first developed, we can be sensitive to how these categories have shifted or remained stable.

Discussion Questions

1. Explain, in your own words, what it means to call art a "stand-alone or autonomous kind of activity. What are some of the historical developments that paralleled this way of thinking? Does it make sense to think about art as a "stand alone" activity today? Why or why not?
2. When Habermas wrote about the importance of the arts for the development of the public sphere, he claimed that people needed to develop new strategies of communication to debate the aesthetic value of the art works of the day. What kinds of strategies do you use to convince your friends that one film is better than another, a certain actor is especially beautiful, or one version of a pop song is superior to another?
3. How and why did the distinction between popular or mass culture, and high culture develop? Does this distinction still categorize cultural products? Are there examples of art that defy easy categorization?
4. Why did Arnold and Leavis take have such a dim view of popular culture during the early decades of the 20th century? How does their view compare to the critique of the culture industry held by Adorno, Horkheimer, and others? Do any of their criticisms remain relevant? Explain.

5. How do Herbert Gans and Richard Peterson defend popular culture? What are the strengths of their arguments? What are the weaknesses?
6. Visit a museum exhibition that you think falls in between categories. Explain why it does not fall neatly into the categories of either "high," "popular" or mass culture.

3
LENSES OF ANALYSIS

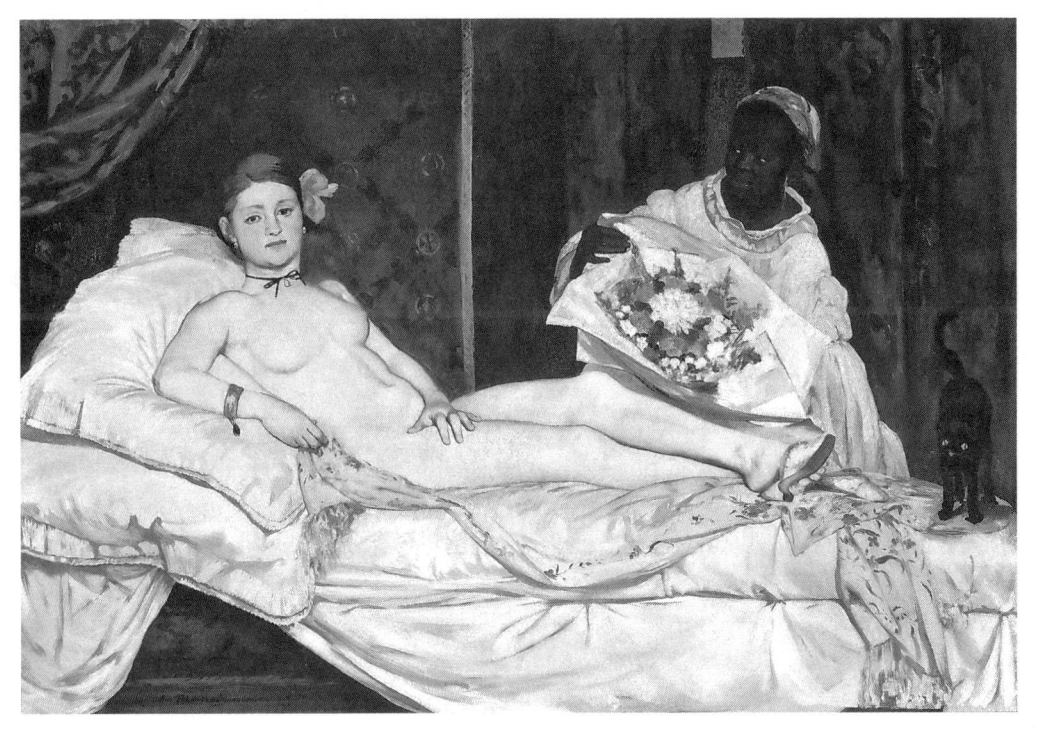

Photo 3.1 **Olympia, Eduard Manet, 1863.**

Olympia Through the Looking Glass

Eduard Manet's painting *Olympia* has attracted the attention of critics and commentators since it was first exhibited in Paris in 1865. The subject of the painting, whom many assume is a prostitute, (see, eg. Flescher, 1985), confronts the viewer with a cold, unflinching gaze. She appears indifferent to the bouquet of flowers from an admirer offered by her maid, as though such symbols of romance and affection have little to do with the economic transaction at the heart of her relationship with her clients. The direct, unsentimental

Photo 3.2 **Venus of Urbino, Titan, 1580.**

look on her face seems like a rebuff to the coy, sensual, and slightly averted glance of the figure in Titian's *Venus of Urbino* (1538) (photo 3.2), the painting to which Manet refers in the pose and composition of *Olympia* (Clark, 1984). It is not only with his twist on the subject that Manet rejects the past. Titian's brushwork, gesture, and color are a reaction against the hard-edged, illustrational painting of the Florentine school that dominated during his time. However, his work still attempts to evoke classical beauty in three-dimensional space. In *Olympia,* Manet emphasizes the vertical and horizontal architecture of the composition by creating a shallow space through the use of harsh tonal contrasts and by dispensing with conventions for rendering rounded objects on a flat surface.

Much happened in Western society from the late Renaissance period, during which Titian worked, to Manet's modern world. *Olympia* captures, through the language of art, many of the key dimensions of these changes. Sociologists who think about large-scale social changes also attempt to capture, in the language of sociology and social theory, broad changes that have occurred in the structure and texture of society.

Social researchers study art worlds using an array of theories, perspectives, orientations, and methods. In this chapter, I will introduce you to three levels of analysis sociologists use to discuss different aspects of these worlds. As I explained in Chapter One, they correspond, roughly, to the three different lenses used by photographers to create wide-angle, middle-range, and close-up images of their subjects. Using wide-angle lenses, classical sociologists like Karl Marx (1818–1883), Max Weber (1864–1920), and Emile Durkheim (1858–1917) studied the changes taking place in modern societies. Like landscape photographers who use a wide-angle lens to capture a broad expanse of visual information, these classical sociologists tried to understand large-scale social questions such as: What caused the sweeping social changes of the 19th and early-20th centuries? How do the systems that govern the distribution of resources and the division of labor shape society? What is the relationship between cultural and economic development?

Macroscopic, wide-angle sociological approaches help us understand the arts in terms of a broader social context. Sociologists of art take up concepts developed by classical sociologists to address similarly general questions about the arts: Why did the arts emerge as a separate and distinct category of cultural production in Western society? What role do the arts play in reproducing the class structure of modern societies? How have technological developments affected the arts in postmodern societies? These sociologists often use empirical data like demographic statistics, economic indicators, and field-notes for descriptive purposes, or to support their conclusions. However, their main focus is on theoretical, or conceptual explanations of large-scale social phenomenon.

Some questions about art worlds are, on the other hand, best explored using a middle-range level of analysis. Photographers use medium-range lenses to capture street scenes or small groupings of people or objects in the context of their environment. In a similar manner, sociologists have developed concepts and tools to describe and understand the development and structure of specific social institutions and organizations and the conflict and consensus within and between them.

Sociologists of art have used this middle-range level of analysis to study, for example, how the development of a commercial gallery system in Paris contributed to the success of the Impressionist painters (White and White, 1993); how and why members of Boston's elite collaborated to take control of nonprofit arts institutions in the 19th century (DiMaggio, 1982); and how the restructuring of the National Endowment for the Arts in the 1990s affected the fundraising strategies of small-scale arts institutions (Smith, 2003). These questions highlight the importance of **empirical,** data-driven investigation. For example, Diana Crane (1989) gathered **quantitative data** in her investigation of the factors that led to changes in the visual arts worlds of New York City from 1940 to 1985. By tracking changes in the number of galleries operating in New York, the price that the works of individual artists received at auction, and rates of museum attendance, Crane made focused arguments about the expansion of the art world, the increasing acceptance of American art styles, and the economics of cultural markets.

Like photographers who use a close-up lens to capture the details of a particular face or the anatomy of a flower, some sociologists focus more narrowly on their subject. Instead of identifying the general qualities of social structures, systems, and institutions, these sociologists study people close up. They ask questions about how meaning, identity, and the self are constructed through social interaction and what "unwritten rules" guide social life. What, for example, do people actually *do* when they are engaged in art-making or in other art-world activities? What are people thinking about as they participate in art worlds? How do members of a particular art world interact with each other to create a shared meaning and context for the work of art? These questions highlight the importance of microscopic, close-up studies of specific art worlds. The microscopic perspective, like a good close-up lens, hones in on the details of social interaction. To gain a close-up perspective, sociologists "get their hands dirty" in the field. They hang out at music clubs and take notes, interview artists and visit their studios, and attend book club meetings to listen to what readers have to say about the novels they read.

Macro Perspectives on Art and Society: Capitalism and Rationalization

As I suggested above, Manet's painting addresses problems of modern society that two founding figures of sociology, Karl Marx and Max Weber, both of whom were from Germany, puzzled over in their work. These social theorists were especially interested in the growth of **capitalism**, or market society, and in the increasing **rationalization** of social life. By depicting *Olympia* as a prostitute instead of a goddess, Manet provides a commentary on the real values of market society. While Victorian women were expected to be chaste and virtuous, their husbands supported a thriving market for prostitution and pornography (Mason, 1994; Marcus, 2008). Manet's modern *Olympia*, a woman who survives by selling both her body and her labor, replaces Titian's idealized goddess, who is shrouded in the sentimental veil of classical mythology. Manet depicts a modern Everywoman, who knows what she is worth. The bouquet of flowers sent by her admirer will not persuade her to forget that "business is business."

Marx on Capitalism

Marx's analysis of economic systems explains how and why modern society differs from the feudal past. His analysis of capitalism in turn helps us understand the characteristic cultural and social forms produced by modern society.

All Societies, according to Marx, have an economic base, or **mode of production**. This base consists of the **means of production,** which includes the technology through which people meet their material needs. (The technology can be as simple as a shovel and hoe or as complex as a computer.) The mode of production also includes what Marx calls **relations of production**, which describe how a society's members organize themselves socially in order to divide up the work and resources that people produce together (more on this in Chapter Four). Those who own or control the means of production get the lion's share of resources. In ancient Egypt, slavery and the institutions that developed alongside it constituted the most important relation of production; during feudal times, mutual obligations between lord and serf tied to hierarchies of blood and custom and in modern, capitalist economies, the private property of capitalists and formally free labor of workers (or, in Marx's terms bourgeoisie and **proletariat**) represented the relations of production.

Marx criticized the industrial capitalism that spread through Europe and the United States during his lifetime because it brought about, among other social ills, the miserable working and living conditions described by Marx's collaborator, Fredric Engels, below (see (Engels [1845] 1993), on working class conditions in London).

> The houses are occupied from cellar to garret, filthy within and without, and their appearance is such that no human being could possibly wish to live in them. But all this is nothing in comparison with the dwellings in the narrow courts and alleys between the streets, entered by covered passages between the houses, in which the filth and tottering ruin surpass all description. Scarcely a whole window-pane can be found, the walls are crumbling, door-posts and window-frames loose and broken, doors of old boards nailed together, or altogether wanting in this thieves' quarter, where no doors are needed, there being nothing to steal. Heaps of garbage and ashes lie in all directions, and the foul liquids emptied before the doors gather in stinking pools. Here live the poorest of the poor, the worst paid workers with thieves and the victims of prostitution indiscriminately huddled together, the majority Irish, or of Irish extraction, and those who have not yet sunk in the whirlpool of moral ruin which surrounds them, sinking daily deeper, losing daily more and more of their power to resist the demoralizing influence of want, filth, and evil surroundings.
>
> Friedrich Engels, 1845

THE LETTER OF THE LAW.

Photo 3.3 **The Letter of the Law, S.D Ehrhart, 1912.** (Library of Congress, Prints & Photographs Division)

On the other hand, Marx had faith in progress and technology. Capitalism, he pointed out, encourages the development of labor-saving technology, innovation, and science because competition forces capitalist enterprises to produce goods more cheaply and faster. In addition, he thought that the market served as a great social equalizer where everyone's dollar is worth the same, regardless of the status or individual characteristics of its possessor.

Capitalism stripped away the illusions of natural superiority that had legitimized the privileges and greed of rulers during feudal times. In *The Communist Manifesto*, Marx and Engels write that capitalist society has

> ...put an end to all feudal, patriarchal, idyllic relations. It has pitilessly torn asunder the motley feudal ties that bound man to his "natural superiors," and has left remaining no other nexus between man and man than naked self-interest.

Marx and Engels, 1848

Marx's emphasis on the organization of economic systems may not seem to be related to the arts in an obvious way. However, vast social, technological, and material resources are needed to fund the elaborate and complex kinds of art worlds that we associate with modern society. Our complex (and expensive!) forms of art and culture reflect, in part, capitalism's ability to generate great amounts of wealth. And, Marx's analysis of how the social meaning and value of objects change when they are sold on the open market for a profit illustrates how works of art differ from—and are similar to—other kinds of **commodities**.

Marx and Culture

Despite Marx's focus on the economy, he had much to say about culture and ideas. In fact, he believed that culture and social institutions are important *reflections* of the economic base of society. According to Marx the social institutions, values, beliefs, and even the art forms that prevail in any society reflect the interests and cement the advantages enjoyed by groups with the most control of the means of production. As he puts it in his preface to the "Critique of Political Economy":

> ...the relations of production constitutes the economic structure of society, the real foundation, on which arises a legal and political superstructure and to which correspond definite forms of social consciousness. The mode of production of material life conditions the general process of social, political and intellectual life.
>
> Marx, 1859

In other words, "He who pays the piper calls the tune." The dominant class may be effective in convincing everyone else that the legal, religious, family, or cultural institutions that they control are the best for everyone. These institutionalized social arrangements, however, are merely those that are most effective at keeping the ruling class in power and reinforcing the values and beliefs that justify the unequal distribution of resources. Just as the official Church dogma of the Middle Ages justified kings' power as a "divine right," modern capitalist institutions, like schools, promote ways of thinking ("hard work pays off" or "competition is natural," for example) that are useful to those in power. Marx refers to the ideas that the dominant groups used to justify and reproduce their power as **ideology.** Cultural institutions and art forms, as well as dominant ideas about artistic value, represent the interests of the dominant class and should be viewed as part of the **dominant ideology**.

Max Weber on Rationalization and Bureaucracy

Max Weber, who experienced many of the disasters of the late-19th and early-20th centuries (including World War I), regarded the consequences of modern forms of technology and social organization more pessimistically than Marx. Neither institutions nor individuals in the modern (as opposed to the traditional) world, according to Weber, determine their course of action based upon tradition, ethical values, or in response to feelings and emotions. Instead, they calculate the most efficient means for attaining desired ends without consideration of spiritual, ethical, or even material consequences, except as they affect immediate goals. Actors (a sociological terms which simply means "people") make calculations as a "mean[s] for attainment of the actors' own rationally pursued and calculated ends" (Weber, 1968: 24). He called this type of logic and behavior **instrumental rationality**, or means/ends rationality, and the process through which individuals and organizations become oriented by this logic and behavior "rationalization". Instrumental rationality guides the bureaucratic organization of modern institutions, where impersonal hierarchies, the division of labor, and standardized procedures are brought to bear so that organizations can achieve narrowly conceived goals. Within a complex bureaucracy, the individual is simply a cog in the wheels of order, and larger goals and ethics are rarely examined. People pay for increased efficiency and technological advances afforded by rationalization with a loss of community, spirituality, and individuality. Weber's characterizations of modern society, bureaucracy, disenchantment, and means/ends rationality provide a context for understanding how modern art worlds emerge and continue to change.

Weber uses the idea of rationalization to explain the growth of capitalism in the West. In *The Protestant Ethic and the Spirit of Capitalism* (1904–1905), he explains that the forms of Protestantism that took hold in northern Europe in the 16th century and in the United States during the 17th century were central to the adoption of instrumental rationality in economic life. Early Protestants were guided by thrift, rational calculation, hard work, and the renunciation of immediate sensual or emotional pleasure because of their strong religious convictions. Not so in the modern world where the habits of rational calculation, divorced from their spiritual meaning, have become an "iron cage" in which we are trapped (Weber, 1930).

> A life of leisure and a life of laziness are two things. There will be sleeping enough in the grave.
>
> Benjamin Franklin, 1774

Photo 3.4 **Benjamin Franklin, "Max Weber quoted Benjamin Franklin for examples of the Protestant ethic," 1868.** (Library of Congress, Prints & Photographs Division)

Rationalization in Art and Music

As part of his project to describe and explain the characteristics of modern Western societies, Weber addressed the subject of music. Much of what Weber wrote about music emphasizes the "sensual-emotional" as well as the intellectual qualities of Western music. He also points out, however, that though music retains much of its expressive and emotional character in modern societies (Weber, 2005), it still tends toward the same kind of rationalization that drives other realms of social action.

The rationalization of Western music, he argued, occurred along with the bureaucratization of the Roman Catholic Church during the Middle-Ages, when monks developed a system of musical notation to standardize liturgical music. Music was further rationalized with the development of more advanced methods for constructing instruments, the invention of the piano in the early 18th century, and its refinement during the Industrial Revolution. Western music's concise system of musical notation allowed for a level of both standardization and innovation not possible (claimed Weber) in cultures (like those of Asia, for example) that do not use musical notation (Weber, 1930: 13–17). Using a standardized system of notation to record what has already been composed, we can more easily develop new and more complex musical ideas and build on what has been done by others. At the same time, precise systems of notation and predictable tonal and harmonic systems encourage rigid standards for performance and interpretation of musical pieces and constrain the personal expression of musicians, composers, and conductors.

The rationalization of art and music leaves unanswered the question: What are the ends of art? Writing about this idea in relation to the French poet Charles Baudelaire, whose work, like Manet's, often reflected the vulgar realities of urban life, Weber noted that "today…we realize that something can be beautiful, not only in spite of the aspect in which it is not good, but rather in that very aspect" (Weber, 1946: 148) In other words, beauty and expression, not goodness or morality, are the special goals of art. Artists in the modern world are not judged in terms of how effectively they illustrate moral or religious sentiments, but only whether they have succeeded with regard to the ends of art.

>
> Like some lewd rake with his old worn-out whore,
> Nibbling her suffering teats, we seize our sly
> delight, that, like an orange—withered, dry—
> We squeeze and press for juice that is no more.
>
> Charles Baudelaire, from "*To the Reader*," 1857

Photo 3.5 **Portrait of Baudelaire, Eduard Manet, 1862.** (Art Stor).

This increased specialization in the arts is captured in Manet's *Olympia* (photo 3.1). Unlike academic painters, he was not trying to create the illusion of three-dimensional form and space. He was instead interested in the abstract play of shapes on the canvass. Like the Impressionist and post-Impressionist painters who followed him, he let the viewer see his brushstrokes, and he wasn't trying to trick the viewer into believing that the painted surface was a mirror or a sculpture. He also wasn't trying to faithfully illustrate a theme from another source, like literature, Greek mythology, or the Bible. Just as science and medicine focus on questions about the natural world and leave questions about spiritual life and ultimate meaning to theologians and philosophers, modern artists like Manet abandoned the tasks of mimicking reality, obeying tradition, and illustrating church or state doctrine. They concentrated instead on developing the vocabulary and technique specific to individual art forms. In the late-19th century, neither the state nor the church was funding Manet. He came from a wealthy family and sold his paintings on the open market, so he could paint whatever he wanted. He rejected the tradition of French academic painting with its illusionistic space and surface. He was more interested in thinking about the unique visual qualities of painting and the relationship between painting and the new medium of photography, which was able to create a more accurate imitation of reality than painting.

Functionalism and the Search for Order

The last wide-angle, macro-perspective that I will discuss in this chapter is **structural-functionalism**, which draws on the work of the classical social theorist, Emile Durkheim. Structural-functionalism (also referred to, simply as

Photo 3.6 **The broom dance at the square dance. Pie Town, New Mexico. The extra girl or man dances around with a broom for a partner. Then drops broom loudly; everyone must change partners and the one left out in the exchange must then dance with the broom, Russell Lee, 1940.** (Library of Congress, Prints & Photographs Division)

"structuralism") emphasizes shared values, social cohesion, and the integration of various parts of society into a stable whole. Even social institutions and aspects of the social structure that might not immediately seem beneficial to society, like inequality (Davis and Moore, 1945) or crime (Durkheim, 1995), might perform important social functions that contribute to the stability of the system overall. From this perspective, the arts have an important role to play in maintaining social cohesion.

Individual members of society, argued Durkheim, are integrated into the social system through a **collective consciousness**, or **social solidarity**, which provides a sort of glue binding people to one another and to the system as a whole. Society ensures that people will not deviate much from social norms by providing means (like the family) for socializing individuals and sanctions (shaming and social exclusion, for example) for punishing norm violators (Durkheim, 1997). Collective rituals and practices like sporting events, religious rituals, rock concerts, dancing, graduations, and so forth provide occasions for individuals to cement a collective identity and experience social solidarity.

In pre-modern societies, Durkheim argued (1997 [1893]), social solidarity was provided through shared customs and traditions and there was less of a range of social types and lifestyles than in modern, urban societies. In modern societies people are held together less through shared customs and rituals (though we certainly still have some of those). Durkheim believed that modern societies still have social solidarity. We achieve this not through similarity and tradition, but through a shared ideology of individualism and the interdependence that goes along with a very complex **division of labor**.

Talcott Parsons' Cultural System

Talcott Parsons (1902–1979) one of the most influential American sociologists from the 1940s through the 1960s explained that society meets its needs by coordinating the actions of what he called the cultural system, the social system, the behavioral organism, and the personality system. These four action systems work together to maintain the social order necessary for the smooth functioning of society (Parsons, 1991, 1968). Art, from Parsons' perspective, is part of the cultural system. We could not coordinate our actions with others if we did not share a cultural framework. In addition, art helps to integrate our personality with the social system (Parsons, 1991 [1951]). For Parsons, the experience of making or appreciating art might feel personal (subjective), but, like Durkheim's social solidarity, art serves a collective function, acting as glue that binds us together.

Parsons's theoretical framework provides insights into the highly expressive, abstract, and specialized qualities of two art movements that coincided with his career as a sociologist: bebop jazz and Abstract Expressionism. Both of these forms of art highlight the specialized elements of their medium. Abstract expressionist paintings refer only minimally, if at all, to objects in the outside world. Instead, they emphasize color, composition, and paint texture—all elements that are internal to painting. Bebop is also primarily concerned with the elements of jazz music itself. It is not intended for dancing, and its emphasis is on the unique sound qualities of individual instruments, innovation, and expression. It does not, like liturgical music, opera, or much pop music, aid in telling a story or providing a background to other activities.

Both Abstract Expressionism and bebop emphasize personal expression and individual innovation. All societies, according to Parsons, have cultural systems oriented toward the satisfaction of expressive needs. In those with highly differentiated systems—that is, systems composed of many different parts that each have very specialized functions—however, the purely expressive needs of the cultural system are satisfied through specialized cultural productions produced by specialized culture producers. According to Parsons "...the creative artist is the person who specializes in the production of new patterns of expressive symbolism." (Parsons, 1991: 275).

MEDIUM-RANGE PERSPECTIVES ON ART AND SOCIETY

European sociology has generally been more inclined toward wide-angle, macro perspectives and social theory. The philosophical underpinnings and disciplinary organization of sociology in the United States (see Smith in Smith 1998: 8) has encouraged instead the development of a more medium-range and empirically-based approach that focuses on the interactions between and within specific social institutions and organizations. Medium-range perspectives start with empirical data, and researchers using these perspectives are reluctant to propose theoretical explanations for social phenomenon without data to support their explanations. For this reason, medium-range perspectives are good for studying phenomenon for which one *can* access sufficient empirical data, such as how rising real estate prices impacted the number of galleries that moved from New York City's SoHo neighborhood to West Chelsea in the early 1990s, or the specific social factors that correlated with a rise in organized crime in Chicago in the 1920s. The medium-range approach is less useful for trying to formulate grand theories about the relationship between culture and the economy, or the social function of the arts.

Production of Culture Approach

One type of medium-range approach is the **production of culture** approach, and many of the sociologists of art whose work I will discuss in later chapters are associated with this perspective. Sociologists in the 1970s drew from a number of other sub-disciplines including the sociology of organizations, institutions, work, industrial sociology, economic sociology, and the sociology of networks to develop this perspective. The production of culture perspective maintains that

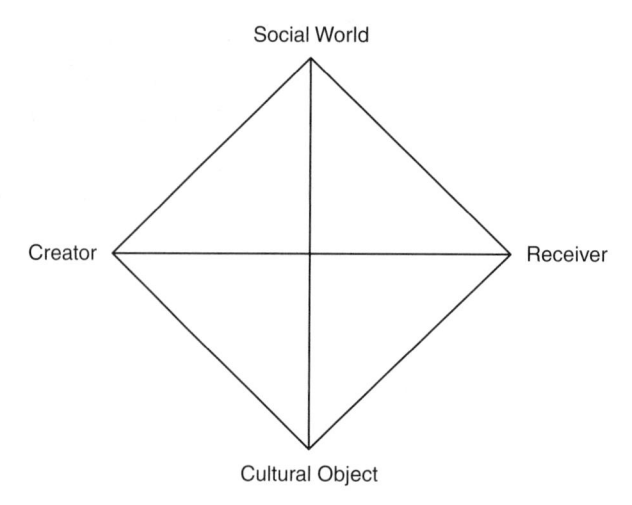

Photo 3.7 **Griswold's Cultural Diamond.**

"the symbolic elements of culture are shaped by the systems within which they are created, distributed, evaluated, taught, and preserved" (Peterson and Anand, 2004: 311). While scholars using this perspective have recently been paying attention to artworks and artists, they have historically given priority to structural, organizational, institutional, and economic factors external to the creation of culture.

The sociologists Richard Peterson and N. Anand (2004) identify six facets of production central to the production of culture approach. The table below lists each of these facets, using the example of the motion picture industry in Hollywood from the 1920s through the 1960s—a period referred to as its "Golden Age." It provides an example of the kinds of research questions that a focus on each facet generates and an example of what findings resulted from asking these questions. You will see how, taken together, a study of these six facets of production sheds light on the social processes through which Hollywood films are produced.

Ideally, a researcher working with the production of culture approach would describe and analyze these components and how they worked together in the social production of Hollywood films during the Golden Age. The point is that products of culture are shaped by the contexts and structures through which they are produced.

Other Perspectives from the Middle Range

The production of culture perspective helps to turn our focus toward the social organizations and institutions through which art worlds are formed. Critics point out, however, that it fails to provide a sociological framework that examines other key dimensions of cultural production, including artists and artworks,

Table 3.1

Facet of Production	Research Question(s)	Examples
Technology	How did technological developments affect Hollywood films?	Development in sound technology transformed acting styles; spread of television led to decline of the film industry.
Law and Regulation	How have laws and regulations shaped the industry?	Threat of government censorship led to development of internal production code (Hays Code) in the 1930s. In 1948 the Supreme Court outlawed the ownership of theater chains by motion picture studios, leading to breakdown of studio system power.
Industry Structure	Through what kinds of structures and institutions were films produced and distributed?	Actors, directors, and other personnel were employees of several large commercial studios (the studio system), which dominated the industry and owned movie theater chains.
Organizational Structure	What organizational forms governed the studio system?	Production of films was highly regimented and followed a series of established formulas. Studio heads had great control and authority.
Occupational Careers	How were high status positions created and maintained within creative fields? What are the reward systems?	Studios, agents, and public relations personnel worked together to promote select actors to quasi-mythical status, creating the "star system."
Markets	What kind of groups consumed Hollywood films? How do industries and producers create demands for their cultural products and shape tastes?	The creation of the Oscars in 1929 helped to bolster the image of films with the American public and to expand audiences. Studios devoted resources to marketing and advertising their products, using new methods of consumer research. The Great Depression brought people to movie theaters in unprecedented numbers as they sought escapist entertainment; industry shaped genres to appeal to large female audiences.

the processes through which audiences and art world members create meaning from cultural objects, and the larger social and historical context in which art worlds and cultural objects are framed.

The contemporary American sociologist Wendy Griswold (2012) offers suggestions for addressing these themes along with the more traditional production of culture emphasis on institutional organization. Griswold urges us to study cultural production in terms of four points of a diamond: producers, cultural objects, recipients, and the larger social world. Each point on the diamond can be connected to any other point through the lines that form its perimeter or through lines that bisect its interior. This diamond, she explains, is a model for studying each dimension of a cultural world and the complex

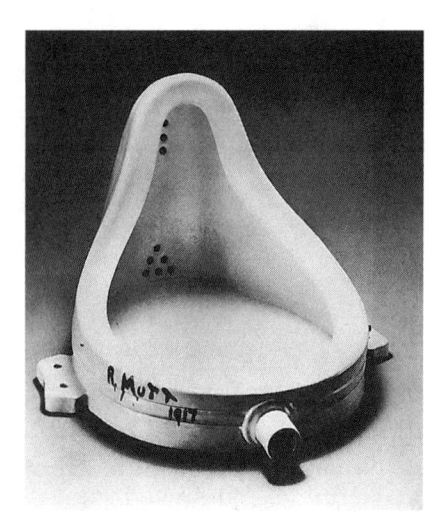

Photo 3.8 **Fountain, Marcel Duchamp, 1950.**

ways in which cultural objects, the people who create and consume them, and the larger economic, political, and social world in which these activities are taking place are linked. The diamond model retains the production of culture's emphasis on social processes as opposed to individual creativity. In addition, it focuses on how cultural objects shape and are shaped by the larger social world as well as the social processes through which both creators and audiences construct and communicate social meaning. Griswold's definition of "cultural object" sums up this relationship well: "A cultural object may be defined as shared significance embodied in form." In other words, "it is a socially meaningful expression that is audible, visible, or tangible or that can be articulated" (Griswold, 2012 [1986]: 11–12).

In 1946–1947, well before Griswold introduced her cultural diamond, the American anthropologist Hortense Powdermaker spent a year conducting fieldwork in Hollywood. I use her book, *Hollywood: the Dream Factory*, to chart the six facets of production in the table above. In her attempt to "understand and interpret Hollywood, its relationship to the dreams it manufactures, and to our society" (Powdermaker, 1950: 15), however, she pays close attention to the rise of consumer society, technology, and mass society. In addition, she conducts a careful study of the norms, taboos, rituals, habits, myths, practices, and social relationships of the producers of Hollywood movies (including the relationships of actors, writers, directors, and so forth), and how all of these left their imprint on Hollywood films. She analyzes how and why Hollywood and its values, norms, and fantasies resonate with American society and how audiences (recipients) use and understand these films in their daily lives. Prefiguring Griswold's model, she links the six facets of production to the larger background features of postwar society and to the films themselves.

Close-up Perspectives on Art and Society

Sociologists and anthropologists observe, describe, and analyze small-scale social interactions, using close-up lenses of investigation, as well. These approaches substitute or supplement microscopic explorations of small-scale interactions for the telescopic investigation of grand macro theory. They appealed to a new generation of sociologists in the 1960s and 1970s (see Calhoun, 2008) who investigated on a smaller scale how human interaction, the exchange of symbols, and self-reflection produce meaning and social worlds.

These approaches, which include symbolic interactionism **social constructionism** are sometimes grouped together as the **interpretive paradigm.** Using this type of lens, interpretive sociologists investigate the small-scale processes through which meaning is created, justified, reinforced, ruptured, and reshaped. Interpretive sociologists championed the use of **qualitative methods** and borrowed fieldwork techniques like **participant observation** and **ethnography,** which anthropologists like Powdermaker and urban sociologists had been using for decades. Instead of searching for correlations between variables based on large, representative samples, they focus on case studies and direct observation. They use fieldnotes, observations, and open-ended interviews and view themselves as interpreters of social life. They place special value on the interpretations or explanations that insiders (members of the group being studied) give for their own actions.

Ethnomethodology and the Breaching Experiment

Social reality operates smoothly, at least most of the time, according to interpretive sociologists, because people collectively attribute predictable meaning and value to symbols and social interactions. Because we attribute good will to a smile or a wave, we are able to use these gestures to greet friends and acquaintances in a mutually non-threatening manner. This collective attribution produces patterns that sociologists can identify and that people who share a culture learn to recognize and reproduce. As a tool for identifying these patterns, the American sociologist Harold Garfinkel (1917–2011) developed a fascinating spin on ethnography. Through descriptions and analysis, ethnographers explain how the culture's various components (e.g. myths, ritual, symbols, architecture, language) fit together in a way that makes sense to members of the culture.

Garfinkel's (1967) body of work follows from his insight that when we study our own culture, we can't see the forest for the trees. In other words, our own habits are so familiar and taken for granted that we are unable to identify the

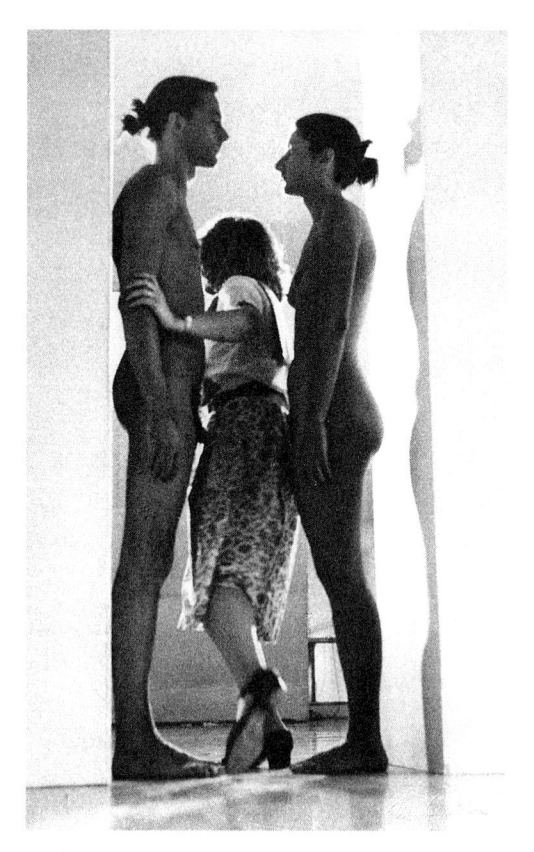

Photo 3.9 **Marina Abramović and Ulay Imponderabilia Performance 90 minutes Galleria Communale d'Arte Moderna, Bologna.** (© 2013 Marina Abramović. Courtesy of Sean Kelly Gallery/(ARS), New York)

social patterns, prejudices, and perceptual schemes that characterize our own culture and shape our interactions. One way, according to Garfinkel, that we can reveal the patterns and perceptions that allow us to coordinate our actions and interactions (and thus make obvious how strange and even distasteful these patterns might be to others from a different culture) is to disrupt or "breach" normal chains of events. Imagine, for example, honestly responding to the greeting, "How are you doing?" instead of politely answering, "Fine, and you?". By intentionally breaching the familiar, we are better able to identify the taken-for-granted assumptions of our own culture's social life.

Interpretive sociology's interests in the social construction of reality, the collective nature of social action, and the use of techniques to shake up our everyday social patterns have been shared by artists since at least 1917. In that year the French Surrealist artist Marcel Duchamp (1887–1968) entered a urinal, which he titled "The Fountain," at an art exhibition and signed it R. Mutt. With this intervention into "normal" art world processes, he forced his audience to think about their taken-for-granted assumptions concerning the distinction between industrial design (the urinal) and art, the lofty goals of art, and the importance of status and reputation in determining whether an actual "artist" has created a work.

In the 1920s, the **Russian formalist** literary critics Viktor Schlovski (1893–1984), Roman Jakobson (1896–1982), and others expressed the view that the main function of poetic language was to "defamiliarize" our everyday modes of perception. The German playwright Bertolt Brecht (1898–1956) employed a similar idea, which he called *Verfremdungseffekt*, or "distancing effect." He deliberately created stereotyped, unrealistic dialogue and staging to prevent the audience from becoming completely immersed in the characters of the story. Instead of helping the audience to "suspend disbelief," he wanted his audience to develop their capacity to be conscious and critical observers of society.

More recently, the performance artists Marina Abromović and her partner Ulay interrupt the normal flow of action in a number of significant ways. These two artists stood facing one another, naked, in the doorway of a gallery through which viewers had to pass to enter an exhibition. With their performance, they created a brilliant example of Garfinkel's "breaching experiment" for the art world. The reaction of visitors as they were obliged to negotiate the narrow passage between the two naked people illustrated the importance of social expectations regarding nudity, gender, genitalia, and art exhibitions.

Performance and the Social Production of Self

For interpretive sociologists, our behavior and identity take place in response to others in an ever-shifting social context, which we in turn help to shape. We do not blindly and unreflectively follow a single set of social routines and conventions. Indeed, we are all in a sense artists, forming our social world and our identities in conscious and creative ways within guidelines that are often fuzzy, fluid, and subject to change. We constantly interpret the actions of, negotiate with, and manage others through symbols that include gestures, language, and material objects.

Canadian-born sociologist Erving Goffman (1922–1982) uses the metaphor of theater (Goffman, 1959) to describe how with the help of others. People construct their identity and create and manage a sense of self. Using **dramaturgical analysis,** Goffman explains that the "front stage" is where, using all of the props, make-up, costumes, and scripts available to us, we perform our formal social roles of professor, student, waiter, lawyer, suitor, or mother. Through the various props available to us, we engage in "impression management" in an attempt to persuade our audience that we are, in fact, who we claim to be. Backstage is where we prepare for and decompress from our performances. Settings like the locker room, student lounge, or restaurant kitchen, where we are away from the gaze of our intended audience, provide a backstage.

Goffman emphasized the collaborative nature of our social performances (they are never solos). For a performance to be successful, everyone has to agree on the nature of the situation. Suppose your friend sees you as "one of the guys", and you define your evening as a romantic date with a potential partner. Both your friend's and your performances are likely to be unsuccessful. In most situations, social cooperation involves an implicit agreement to ignore or correct mishaps, mistakes, or inconsistencies. You might, for example, subtly help out an acquaintance who is introducing you to his friend but seems to have forgotten your name. Or you might try to ignore the spinach in your professor's teeth as she goes over your paper in her office. To call attention to these lapses would upset the fragile web of meanings and expectations that we have of others and ourselves.

Goffman's dramaturgical analysis can be used fruitfully by sociologists to study actual art worlds, especially since art world actors are especially cognizant of, and articulate about, the importance of meaning and meaning-makers (Rothenberg and Fine, 2008). At the same time, artists, especially recently, have played with the ideas of the social construction of the self and "impression management" that interest sociologists like Goffman. The photographer Cindy Sherman, for example, carefully chooses make-up, costumes, props, and facial expressions to create portraits of various social "types," using herself as a model. These photographs suggestively comment on how carefully we craft our impressions of ourselves even in everyday life.

Subcultures and Deviance

While a focus on patterned social behavior helps identify the processes through which people conform to social rules, norms, and expectations, sociologists like Howard Becker also investigate the processes through which individuals and types of activity are labeled as "deviant" (1963). Becker and others stress that social norms are created and enforced not because some behaviors are inherently more or less desirable than others (or deviant). Instead, it is through instituting social norms that those with more power can enforce their definitions of "normal" on those with less power. Furthermore, once people have been labeled deviant, their subsequent life history has less to do with whether or not they are violating or have violated social norms than it does with the label they have acquired (see Chambliss, 1973).

Understanding how deviance categories are socially constructed explains why, for example, parents in the 1960s, while sipping their evening martinis, could warn their teenagers that smoking pot would lead to a life of crime. Marijuana is not inherently more damaging to one's health than alcohol, but rather, the Federal Bureau of Narcotics, for reasons that had little to do with public health and safety, waged a moral crusade against marijuana use in the 1930s. They drew on public anti-immigrant sentiments and fear of youth culture by saturating the media with images of crazed Mexican immigrants on pot and stories of marijuana-induced rape and mayhem (Reefer Madness http://www.youtube.com/watch?v=Y-BvEEQDxDU). Alcohol consumption, on the other hand, was depicted as a social practice followed by respectable middle-class people.

Many artists' communities share characteristics of deviant subcultures. Becker illustrates this point in a participant observation study of the lives of Chicago dance musicians, whose members subscribed to norms and values (late hours, use of marijuana, for example) that mainstream society but also those who controlled the cultural field at the time labeled as deviant. The labeling process isolates member of the community from outside society and cements the identity of community members, who now seek to maintain that isolation through strategies of self-segregation (Becker, 1963). Later, as mainstream culture changed, the same movements and artists often lost their "deviant" label.

Networks and Scenes

Interpretive sociologists analyze the group interactions that give meaning to the social world. They study smaller groups to unpack the social exchange and collective interpretations of complex symbols that make for rich and detailed micro-sociological analysis. Their insights apply to artistic communities and groups of arts consumers, as well. For instance, Becker, in his study of marijuana users (1963), observed that novice users learned to interpret the physical effects of pot as desirable and pleasurable through their interaction with experienced users in their peer group. In a similar way, our friends often introduce us to musical forms, books, and art styles that we do not immediately understand or appreciate. Peer groups (people with whom we have strong ties and share relatively equal status) are especially important in shaping our cultural tastes, attitudes, behaviors, and the meanings that we attach to activities and objects. When our friends consume, discuss and appreciate Punk music, we are likely to learn to recognize the subtleties in the way that different punk musicians utilize, break with, or expand on the conventions of Punk. We will also learn the specialized vocabulary, references and judgment criteria that go along with Punk music and culture and these will bind us more closely to our peer group or social circle.

In this way, through peer group interactions, new cultural forms and ideas spread through the larger population. Sociologists have explored **social networks** (Kadushin, 2012), that is, the pathways and patterns through which people are connected to one another through some type of social relationship, and found that the types of networks in which people are embedded have important consequences. It is through networks that cultural knowledge and tastes form and are spread. Sociologists (and, not surprisingly, market researchers) have studied the impact of word-of-mouth communication on the success of fashions, films, and retail strategies, as well as on the spread of rumors, information, and gossip (e.g. Lin, 2001; Rosnow, 2001). Researchers also study the processes through which early users (pioneers) can influence the spread of fashion trends simply by appearing in public in their five-fingered shoes, demonstrating the features on their tablet to their curious friends, or trying out an unusual dish in a restaurant. Marketing firms, in fact, draw on research into social networks by employing "stealth-marketing" techniques, like hiring good-looking models to wear certain brands of shoes in public or to order a particular brand of vodka in a bar (see e.g. Kaikati and Kaikati, 2004). In a more specialized take on stealth marketing, author Jennifer Belle, dissatisfied with the efforts of her publicist, hired professional actresses with particularly engaging laughs to read her book *Seven Year Bitch* on subways and at New York City landmarks (Belle, 2010). The advent of social networking tools like Facebook, blogs, Internet communities, and product review Web sites have, of course, increased the density of social interaction and the speed with which cultural knowledge and objects and the ways of attending to and talking about those objects circulate through networks.

The contexts in which culture and the arts are created, popularized, and consumed through social interaction within social networks and peer groups are sometimes called **scenes**. Scenes are similar to subcultures, in which the participant's identity is closely tied to a shared, display, creation, practice, or consumption of a particular type of culture. Sociologists have talked about roller derby subculture (Beaver, 2012), sports subcultures (Wheaton, 2000), ethnic subcultures (Park, 1997), hip-hop subculture (McLeod, 1998), and so forth. Scenes include all of the characteristics of subcultures, such as clothing styles, specialized terminology, and rituals. They also place emphasis on the physical setting, or space, in which the exchange of knowledge, social networking and the characteristic modes of interaction take place. When we talk, for instance, about the birth of hip-hop in New York City, we imagine not only the characteristic fashion, dance styles, and music of the early hip-hop scene, but we also imagine the streets of the Bronx where the outdoor dance parties took place. When we think about the French art scene during the period of high modernism in the 1920s, we can visualize the cafés where artists and writers exchanged information and ideas and the small galleries where buyers met art dealers. For this reason, we ask about the spatial dimensions of social interaction in art worlds: "what role did the café have on the Parisian art culture of the late-19th century?" "How did the end of cheap rents in New York City affect the move of writers into the academy?" "Why do the premier film festivals occur in resorts like Cannes and Park City, Utah?"

Table 3.2

Type of Lens	Emphasis of Analysis	Type of Questions
Wide-angle, macroscopic	Broad-scale social change, historical patterns, identifying general characteristics of different types of societies, social structure and the relationships of different dimensions of the social structure.	Why did the arts emerge as a separate and distinct category of cultural production in Western society? What role did the arts play in the formation of the class structure of modern capitalist societies? How have the arts been affected by economic and technological developments in postmodern societies?
Mid-range	The development and structure of social institutions and organizations, and communities; conflict and consensus within and between organizations, institutions, and communities.	How did the development of the commercial gallery system in Paris influence the success of Impressionist painters? How and why did members of Boston's elite collaborate to take control of nonprofit arts institutions in the 19th century? How did the restructuring of the National Endowment for the Arts in the 1990s affect the fundraising strategies of small-scale arts institutions?
Close-up, microscopic	The social construction of meaning and identity, the social self, the "unwritten rules" that guide social interaction and social life, small-scale webs of interaction, everyday life.	How do audiences at poetry slams communicate their appreciation to poets? How do commercially successful artists construct their self-presentation to manage their reputations? Through what processes is "insider status" granted and conferred in the avant-garde dance world?

Structure and Agency

Smaller-scale, more empirically-based studies using a close-up lens help us make sense of why and how the arts change. Social structures are not simply blueprints that are imposed on human beings through socialization. People are not empty, static vessels into which their culture is poured during childhood. Instead, as British sociologist Anthony Giddens (1984) has explained, **social reproduction** reflects a complex feedback loop between social context and **social structure**, and the actions of conscious and reflective individuals. Culture and social structure only happen because of people's active engagement with one another and with their own cultural traditions. In modern societies, where we highly value change and innovation, traditions are often rapidly overturned. Even if we aren't consciously trying to do things differently from those before us, we inevitably make changes to tradition because of the collective and temporal nature of art worlds (Becker et al., 2006). Thus, a complex combination of what sociologists call **agency** (the ability or intention to push through one's own interests or agenda), **constraint** (social or material conditions that restrict or determine outcomes), negotiation, and **contingency** (accident) determine the outcome of any particular art-world situation. Studying topical cases using empirical data reveals how patterns of artistic invention and reception are reproduced and how they change. Medium-range lenses help us understand how institutions and organizations enable and constrain the type of cultural products that are produced, how they are circulated and how they are received by audiences. At the same time, the large-scale macro lenses discussed earlier provide us with powerful analytical tools for understanding why and how these patterns matter to society.

Discussion Questions

1. What, according to Marx, is the relationship between economic systems and culture? How might this relationship relate to the arts?
2. Can you provide some examples of ideology in contemporary culture?
3. Weber explained how rationalization affected modern society and the development of music. Discuss some examples of rationalization in contemporary society. What about in the arts?
4. How do Adorno's ideas about the special qualities of art echo Weber's claims about modern society's tendency toward increased autonomy, or specialization in different spheres of activity?
5. What is the social function of the arts, according to Parsons? What do you think are some of the social functions of the arts today? Provide specific examples.
6. What are the advantages and limitations of each level of analysis (macro-, mid-range, close-up)? Take a specific art world and jot down some questions you might want to ask about that world. Which lenses are most appropriate for each question?

4
SOCIAL CLASS AND THE ARTS

Photo 4.1 **Wife of a homesteader with her WPA (Work Projects Administration) music class. These children walk eight miles for their music lessons. Pie Town, New Mexico, Russell Lee, 1940.** (Library of Congress, Prints & Photographs Division)

While perusing the Library of Congress image collection archives, I came across this fascinating photograph, probably taken in the 1930s, with this title: "Wife of a homesteader with her WPA (Work Projects Administration) music class. These children walk eight miles for their music lessons. Pie Town, New Mexico." This was the only information available on the library site about the content of the photo or the circumstances surrounding its creation. As I examined the picture, however, I wondered about those children, whose bare feet and worn clothing testified to the modest economic circumstances of their families. It must have been very important to their parents that they learn music. After all, it can't be that easy to get a child to walk eight miles for a piano lesson. Also, the teacher was part of the Works Progress Administration (WPA), a federal program that employed out-of-work citizens during the Great Depression. It testifies to the value that society placed on arts education during that time. Many Americans must have believed that even the poorest children should have access to the arts.

Judging from a 2008 Nation Endowment for the Arts study, arts education and participation don't follow the same public ideal concerning equal access today. The percentage of children attending art classes whose families make over 150K a year (19.2 percent) is almost eight times that of children of families whose income is below 10K a year (2.5 percent) and roughly twice the percentage of children from families making 75–100k a year (10.9 percent). Roughly 21 percent of children whose parents were high school graduates had attended an arts performance outside of school, while 56 percent of children whose parents attended graduate school had done so (Iyengar et al., 2009).

The concept of **social class** helps us talk about social inequality in modern societies and to consider more carefully what this inequality has to do with the arts. **Social inequality** refers to the unequal distribution of social resources including wealth, power, status, health, education, leisure time, housing, and so forth within a society. The distribution of such resources, sociologists note, typically follows distinct and identifiable social patterns whereby members belonging to some social groups are systematically favored over members of others. Social class refers to the axis of inequality primarily concerned with the division of economic resources. Access to economic resources is tied to access to educational resources in complicated ways in modern societies, so it is difficult to study economic groupings without also studying their educational attainment.

Members of different economic classes have different shares of economic resources at their disposal. Access to economic resources has obvious consequences for how one consumes and creates art and culture. Groups with more resources can afford to purchase more concert tickets, collect more art, and pay for music and art lessons for their children. They can also provide their children with the kind of formal education through which they will learn to appreciate and talk about art and culture. In addition, economic group membership is linked to other aspects of artistic practice and consumption. To think about the relationship between social class and the arts, we first have to explore various ways of conceptualizing class and the relationship between class and culture more generally.

Marxist Theories of Class

Class as a Social Relationship

Karl Marx, with whom you are quite familiar by now, devoted much of his work to the study of social class. For him, social classes are social relationships organized around the production and distribution of material resources. Class membership, according to Marx, is determined by one's relationship to the means of production, which include tools, factories, land, technology and other non-human things that are necessary for creating goods and services (see Chapter Three). Marx divided members of capitalist societies into two main classes: the working class (proletariat) and the capitalist class (bourgeoisie). The working class does not own the tools and technology through which wealth and material goods are created. They may own their apartments, cars or even designer clothing but not the factories, land, or laboratories where they work and where the things they buy are produced. They do, however, own their own labor power (a necessary ingredient for creating wealth). In a cash economy, the working class has no choice but to sell its labor to the capitalist class in exchange for wages to survive.

Workers, according to Marx, are disadvantaged in capitalist society because they don't have control over what they make, the tools and technology with which it is made or the profit, or **surplus value**, created by their labor. Surplus value is the value of an item, or commodity, above and beyond what it costs to produce that commodity. What you pay for a cell phone is more than the cost of materials, labor, transportation, marketing and so forth that went into creating the phone. That extra goes to the owner, or capitalist, to reinvest in the company and to spend on a luxurious lifestyle. In this way, according to Marx, workers are **exploited** by a system in which they are not being paid the full value of their labor (Marx [1835], 1965). Because workers are exploited, and because they have little, if any, control over the labor process, they are **alienated** from their labor and from the goods that they produce (Marx, Karl. *Economic and Philosophical Manuscripts of 1844*. "Estranged Labor." 1844 available at: http://www.marxists.org/archive/marx/works/1844/manuscripts/labour.html) Though they have created these goods with their own labor power, they don't feel any sense of connection or real ownership to the things they have made, and they don't reap the rewards of the real value of these goods. Without the capitalist acting as a "middleman," according to Marx, workers would be able to distribute the wealth they create among themselves and for the good of society more generally.

This is still true today even though workers in developed countries like the United States can afford to purchase luxury items such as Nike sneakers and flat-screen televisions. The purchasing power of workers in richer countries comes at the expense of workers in countries where these goods are produced like China and Indonesia where workers are paid very little. Factory workers in China work long hours and produce millions of sneakers, but will never be able to own those sneakers themselves. Nonetheless, regardless of how many burgers you flip in an hour working at McDonald's, your full-time wages will never amount to a fraction of what the chain's shareholders and upper management will earn from your increased productivity. You might be able to purchase a pair of Nikes with your wages because the workers who produced them were paid so little compared to you, but you won't be able to buy a large house in an exclusive neighborhood, a private jet, or a painting by Andy Warhol no matter how hard you work at McDonalds, the Gap, or even in one of the few remaining factories in the United States.

In Marx's day, the prototypical proletarian was a manual worker or factory hand. Today, 63 percent of Americans in the labor force make up what economist Michael Zweig calls the "working-class majority." Almost 70 percent of them work outside of typical blue-collar occupations in sales, the service economy, or office and administrative support (Zweig 2000: 30). Between workers and capitalists Marx identified a middle-class of small-business owners, skilled workers, and intellectuals (scholars, artists, lawyers and other professionals) who served the bourgeoisie (Marx, Karl and Friederich Engels. *The Communist Manifesto*. Chapter 1, "Bourgeois and Proletarians." 1848. available at: http://www.marxists.org/archive/marx/works/1848/communist-manifesto/ch01.htm). These groups, he thought, would eventually be absorbed into either the bourgeoisie or the proletariat. On the other side, the capitalist class today consists of CEOs and major shareholders of industry and property.

What is the class position of artists in contemporary society? Are painters, sculptors and musicians members of the proletariat? How much control do they have over the production of their art? Are the prices they earn for their work a true measure of their talent? Under what conditions are they likely to maintain control over their products? Do artists share with workers a sense of exploitation when they can't keep the profits generated by their labor (or their ideas)? To what extent are artists alienated from their work once it becomes a commodity and takes on a monetary value? And, are music and film studios, cameras, editing programs and so forth part of the means of production? How do works of art differ from other kinds of material resources? These are questions that scholars working in the Marxist tradition have asked about the arts.

Class-Consciousness

In modern, Western societies that stress individual rights and achievements, many people see few direct connections between their life chances and those of others who occupy a similar social position. Marx, on the other hand, emphasized two aspects of class membership: its *collective* and *antagonistic* nature. For Marx, people who share a relationship to the means of production (i.e. workers or owners) also have a shared interest in how society should be organized.

Classes are also in conflict with each other. According to Marx, the bourgeoisie, or owner-class became conscious of their shared class position when they opposed the aristocracy in the 18th and early-19th centuries (see Chapter Two) and sought to gain greater political power. As we saw in Chapter Two, this consciousness found cultural expression in the arts of the day, and was fostered through arts participation, debate and discussion. Ideally, Marx thought, like the bourgeoisie of the 18th and 19th centuries, workers would become conscious of their shared interest in wresting power from the bourgeoisie and would unite as a group to take over the means of production.

The idea of **class-consciousness** has generated much discussion since Marx's time. One of the founding fathers of cultural studies, British Marxist historian E. P. Thompson (1924–1993), stressed the importance of popular culture and arts in the formation of a conscious and shared identity for the new industrial working class of England in the early-19th century (Thompson, 1963). Thompson and others argued that the rich community life and popular song of the working classes in England represented a site of resistance to the social fragmentation caused by the Industrial Revolution.

> I belong to Glasgow,
> Dear old Glasgow town;
> But what's the matter wi' Glasgow,
> For it's goin' roun' and roun'!
> I'm only a common old working chap,
> As anyone here can see,
> But when I get a couple o' drinks on a Saturday,
> Glasgow belongs to me!
>
> Written by Will Fyff, Scottish Music Hall entertainer, 1920

Whether working-class culture continues to offer an expression of social solidarity is debated by scholars and critics. In the post-World War II era, critics have noted that an individualist and passive culture of consumption, which Adorno and others associated with mass culture, began to dominate working-class life (see Storey, 2003: 65) (see Chapter Two). Other Marxist scholars have noted that urban-based art forms rooted in the culture of the industrial worker represent collective responses to a world fashioned by social conflict. The historian George Lipsitz, for example, argued that rock and roll grew from the intersection of country music and rhythm and blues. When Whites and Blacks started working together in munitions factories in northern cities during World War II, they combined their musical traditions to form a new kind of music, which reflected their shared working-class culture and experience (Lipsitz, 1994).

Photo 4.2 **Metro Pictures, Cindy Sherman.** (Permission granted from Sean Kelly)

From a Marxist perspective, a common class position and interests generate a shared understanding and experience of the world, which is expressed in artistic forms and practices. These forms and practices serve to produce and reproduce class-consciousness in their participants. To understand the influence class consciousness has on art worlds we need to know something about the class position of its participants and about the degree to which participants are consciously acting on a sense of class membership when they engage in cultural activities.

Some Problems with Thinking about "Class-Consciousness"

The idea of class-consciousness is problematic, especially in the context of American society. Americans have long been reluctant to identify class as a constraining force or a strong component of self-identity (Zweig, 2000). In other words, we are much more likely to attribute an individual's success or failure to personal characteristics like intelligence, laziness or attitude than we are to consider how an individual's life chances were enabled or constrained by their position on the class ladder. And, despite rising levels of inequality in the United States and other post-industrial, capitalist societies, recent surveys indicate that 90 percent of Americans say that they are "middle class" (Kingston, 2000; Devine, 2008; Moskowitz in Cahill and Johannssen 2007:13).

Class-consciousness suggests a linkage between class identity and cultural expression and taste. In line with their individualistic, middle-class orientation, Americans are inclined to view their cultural tastes as a matter of personal choice rather than as badges of class allegiance. In Europe, and elsewhere, a long history of **caste-based stratification systems** normalized social divisions with regard to culture and status displays. In such societies, sumptuary laws

Photo 4.3 **Street musicians in Harlem, Roger Smith, 1943.** (Library of Congress, Prints & Photographs Division)

regulated consumption and displays of luxury by social status. Louis XIII of France, for example, issued edicts that prohibited anyone but the nobility from wearing clothing with gold embroidery (Köhler and Sichart 1963: 289). Note that in the portrait of King Louis XIII below, he proudly displays his gold-studded suit of armor, lace collar, white kid gloves, and silk sash. These accessories denote his high status, and it was forbidden for commoners to sport similar styles, even if they could afford to purchase them.

Photo 4.4 **King Louis XIII of France and Navarre 1601–43, Egmont, Justus Van (1601–74).** (Alfredo Dagli Orti/The Art Archive at Art Resource, NY)

Photo 4.5 **The streets of New York—running the gauntlet of horrors, 1879.** (Library of Congress, Prints & Photographs Division)

Photo 4.6 **There is one class which feels competent to appraise social position; these are head waiters, George Hand Wright, 1919.** (Library of Congress, Prints & Photographs Division)

Conspicuous consumption and status-displays also played a large part in erecting and maintaining class boundaries in the United States (see Lamont and Fournier, 1992; Veblen [1899] 2005), but those boundaries were the result of the accumulation of wealth and not frozen into law or tradition.

On the other hand, the ideals (and to a certain extent the reality) of class mobility and equality of opportunity in the United States (see Lipset, 2001; de Tocqueville and Goldhammer [1840] 2003; Erickson and Goldthorpe, 1985) have worked against the claim that there is a direct and visible link between class and culture. If a poor farmer could become a wealthy industrialist, or if the son of a working-class single mother can become president and maintain his down-home tastes for BBQ and beer, how important could high culture pretensions really be? In the United States, we learn that an individual's class position is achieved through hard work, entrepreneurial savvy, and luck. And, the outward markers of class status can be displayed by anyone with enough money to purchase expensive cars, designer clothes, blue-chip paintings, or ski camp for their children. And, knock-off imitations of some of these items can be purchased by people who don't have much money. Furthermore, without the insurance of inherited titles and honors, these cultural symbols of status can be easily lost with fluctuations in the economy.

The post-war expansion of the middle-class played an important role in weakening other kinds of class identification. In the 1950s in the United States, levels of inequality went down and opportunities for class mobility increased (Shammas, 1993). After World War II, wartime production and new industrial and management technologies brought unprecedented economic growth, home-ownership and material plenty to increasingly large sectors of the

Photo 4.7 **Dance Scene at the Palladium, 1980.**

American populace, including members of the working class with strong labor union representation, like industrial workers, members of the skilled trades, and longshoremen (Harvey, 1989). As income inequality decreased and previous sources of working-class solidarity and identity lessened, working-class Americans increasingly identified with the middle and upper classes. And, with increased funding for education and scientific research and a more complex organization of industry, the proportion of Americans who could legitimately claim middle- and upper-middle-class status swelled (Mills [1951] 2002).

The growing culture of consumption also helped to level class differences and democratize culture. Developments in marketing and advertising technologies (Ewen [1972] 2008)) and commercial television (Barnow, 1990) and radio (Sterling and Kitross, 2001), combined with increased prosperity and a population hungry for new consumer goods after war-time rationing helped to foster this new culture. In a highly standardized consumer culture an ethnically and economically diverse populace could find common ground (Ewen, 2008). By the 1960s, advertising, television, the music industry, and other forms of mass entertainment and communications began to compete with manufacturing as economic pillars of U.S. capitalism, and American popular culture began to dominate the globe (Glynn, 2006). The explosion of youth demographics and culture, epitomized by the birth and rapid commercialization of rock and roll, brought an even greater social relevance to popular culture, which was consumed across class boundaries (Lipsetz, 1990).

Even the world of cutting edge high art was permeated by the consumer culture of the 1960s. With the growing popularity of **Pop artists** like Andy Warhol, gallery openings evolved into parties, where media celebrities mingled with artists,

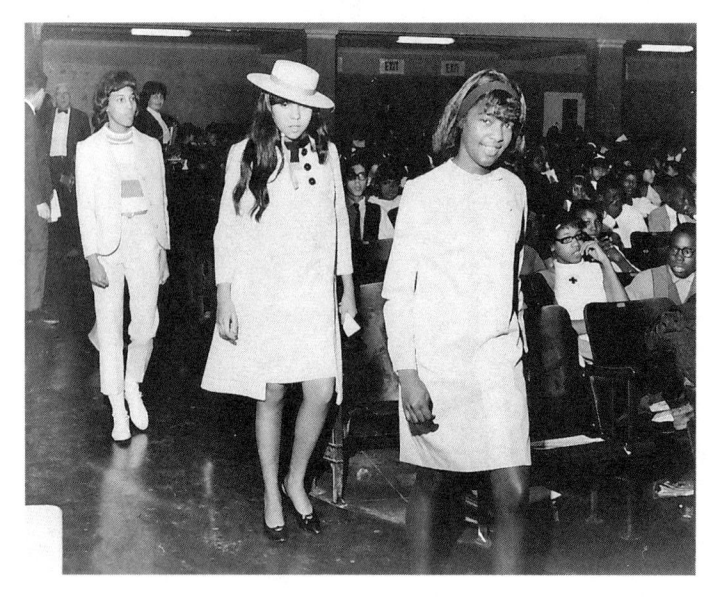

Photo 4.8 **Three African American teenage girls modeling clothing for the "Teen-age Consumer a Go-Go" promotion at J.H.S. 164, New York, New York, 1967.** (Library of Congress, Prints & Photographs Division)

hangers-on and smartly dressed middle-class or nouveau riche collectors like Robert and Ethel Scull (Wolf 1968). These gallery-goers' clothing matched the art on the wall, which included Warhol's silk-screened series of celebrity icons (notably Marilyn Monroe, James Dean, and Elvis Presley) and his commissioned "Society Portraits" in which some of the attending public literally viewed images of themselves.

The populist style and content of these works helped integrate the growing class of newly moneyed professionals by providing an entrée into the world of art and culture traditionally reserved for more established elites (Jones, 1998, also see Crane, 1989). They also helped to blur the distinctions between elite and mass styles of cultural consumption.

Influential sociologists Peterson and Simkus (1996) and Gans (1999) argue that in today's consumer culture, class-consciousness, at least as Marxists use this term, plays little role in shaping people's cultural identity and artistic tastes and dispositions. Because of rapid fluctuation in the type of work skills needed by the labor market, geographical mobility, and the development of consumer products oriented toward a diversity of lifestyles, people are constantly in the process of self-creation, and coalitions between different groups are formed and reformed in different situations (Beck, 1992: 100). Society is characterized by both affluence and precariousness and any kind of collective culture has little enduring meaning or permanence.

Although researchers continue to find objective correlations between class position and arts consumption and participation (see e.g. entries in Torper and Ivey, 2008), there is less empirical evidence on which to establish a clear

Photo 4.9 **Party at The Sculls, Fred W. McDarrah, 1975.** (Fred W. McDarrah/Premium Archive/Getty Images)

relationship between people's self-understanding of a shared class position and the arts. For example, when researchers delve into the question of class-consciousness through in-depth interviews and ethnographies, they often find that respondents provide complex and contradictory accounts regarding their understanding of their own class position and the relationship between their cultural practices and class position. In a fascinating study, sociologist David Halle (1996) used ethnographic methods to gain a close-up perspective on how people from different social classes use art to decorate their homes. He interviewed people in four different neighborhoods in the New York City area—ranging from upper class to working class—in their homes. He found that people in all neighborhoods favored images of calm landscapes because they helped people relax. Each household displayed family photos, but only elites favored abstract art. Halle also found that household decoration varied by race, religion, political affiliation and ethnicity. Catholics were more likely to display religious iconography, while African Americans were more likely to decorate their homes with African masks and statues than Whites, and Whites who collect tribal arts are more likely to be left-of-center politically (Halle, 1996: 201). These accounts suggest that some degree of class-consciousness is at play in people's everyday understanding of their cultural practices.

Class and Status

Weber on Class and Status

Max Weber's (see Chapter Three) ideas about class have been more influential in the United States than those of Marx. Marx viewed class—defined in terms of property relations—as the most significant dimension of inequality and social identity. For Marx, all other aspects of society, including identity, action and culture, were tied to the underlying class structure of society. Weber viewed social inequality in terms of power, access to which is determined by ones' ranking on three different axes: market position, status group, and political affiliation. The axis that most closely resembles Marx's concept of class is **market position**. Instead of emphasizing people's position in relation to the means of production, for Weber people occupied the same class rung if they had similar positions in relation to the market (Weber, [1946] 1973: 181–186). For example, a highly paid factory worker may share a market position with a small business owner and thus may have a shared economic interest in, for example, lowering taxes on the middle-class ([1946] 1973: 186). Weber did not, however, think that market position was the most important basis for understanding cultural identity, social action, or power. For Weber, members of the same class (or market position) did not necessarily share a collective identity or strong sense of group affiliation. In fact, little more than shared life chances and economic interests linked them. What really linked people together and shaped group identity, community and action was a rung on a different ladder: the ladder on which status, or honor rankings, is organized.

These status groups *could* intersect with property relations (CEOs of major occupations also form a shared status group, as might construction workers, or small business owners) but status groups could also form around ethnicity, caste, gender, academic prestige, professional fields, or Hollywood celebrity. University professors, for example, might form a relatively powerful and privileged status group based on the shared honor conferred by degrees and titles, although most don't own means of production and only a few are wealthy. This group membership ends up being important in terms of shared lifestyle and cultural preferences. As we saw at the beginning of this chapter, graduate degrees are strong predictors of arts participation. The children of university professors may attend music academies and theater events at a rate similar to the children of corporate lawyers and Wall Street executives, even though university professors don't have nearly the same market position as these folks. Other groups share a status affiliation based on ethnicity, religion and other ranked categories, but they also don't necessarily share a market position. In the United States, Jews, African Americans, Asians, and WASPS (white, Anglo-Saxon Protestants) may consider their ethnic or religious affiliations to be much more central to their identity, political views, and cultural tastes than their market position.

Status groups and classes overlap but they are not the same, and the importance of each type of group membership varies in different times and places. In addition, status groups are infinitely divisible and amorphously defined. Marx's theory of class suggests that aesthetic taste and the social position and prestige of various kinds of art must be understood in terms of the socioeconomic relations that structure society. Weber's theory, in contrast, suggests that artistic production and consumption plays a role in a complex hierarchy of status identity, which is often in a state of flux as members jockey to improve their position through outward signs of group affiliation.

In addition, people use art and culture to signal their class *aspirations*. A service worker who earns 10 dollars an hour might, for example, scrimp on other things in order to purchase a Coach bag. Carrying such a bag symbolizes an affiliation with the class and status groups she desires to occupy rather than her actual market position. Members of the middle-class might in the same way save up to buy opera tickets, or pay for music lessons for their children, since this kind of high-cultural display allies them symbolically with members of a higher class. Sociologist Wei-Ting Lu's work on Western, classical music schools in the Chinese and Taiwanese immigrant communities of New York City illustrates how outsiders (in this case ethnic minorities) use the fine arts to assimilate to the dominant culture and increase access to valuable educational opportunities (Lu, forth coming).

Photo 4.10 **Arab American Museum in Dearborn, Michigan.** (Bruce Harkness/Courtesy Arab American National Museum)

Alternatively, status groups also form around ethnic affiliation. In this case, cultural displays help immigrant groups to maintain and express their ethnic identity in the face of pressures to assimilate to a new society. As Amaney Jamal (in DiMaggio and Fernandez-Kelly ed. 2010) has shown, the Arab American community in Michigan shows a high degree of arts participation and activity, both in terms of traditional forms of Arab arts and incorporating Arab politics, culture and identity into Western art forms. For these arts producers and consumers, participation in arts festivals and support of community based artists and institutions are part of a shared expression of ethnic solidarity and cohesion in the face of negative stereotypes.

Weber's Influence in Theories of Class and Culture

Weber's theory of power and privilege offers a less elegant explanation for the relationship between class and culture than does Marx's, but it is more directly applicable to contemporary, complex societies like our own, in which race, ethnicity, professional memberships, and education are just as important in determining an individual's access to power as her relationship to the means of production. In addition, in modern societies, there is a considerable amount of class mobility—that is—people are likely to move up or down on the class ladder in their lifetime, and their children and grandchildren are even more likely to occupy a different position on the ladder. For this reason, among others, individuals or even groups may well have come to occupy a relatively high class position, but lack higher status group affiliations.

Most American sociologists have adopted some version of Weber's approach to describe a multi-runged class ladder as opposed to Marx's relational one, using models based on a combination of wealth, income and education to describe the class structure of contemporary capitalist society. Working from this type of model, sociologists can then design empirical studies to investigate the relationship between class status, cultural consumption, arts participation, political views and a host of other variables.

Pierre Bourdieu: Linking Marx and Weber

Cultural Capital and the Reproduction of Class

The French sociologist Pierre Bourdieu combined Marx's insights into the relationship between social class, power, and domination with Weber's emphasis on the importance of status and culture in understanding the structure of inequality. He was especially interested in the mechanisms through which class positions were transferred from one generation to the next. We know that if our parents are rich, we will likely inherent wealth, while if they are poor, we will likely have to spend our own resources caring for them in their old age. Bourdieu was interested in explaining the role played by socialization and culture in the transfer of class position from one generation to the next. In his book *Distinction: a Social Critique of the Judgment of Taste* (1984) he explains how and why artistic tastes correlate so highly with social class and what this correlation has to do with social power and the reproduction of class structure. His insights into relationship between cultural tastes and the reproduction of class status from one generation to the next provide an important explanation for why culture and the arts matter so much if we want to study the reproduction of inequality.

Bourdieu developed an analysis of **cultural capital**. Cultural capital refers to valuable cultural knowledge, sensitivities, and resources. Examples include the ability to distinguish one variety of red wine from another, to know and explain how Mozart differed from other composers from his time, to identify the work of a particular Manga cartoonist, or to speak a second language. This knowledge differs in a number of obvious ways from economic capital, or financial investments. It is difficult to quantify cultural capital. Cultural capital is less able to predictably yield rewards like more money, power, or status. It is symbolic rather than material. Cultural capital *can*, in the long run, however, be converted into economic capital by granting its possessor access to the social circles inhabited by elites (Bourdieu, 2008). With inclusion in these circles comes greater access to opportunities to enhance status, money, etc. Here is an example of how this works: you are having an important job interview for a management position in a major bank, and your potential employer asks you to choose the wine at lunch. By making the right choice, and demonstrating to her that you have experience evaluating and choosing fine wines, you assure her that you share her values, education and cultural knowledge. You have demonstrated *symbolically* (you didn't need to spend any money to do this—in fact, the potential employer paid for the lunch) that you are suited for membership in the exclusive circle of financial elite. If you can make small talk by chatting about all the new art galleries you discovered on your latest trip to Berlin, you will gain extra points for your worldly sophistication. For this reason, groups that seek upward mobility will often invest precious resources in providing their children access to certain kinds of cultural knowledge and milieu (music lessons, travel, private school, etc.) so that they can have a better shot at upper-class membership when they grow up. My mother's parents, for instance, were poor, uneducated immigrants from central Europe. They would, however, save their pennies to provide my mother with piano lessons and cashmere sweaters in the hopes that these symbols of cultivation and taste would help her to move up the class ladder in the United States.

Some groups have fewer possibilities for becoming fluent in the forms of culture that upper-class people use to distinguish themselves and identify each other. For example poor, urban African Americans who have little access to European vacations, violin lessons and expensive wine are automatically

Photo 4.11 **Pretty Woman, Buena Vista Pictures, 1990.** (Buena Vista Pictures/Photofest)

excluded from competing for upper-class positions because they don't possess the cultural capital that they need to prove their membership in elite circles. They do possess other forms of cultural capital, knowledge and tastes that matter in their communities, but these won't necessarily be "transferable" to economically profitable job or marriage opportunities. In the blockbuster film *Pretty Woman*, starring Richard Gere and Julia Roberts, a wealthy businessman played by Gere falls in love with a prostitute played by Roberts. To take her out in his social circle he has to buy her more elegant clothing to replace her immodest "hooker" outfit and instruct her in dinner table etiquette. The sociological point of the movie is that while cultural capital may not guarantee access to elite circles, it is a requirement for success in them.

Habitus and Aesthetic Disposition

Bourdieu is not trying to say that the cultural tastes of the dominant class are superior to those of the less powerful, or "dominated" classes. They serve as a mechanism for establishing boundaries between classes, though. They are effective mechanisms for doing this because acquiring an upper-class **habitus,** or "**disposition**"—which he defines as the "matrix of perceptions, appreciations and actions" (Bourdieu, 1977:82–83) that allow individuals to feel at ease with elite culture, and to demonstrate this ease" requires a complex system of socialization. This socialization is accomplished in part through the educational system. In elite schools, students are trained to be familiar with high culture and to be self-directed, creative problem solvers—qualities they will use in their adult social and work lives, while curricula geared toward working-class kids emphasizes rule-following, practical skills, discipline and rote learning. As the sociologist Paul Willis (1977) suggested in his classic work on class and education, such schools teach working-class kids to get working-class jobs (also see Bowles and Gintis, 2002). According to Bourdieu, however, the most important part of cultural education takes place in the home. Wealthy families train their children on an ongoing and informal basis to appreciate and to feel comfortable with the forms of culture that signify elite status and to develop complex verbal skills and to feel entitled to assume a position of authority (Lareau, 2011). It is possible to learn these things later on, and many people do, but like learning a second language as an adult, mastering the subtleties of expression, accent and confidence of a native speaker will always be allusive. When Eliza Doolittle—the working-class flower seller in George Bernard Shaw's classic play *Pygmalion* from which *Pretty Woman* borrowed its main theme—lost her temper, she abandoned the refined, upper-class English in which Henry Higgins had patiently tutored her, and fell into the cockney dialect with which she could more easily express her emotions. In doing so, she revealed her working-class origins and the weakness of her claim to membership in "polite" society. To master the cultural codes of the elite, one needs more than a crash course.

The habitus of the dominant class, according to Bourdieu, consists in a way of consuming and evaluating culture that he calls the **aesthetic disposition**. This disposition is closely related to ideas introduced by Immanuel Kant (see Chapter Two) at the end of the 18th century. If you remember, Kant opposed "pure" aesthetic judgments, based solely on a disinterested, impartial, yet highly attuned awareness of the unique properties of aesthetic experience to judgments based on desire, greed, or sensuous titillation. According to Bourdieu (1984), the

Photo 4.12 **Finnish construction workers from New York, drinking beer and spending their leisure time in a new cafe near Camp Blanding. They were unable to work because of the heavy rains. Starke, Florida, Marion Post Wolcott, 1940.** (Library of Congress, Prints & Photographs Division)

Photo 4.13 (Shutterstock)

adoption of Kant's definition of a "pure" aesthetic disposition allows the dominant class to claim a sort of "natural superiority" because they are able to put aside vulgar, material desires and to appreciate cultural objects, for example abstract paintings, which are created according to complex sign systems that have little meaning to those who have not been trained (through family and school) to understand them. The dominated classes, Bourdieu argues, without training in these sign systems or in the habits of "aesthetic distance" will prefer culture that has a more obvious "function"—music that can be sung along with or danced to, broad comedy that provokes the public pleasure of laughing together with others, sexually arousing images, or drama that has a clear moral message. The appreciation of "pure" art, on the other hand, requires specialized training because this art is not moored in any kind of knowledge or experience outside of art. As such, aesthetic disposition is the "distinctive expression of a privileged position in social space" (Bourdieu, 1984:56). It is the product of the conditioning of particular class and unites them while distinguishing from members of less privileged classes.

Bourdieu makes another point about habitus and economic power, revealing an important link between cultural and economic capital. "Economic power," he explains "is first and foremost a power to keep economic necessity at arm's length (Bourdieu, 1984: 55)." In order to develop the "aesthetic disposition" one must be able to "neutralize ordinary urgencies and to bracket off practical ends" (Bourdieu, 1984: 54). Again, the example of wine connoisseurship is useful here: people who are hungry or thirsty consume beverages that will satisfy their thirst and supply some immediate energy and appealing flavor. Many people come home from a day of stressful hard work and drink alcoholic beverages in order to relax and forget their troubles. Beer, wine, and spirits are often served at social gatherings because of the notoriously disinhibiting effects of alcohol. The wine connoisseur, on the other hand, not only pays a hefty entrance fee to a wine tasting, but also upwards of $100 for a bottle of fine wine that will probably be consumed in one sitting. These are economic investments. Once at the wine tasting event, true connoisseurs do not even swallow the wine: They take small, careful sips, rolling the liquid around on their tongues, and then spit it out! By doing this, they can focus on the complex flavors of each wine without becoming full or drunk. They can then discuss and describe these flavors using a specialized vocabulary that they have acquired through reading books, taking courses, and listening to friends, family, and colleagues. In this way, wine becomes anything but a means toward the satisfaction of a directly material need. The appreciation of wine serves as a symbolic demonstration of the degree to which the connoisseur is free from the hunger, thirst, and the daily grind that shape the tastes of ordinary folks. Wine, like high art, has become the object of an aesthetic disposition freed from material needs.

Criticisms of Bourdieu

As elsewhere, high culture and class status have been tied together in the United-States. In the early-20th century, White, Anglo-Saxon elites banded together to create a distinction between popular and high culture through which they could demarcate themselves from working-class Catholics. They gained control of the arts by establishing a new form of cultural control through "non-profit" organizations (DiMaggio, 1982). Even today, the board of directors of operas, museums, theater and other high-culture institutions are composed of members of the economic elite, and members of the upper class organize and attend fundraisers, gala openings, and other high-arts related events as a regular part of their social life and self-identity (Ostrower, 1997, Ostrower 2004) and thus, they continue to have control over high culture, at least in the United States. In her study of philanthropy, Francine Ostrower interviewed 76 board members of major cultural institutions. Virtually every trustee she interviewed was a millionaire and the percentage of millionaires on individual boards ranged from 94–100 percent, and most of these were multi-millionaires (2004: 3). Her research also revealed that elites are attracted to boards for class related reasons of prestige (1997).

Nonetheless, Bourdieu's work on class and culture has drawn criticism on a number of counts. The most glaring problem is that his conclusions are drawn from survey data gathered in France in the early 1960s. France's long history of rigid social hierarchies and the relationship between status and the mastery of the codes of high culture cannot be generalized to the United States or even to contemporary French society (Lamont, 1992; Lamont and Lareau, 1988; Halle, 1993; Erickson, 1996), where possession of cultural capital is no longer as important for achieving power and economic success. Indeed, the structure of social stratification has changed everywhere since Bourdieu's writing. Museums and other fine arts institutions and events have sought out (and achieved) a broader audience through blockbuster exhibitions, family events, and the like. **Middle-brow** culture—like the wildly popular Broadway musical production based on Victor Hugo's great 19th-century novel, *Les Misérables*—provides mass audiences with access to works of art that might otherwise have been reserved for the highly educated elite. While Bourdieu's critics have some fair points, his analysis of the relationship between taste, education, and power continues to help us make sense of the role that the transmission of elite culture plays in maintaining and reproducing class distinctions.

Conclusion: The Declining Significance of Class?

> We are proud of those facts of American life that fit the pattern we are taught but somehow we are often ashamed of those equally important social facts which demonstrate the presence of social class. Consequently, we tend to deny them, or worse, denounce them and by doing so we tend to deny their existence and magically make them disappear from consciousness.
>
> W. Lloyd Warner, (1960) *What Social Class Is In America*

Much of the research that we have considered suggests that arts preferences, participation and value are not neatly linked to class position today. Mass consumption, the rising status of popular culture, the declining importance of high culture for establishing class boundaries all help to weaken hard and fast linkages between class and cultural preferences. So does class still matter for sociologists of art and culture? The evidence and theories that connect class position to the arts and to culture more generally reveal a complicated picture of this connection. However, I believe that class and the arts are still undeniably linked.

Although critics are correct in pointing out that a mastery of "high culture" does not play the same role in establishing and maintaining class position that it once did, other studies reveal that particular cultural dispositions, learned in the family and through the educational system, still help to reproduce the class structure of contemporary societies (Lareau, 2011; Lareau and Weininger, 2003). As these researchers show, participation in "high culture" requires education and leisure and usually money and thus the category itself serves as a segregating, boundary-creating device. This does not imply, of course, that groups of people with less access to these resources do not create and consume cultural products. The very process of categorization that Bourdieu described, however, still ensures that aesthetic forms produced by and for working-class and lower-middle-class people are classified as popular or folk, or sub-culture (or, later, if they are appropriated by culture industries, mass-culture). While "fine" artists freely appropriate themes and forms from popular culture, and popular culture likewise borrows from fine arts, the worlds in which cultural objects are evaluated and accrue value are still controlled by economic elites (Skeggs, 1997). Andy Warhol, for example, used images of everyday consumer items like Campbell's soup cans and well-known popular culture icons like Marilyn Monroe and Mick Jagger in his work. He achieved his fame and financial success, however, by appealing to wealthy collectors and powerful curators and critics (Koestenbaum, 2001). His work may resonate with a larger public, but only members of the highest socioeconomic strata can afford the 63 Million dollars that it cost to purchase his 1962 "Men in Her Life", a silk-screen painting honoring Liz Taylor that was sold at auction in 2010 (Cohen, 2011).

Levels of economic inequality have been on the rise in the United States and elsewhere over the past decades (Seaz, 2013) and the gap between the quality of health care (Barr, 2008, also see NYT Class Matters), housing, education, income, job opportunities, and other social resources that are available to the wealthiest groups and those available to middle- and working-class people continues to grow. The austerity measures and tax cuts for the wealthy that have accompanied economic restructuring in post-industrial societies have led to a loss of government funding for the educational and cultural programs through which culture might reach members of classes who occupy the bottom rungs of the socioeconomic ladder (http://www.nea.gov/research/ResearchReports_chrono.html).

Familiarity with high culture as it has been traditionally conceived may not be a crucial passport for entry into the privileged class. But without access to cultural resources like musical instrument lessons, exhibition spaces and art supplies, people with few economic resources are denied important opportunities for self-expression and community. Without resources to produce and promote autonomous artistic expression, lower-class people are more dependent on commercially produced and distributed forms of culture. Thus, as material disparities between classes continue to grow, we might expect to see an even stronger correlation between class, as measured by socioeconomic status, and artistic consumption and production (Iyengar et al., 2009).

Discussion Questions

1. How do Marx and Weber's view of social class differ? Which one do you think is most helpful in understanding the relationships between social class and the arts?
2. How has your class position impacted your participation in the arts (think about consumption and production)? What other kinds of group memberships explain your own arts participation?
3. What role has education played in your arts participation? Do any of Bourdieu's ideas explain the relationship between the socialization you received in your family, your experiences with education, and your arts participation?
4. What sorts of questions might you ask someone if you were interested in how their range of cultural practices intersects with their social class?

5
GENDER AND THE ARTS

Photo 5.1 **Pas de Quatre, Les Ballets Trockadero de Monte Carlo.** (Courtesy of Les Ballets Trockadero de Monte Carlo)

Les Ballets Trockadero de Monte Carlo has been entertaining audiences around the world with their productions of classical ballets like *Swan Lake*, *Les Sylphides*, and the *Nutcracker* since the 1970s. Like other internationally acclaimed ballet troupes, Les Trocks (as fans refer to them) bring these aging masterpieces to life with their acrobatic dance moves, frothy costumes, and expert choreography.

Les Trocks, however, is markedly different from other ballet troupes in one important respect: all of the dancers are male. By casting male dancers, body hair, big muscles, and all in roles and costumes (including tutus and toe shoes) that we typically associate with delicate female bodies, they turn serious traditional ballet—a dance form that relies on highly stereotyped ideas of masculinity and femininity—into broad comedy. At the same time, their performances reveal the highly scripted nature of all gender performance.

Gender, like class, plays a key role in structuring social life. Even in a relatively gender-equal society like our own, by almost every measure (wealth, political power, division of labor in the family, control over cultural resources and industries, victimization by sexual violence) women remain disadvantaged. Like class, gender classifications are not stable or transhistorical. Gender categories, and the kinds of meanings people attach to them, fluctuate over time and place and respond to larger historical and social events. Gender is different from class, however, in several regards. One difference is that gender is achieved under much more restricted conditions than class. In class societies, class positions are partly inherited (being born into a wealthy, poor, or working-class family will provide you with a set of advantages, orientations, disadvantages and so on—see Chapter Five). But class position is also achieved through luck (or lack thereof), individual characteristics, and historical and political circumstances. As I discussed in the previous chapter, the relationship between class position and cultural identity and practices is complicated by people's expectations of class mobility. In class-based societies, people expect that they, or at least

Photo 5.2 **Kennedy wedding–Jackie throwing the bouquet, Toni Frissell, 1953.** (Library of Congress, Prints & Photographs Division)

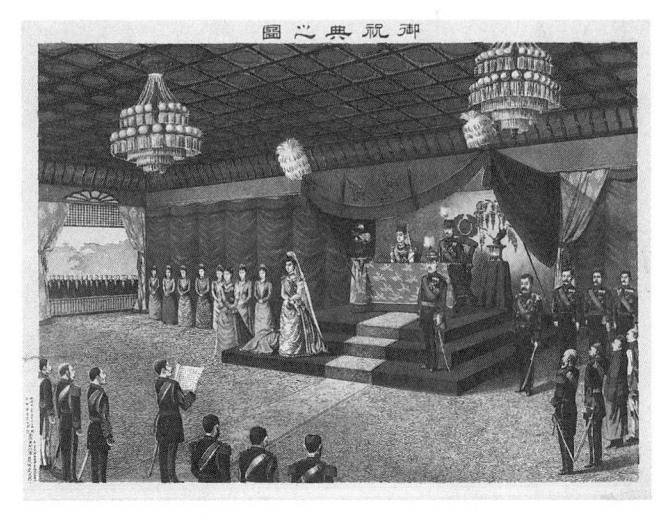

Photo 5.3 **Wedding reception of Crown Prince Yoshihito and Princess Kujō Sadako, Torajirō Kasai, 1900.** (Library of Congress, Prints & Photographs Division)

their children, will move up (or possibly down) on the class ladder. Sociologists argue that gender, like class, is also achieved (see Butler, 1999; West and Zimmerman, 1987; Garfinkel, 1967; Lorber, 1994). We may be born with male or female genitalia, but the behavior, rituals, and cultural displays that go along with gender norms must be continually learned and performed by society's members. These gendered behaviors and displays structure our everyday lives on the level of the mundane: when you get ready to leave the house in the morning your decisions about what type of clothing to wear and what sorts of cosmetics to use are determined at least in part by what you know about gender norms and expectations. More formalized settings such as sporting events, weddings, and holidays involve fairly predictable kinds of gendered performances (see Chapter Three for a discussion of the performative aspects of social life). And, not surprisingly, many forms of artistic expression such as ballet or tango dancing involve highly scripted and inflexible gender performances. Part of the appeal of a group like Les Ballets Trockadero de Monte Carlo, is their deliberate reversal of gender expectations.

In addition, gender norms and expectations, like those associated with other status positions, vary by culture and time period and even by social class, race, ethnicity, and religion within a society (Brettel and Sargent, 2009; Brodkin, 1998; Pascoe, 2011). Sociologists, anthropologists, historians, and psychologists have identified the importance in all societies of gender roles, the gendered division of labor, gender socialization, gender display, and so on. It makes sense that gender intersects with the arts on a number of levels.

Before the 1970s, most studies of the arts adopted a "gender blind" perspective. Art critics and historians agreed that great works of art expressed universal aspects of social experience or possessed transcendental aesthetic value. Marxists understood art and culture more generally as a reflection of class relations and class inequality (Chapter Three), and sociologists tended to minimize the importance of gender across the board. In other words, few people investigated the manner in which works of art, their production, and their consumption were a result of—and contributed to—how gender inequality and identity was produced and reproduced in society. With the advent of the second-wave feminist movement in the late 1960s, scholars, artists, and activists investigated the relationship between the social construction of gender roles and relations, cultural forms, and sex and gender norms. Artists and scholars sought to reveal and challenge traditional gender-blind views of the arts and produced new interpretations of history and new kinds of art. In this chapter we will investigate some of the research and the ideas about gender and the arts that emerged during that period and after. Like class and race, studies of gender have responded to political, economic, and social developments.

The Victorian Family and the Separation of Spheres

Although many women, especially artists, resisted restrictive gender norms, women in the 19th century were considered politically, morally, physically, and intellectually inferior to men. The first organized social movement for women's equality (**first-wave feminism**) began in the late-19th century in the United Kingdom and United States and was concerned primarily with securing voting and other legal rights for women (Flexner, 1996; Dubois, 1999; Stansell, 2011). Many first-wave feminists, who themselves were mostly upper-class, were also involved in other social causes meant to better the plight of poor and working class women (Kenneally, 1973). As we have seen already, the growth of market society and ideas about democracy, equality and "the rights of man" had helped dismantle traditional systems of caste privilege in the United States and Europe. By the mid-19th century, throughout Europe and the United-States, a greater swath of the population now had the opportunity to receive professional training and education, own property, start a business, and participate in politics. Unfortunately, these gains in personal autonomy did not extend to all groups. Women and African Americans were explicitly denied the rights and privileges of full inclusion in the 19th century.

In fact, Western society in the 19th and early 20th centuries developed alongside new ideas about gender and the family practices that *stifled* women's cultural, economic, and social participation in modern society (Coontz, 1992, 2005). Before the Industrial Revolution, families worked together on farms or in workshops that were based in the home. Women, men, and children participated in producing the goods that were sold in markets and used at home. These families were **patriarchal** (controlled by men), but both fathers and mothers contributed to the family economy and training and educating children. By the middle of the 19th century, with industrialization and urbanization, economic activity increasingly took place outside the home, in factories, offices, and public institutions. While working-class women (and children) worked in sweatshops, factories, and as domestic workers in the homes of the wealthy, women of the middle- and upper-classes, barred from professional training and financial activities by active exclusion and gender norms, were increasingly relegated to the domestic sphere (Cowan, 1983). This new, gendered, **separation of the spheres** of private domestic life and public, political, and economic life was reinforced through ideas and material culture (Wolff, 1989). Though some writers and philosophers (Marx and Engels, [1884] 1980; Mill, 1869; Wollstonecraft, 1792) called for gender equality, other influential figures of the day, like prominent British art critic John Ruskin (1819–1900) and Scottish social commentator Thomas Carlyle (1795–1881) asserted that women's "natural" place was in the home, providing love and guidance to their children

Photo 5.4 Madame Georges Charpentier (Marguérite-Louise Lemonnier, 1848–1904) and Her Children, Georgette-Berthe (1872–1945) and Paul-Émile-Charles (1875–1895), Auguste Renoir, 1878.

and support for their husbands in the form of a comfortable, cozy, "haven in a heartless world" (see Wolff, 1989). They argued that men were by nature competitive, rough, rational, and brave and thus suited for the cruel world of commerce. The ideal bourgeois female, on the other hand, was weak, irrational, delicate, and pure, in need of male protection and guidance (see Poovey, 1985).

This painting (photo 5.4) by the late-19th century French impressionist painter Pierre Auguste Renoir, depicts Madame Charpentier, one of Renoir's prominent supporters, and her two children and dog in their luxurious but cozy home. This sort of scene of domestic serenity, despite the loose brushstrokes, saturated color, and flattened space, all characteristic of the radical new painting of the period, represents the gender norms of the Victorian family.

Publishers and critics actively suppressed literature that presented women as anything other than loyal and demure wives and mothers. Paintings and theatrical productions often centered on themes of happy domesticity or dire warnings concerning the fate of the "fallen woman" who let herself be guided by sexual desire or the desire for independence (Wolff, 1989). The sex industry was, of course, off-limits for respectable women, and the extra-marital sexual lives of men remained largely a taboo subject within the sphere of the family. Nevertheless, as we have seen, avant-garde painters and poets like Henri de Toulouse-Lautrec, Eduard Manet, and Charles Baudelaire were free to represent and take part in this sexual underworld (Photo 5.5), which provided much inspiration in the development of modern painting, poetry, and other arts.

Photo 5.5 The Sofa, Henri de Toulouse-Lautrec, 1894-6.

Because of middle-class norms of propriety, Victorian women did not attend theater, opera, or musical performances unattended by a male chaperone. An unattended female would be considered a prostitute, a status assigned also to female performers (Pollock, 1988). The popular culture produced and consumed by the working class in the dance halls and pubs of the Victorian city was less restrictive to women in terms of its content, production, and audience participation (Bailey, 1998).

Thus, middle- and upper-class men and women in Victorian life inhabited separate spheres in their work and leisure activities, which served to exclude women from much of the cultural life of the period. Although wealthy and middle-class women learned drawing, music, and dance as part of their preparation for marriage and domestic management, they were not allowed to study in official academies or to participate in life-drawing classes where they would be exposed to nudity (Nochlin, [1971] in 1988). Less privileged (or un-marriageable) women might be professionally trained in the more practical arts like weaving or embroidery, where they could hope to earn a living. More prestigious fields like painting and sculpture, however, were reserved for men. Some female painters and sculptors, like Mary Cassatt, Camille Claudel, and Berthe Morisot, managed to create powerful work despite the barriers they encountered (see Pollock, 1988) Cassatt (1844–1926), who in the example here incorporated design elements from Japanese prints that were in vogue at the time and used lively and expressive brush strokes, often depicted mothers and children and other "feminine" subjects in her painting (photo 5.6). Nonetheless, while much of her work rivals that of her male contemporaries, she and other female artists were usually considered lesser talents

Photo 5.6 **The Child's Bath, Mary Cassatt, 1893.**

at the time and continue to be marginalized in official accounts of art history (Mathews, 1998).

The French sculptor Camille Claudel (1864–1943), who was Rodin's mistress, assistant, and inspiration, died in obscurity in a mental institution where she had lived for 30 years. Her powerful work has only recently received acclaim. Many women like the American photographer Gertrude Käsebier (1852–1934), pictured, (see photo 5.7). however, entered the new field of photography, where their presence was accepted because photography had a tentative status as a utilitarian craft with a very short history (Rosenblum, 1994; Sandler, 2002).

Photo 5.7 **Gertrude Käsebier, Frances Benjamin Johnston, 1905.** (Library of Congress, Prints & Photographs Division)

Women writers in the 19th and early-20th centuries faced fewer challenges because writing can be done in the private space of the home and required few materials. Nonetheless, many women writers, like the English novelist George Eliot (Mary Anne Evans, 1819–1880), deliberately adopted male pen names and personas in order to publish their work. Others, such as the English writer Virginia Wolff (1882–1941), addressed the challenges faced by women who wished to create art in their work. Her novel *Orlando* (1928), which was the basis for a successful film starring Tilda Swinton and Quentin Crisp in 1992, casts a wry look at gender roles through the story of an English nobleman who lives for three centuries and turns into a woman while asleep on military duty in Constantinople. Orlando then lives the rest of her life as women keenly aware of the advantages and disadvantages of both gender roles. As novel writing gained in prestige, though, women were increasingly excluded from the field (Tuchman and Fortin, 1984).

The ratification of women's right to vote, urbanization, and the spread of consumer society brought more relaxed gender norms to the 1920s. The "flapper" look of the period featured short, bobbed haircuts and knee-length skirts, and the new, more liberated urban women drove cars, rode bicycles, smoked, drank, and danced with men at prohibition era speakeasies and jazz clubs (Connor, 2004). Many young women (and men) embraced more relaxed sexual standards, and an atmosphere of bohemian hedonism prevailed among many during the roaring twenties (Alberti, 1994). Women like the American anarchist Emma Goldman (1869–1940) and the American birth control pioneer Margaret Sanger (1879–1966) advocated sexual liberation, birth control, and the abolition of the traditional family as part of their vision for a utopian society. Others, such as Gertrude Stein (1874–1946) and Mabel Dodge (1879–1962) were central patrons and critics for modernist art movements. And, in part because artists existed on the fringes of "respectable" society, they were granted more latitude (at least by their peers) concerning conventional gender and sex norms (Reed, 2011). Gertrude Stein, for example, lived openly as a lesbian with her partner Alice B. Toklas (1877–1967), and the French writer Andre Gide (1869–1951), wrote an eloquent series of dialogues concerning the naturalness of homosexuality in *Corydon* (1924). The Weimar graphic artist, Christian Schad (1894–1982), though himself heterosexual, included among his subjects erotic paintings and drawings of the homosexual underworld of his period.

The birth of commercial radio and the growing popularity of blues and jazz music during the 1920s Jazz Age also brought opportunities to African American, female vocalists and performers like Bessie Smith (1894–1937), Billie Holiday (1915–1959), and Josephine Baker (1906–1975). Like today, female performers had to utilize their sexual appeal—and appeal to racialized stereotypes—to gain a mass audience. Many female performers, however, were able to direct their own careers and musical production in ways that would not have been possible in the 19th century.

Photo 5.8 Entertainment. Circa 1930's. Josephine Baker, (1906–1975) African American dancer, actress and entertainer, famous for her Paris stage shows and her scanty costumes, Bob Thomas, 1975. (Bob Thomas/Popperfoto/Popperfoto/Getty Images)

Women, including Frida Kahlo (1907–1954) (photo 5.10). Gertrude Stein, and the American painter Georgia O'Keefe (1887–1986), played central roles in the development of the visual arts in Latin America, Europe, and the United States in the first decades of the 20th century (Deepwell, 1998). Georgia O'Keefe and the Mexican artist Frida Kahlo were both married to very prominent artists, whose reputations at the time far exceeded their own. Today, many of us are more familiar with Kahlo's moving Self-portrait with Thorn Necklace and Hummingbird than the political murals of her husband, Diego Rivera (1886–1957), and O'Keefe's hauntingly sensual paintings of flowers, skulls, and landscapes are certainly as recognizable as the elegant, somber photographs taken by her husband, Alfred Stieglitz (1864–1946), who was a major figure in American modernism. These women are especially relevant to us today because their work reflects the artistic concerns of the day through the lens of women's experience. Kahlo, for example, in the self-portrait below, refers to the pain of her bodily experience (she spent much of her life suffering from the effects of a childhood traffic accident and polio) as she maintains her cool dignity despite the necklace of thorns she wears. Although the apparent subject of Kahlo's work is the artist herself, her own physical and emotional experience serves as a metaphor for the turbulent political times—the Mexican Revolution, two world wars, and the Great Depression—through which she lived.

Explicit references to women's bodily experience have become common in art because of these pioneering artists. The young Guatemalan performance

Photo 5.9 **Self-Portrait with Thorn Necklace and Hummingbrid, Frida Kahlo, 1940.** (© 2013 Banco de México Diego Rivera Frida Kahlo Museums Trust, Mexico, D.F./Artists Rights Society (ARS), New York)

artist, Regina José Galindo (1974–), for example, used her body to comment on the nature of violence against women in her native country in her piece *¿Quién Puede Borrar Las Huellas?* In this performance piece, created in memory of the victims of armed conflict in Guatemala, Galindo walked from the Court of Constitutionality to the National Palace of Guatemala, leaving a trail of bloody footprints.

Photo 5.10 Regina José Galindo, Quien puede borrar las huellas?, 2003, performance. Photo: Victor Pérez Video: Damilo Montenegro, 37' 30". Courtesy prometeogallery di Ida Pisani, Milan/Lucca.

Gender, Post-war Society, and the Arts

The feminist movements of the late 19th and early-20th centuries dissolved after achieving their primary goal of women's suffrage in the first decades of the 20th century (see Cott, 1987). This did not, however, mean that women had achieved real cultural, economic, or political parity with men. While women became more active in the public sphere of educational, cultural, and political institutions, men continued to dominate the workplace and even family life. Despite the rapid cultural developments of the first three decades of the 20th century, by the end of the Second World War, the media, government, and employers pressured women to adhere to a new, updated version of Victorian-era gender roles in the family and economy. Many women, like the famous "Rosie the Riveter" had found new independence in the wartime economy, where their labor was needed to replace the male work force now at war. After the war, working women were accused of being unpatriotic, if they did not relinquish their jobs to returning servicemen. The inflexibility of proscribed gender roles was encouraged by suburbanization, which physically enforced the separation of men's work in the money economy of cities and women's isolation in the suburban home. Television shows like *Leave it to Beaver* (1957–63), Hollywood films, and advertisements reinforced stereotyped versions of masculinity and femininity and the security of domestic life. They and other forms of popular culture instructed women and men in how to use new technology and consumer

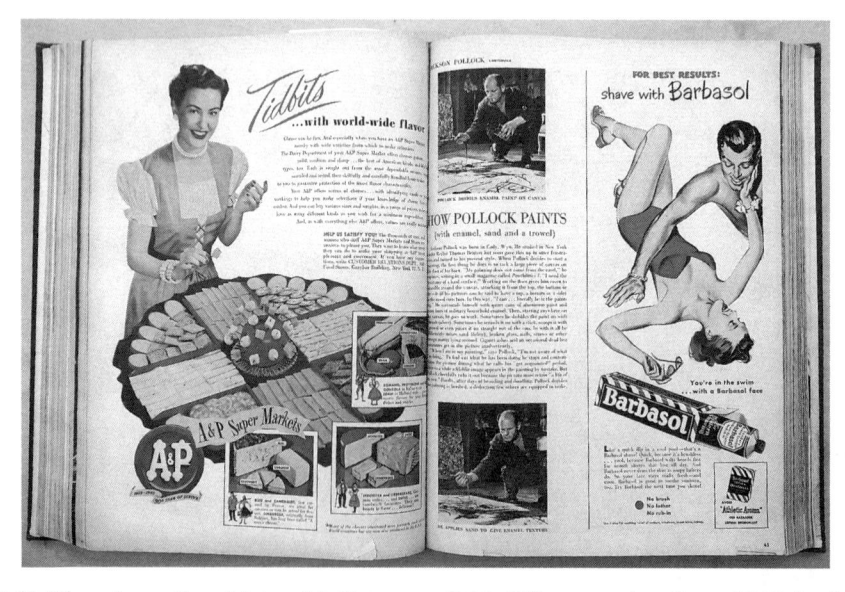

Photo 5.11 **The ads on the right and left pages of this Life magazine from 1949 depict idealized gender norms of the era. The smaller images in the middle accompany an article about the artist Jackson Pollock. Pollack is the iconic example of the "bad-boy" masculinity that acted as a counterpoint to more conventional masculine role models.**

goods to construct a socially desirable heterosexual, gender identity see photo 5.11.

Avant-garde art worlds of the period like the **Beats, Abstract Expressionism,** and jazz glorified the rebellious, individualist, artistic genius—hard-drinking, drug using, and unhampered by family obligations (see Savran, 1998, Penner, 2011, Leja, 1993). Beat writers and artists experimented with their sexual identity, and some, like the poet Alan Ginsburg (1926–1997) and the writer William S. Boroughs (1914–1997) were openly gay. The Beat movement cultivated a posture of bad-boy rebelliousness and privileged male-to-male relationships, and their work often contained misogynistic over-tones. For example, Jack Kerouac's (1922–1969) well-known novel of the Beat era, *Dharma Bums* (1958) chronicles male relationships and characteristically masculine adventures like mountaineering, fire-fighting, and hard drinking. Women in this and other Beat classics are represented as sexually alluring and available, but bearing the shackles of marriage and childrearing, they are ultimately dangerous to the true artist (Knight, 1996). As the main character in *Dharma Bums* says "Pretty girls make graves."

Women who participated in these movements were often marginalized. Painter Lee Krasner (1908–1984) devoted more energy to promoting her husband Jackson Pollock (1912–1956) than to her career, and the Beat poet Joan Vollmer Adams (1923–1951) was shot to death by her former husband, William S. Burroughs during a drunken reenactment of William Tell. Except for vocalists, jazz musicians were almost exclusively male. Art movements of the 1940s and 1950s helped to construct an important alternative to the mainstream masculine ideal of the loyal husband and provider in the rebellious, angry, and non-conformist male artist, but they did so in part by implicitly and explicitly excluding women from their ranks. Social research on post-war art worlds has become increasingly sensitive to the importance of understanding the prevailing organization of gender of the era.

Feminism Returns

Second-wave feminism grew out of the social ferment of the 1960s. Young women who had become active in the anti-war and free speech movements that coalesced around colleges and universities resented being treated like second-class citizens by male activists. These men opposed racism, US imperialism, and consumerism but were blind to sexism in their ranks and underplayed the importance of gender oppression (Freedman, 2002; Mclean, 2009). At the same time, middle-class, married women who had attained high levels of education became increasingly dissatisfied with the narrowness and isolation of suburban family life and their continued role as unpaid domestic workers. The writer Betty Friedan (1921–2006) famously captured this sense of dissatisfaction when she described "the problem with no name" in her influential 1963 book, the *Feminine Mystique*. An energetic and rapidly expanding women's movement soon grew, and few artists and scholars who came of age during the 1960s or 1970s remained unaffected by the movement (Broude et al., 1994)). Though feminism didn't (and still doesn't) provide a unified view of the causes, consequences, or remedies for gender inequality, the frameworks developed through second-wave feminism continue to have a profound effect on the way in which sociology, the arts, and other disciplines are practiced today.

Varieties of Second-Wave Feminism and the Arts

Feminists and Inclusion

Feminists expanded on the rights-based, inclusion model presented by first-wave feminism (Nicholson, 1990), focusing their activity and analysis on reforming existing institutions through legal reforms, reproductive rights, affirmative-action, and anti-discrimination policy. Scholars and activists in the arts and academia fought for women's inclusion in academic departments, museum exhibitions, and performance spaces. They also sought to redress the **canon** (the body of knowledge considered important by scholars and taught in schools) by conducting research and producing scholarship on women philosophers, artists, composers, and scientists whom male-dominated disciplines had written out of history. Feminists have made great strides in promoting greater inclusion and visibility for women in the arts and in society more generally. Over 5,000 colleges and universities in the United States alone (U.S Department of Education, 2010) offer programs and courses in women's studies, and sociology, anthropology, economics, and other fields now identify gender and the experience of women as important areas of research. Nonetheless, women continue to be underrepresented in the arts professions and in major literary journals (http://vidaweb.org/the-count-2010), film and television production (Bielby and Bielby, 1996; Beilby, 2009), museum and gallery exhibitions (Dumlao et al., 2007; Saltz, 2007), and most genres of music (Bayton 2006; Peterson 1997). As with other professions and occupations (Epstein et al., 1999; Fraad et al., 1994, 1990), women's opportunity structures in the arts are affected by glass ceilings, gender bias, and exclusion from male-dominated social networks. For example, research provides evidence for gender bias in classical music. During the 1970s and 1980s, the number of female musicians significantly increased after orchestras adopted blind auditions in which players perform behind a screen for juries (Goldin and Rouse, 2001). From the perspective of inclusion, women have made strides in the arts, but gender inequality continues to be a significant factor in the constitution of art worlds.

Other feminist artists and scholars sought to enhance the status of traditional women's forms of culture making, like quilting, embroidery, diaries, and ceramics (see e.g. Parker, 2010; Dempster and Bodman, 2001). The American artist Judy Chicago rejected the view of the artist as a privileged but isolated genius/creator and the denigration of the crafts that women traditionally practiced collectively. Chicago created her installation piece *Dinner Party* (1973–1978) in collaboration with teams of craftswomen from around the country. Under her direction, they created a giant, triangular table with 39 place settings, each meant to stand in for a notable female historical figure. Each of the plates, in addition to referring to the biography of one guest, was molded or painted with explicit vaginal imagery. See,

http://www.brooklynmuseum.org/exhibitions/dinner_party/

Her use of vaginal or womblike imagery in *Dinner Party* provides an example of another strategy adopted by early feminist artists who sought to express what they believed was the *essential*, or unique, nature of women's sexual and physical experience.

The Great Artist as a Figment of Gender

Some feminist of the second wave, however, doubted that the institutions and structures of patriarchal society could be transformed through greater inclusion and minor tinkering. They believed that a much more radical analysis and upending of the ideological and structural impact of male dominance were in order. The art historian Linda Nochlin pointed out in her famous essay (1971), that problem of "why have there been no great women artists" cannot be solved simply by rediscovering women forgotten from history. Feminists, she argued, have to understand how the very manner in which that question is phrased conceals the complex and institutional history of patriarchy. As in Bourdieu's analysis of class and culture (see Chapter Two), Nochlin explains that the educational institutions through which the expert knowledge of the arts necessary for "greatness" were transmitted were closed to women (Nochlin, 1971). In addition, she explains that the very idea of the "Great Artist" is based on a mythical idea that one person imbued with supernatural powers of genius individually and autonomously produces art. In fact, as, Howard Becker argues (see Chapters One and Two), success in the field requires the coordinate action of a multitude of people and a social structure that supports a particular definition of success. In this case, the unwavering, obsessive devotion to one's art required to be a great artist presupposes a gendered division of labor that leaves men free to pursue their talents unhampered by the gritty (and collective) reality of child-rearing, housework, and the constant reassurance and devotion that traditional forms of romantic companionship have provided men. If adherence to socially accepted gender roles means that women must be married and have children, that even a few have managed to become great artists is astounding indeed! Here, ideologies about artistic greatness, by naturalizing the powers of the male artistic creator, support the very social structures that produce gender inequality.

Tia DeNora's work on the rise of Beethoven's (1770–1827) music and his reputation as a "genius" in the 19th-century music world of Vienna demonstrates that the ideology of genius was both a produce of and helped to produce gender divisions in art and the larger social world. DeNora (1995) explains that prior to Beethoven's entrance on the musical scene, female keyboardists were well represented in the music world of 18th-century Vienna and performed the same pieces as their male counterparts. Beethoven's rise to fame coincided with and drew upon new ideas about aesthetics that were gaining ground in 18th-century Europe. The philosopher Immanuel Kant, whom you met in earlier chapters, contrasted the idea of the sublime with that of the beautiful in relation to aesthetic experience (DeNora, 1995). According to Kant, the sublime, in contrast to the beautiful, was that which inspired awe, a sense of boundlessness, and maybe even terror. Examples of the sublime can be found in nature, like the vastness of the ocean, the power of an earthquake, or the magnificence of a sunset. Eighteenth and 19th-century philosophers and art critics increasingly came to value works of art that incited this kind of experience, and artists who conjured up such experiences were associated with genius. At the same time, new ideas about masculinity and femininity were taking hold in Europe—ideas which associated femininity with weakness, passivity, and charm and masculinity with strength, activity and even violence. Beethoven and his supporters used these fashionable ideas about the sublime to promote Beethoven and his music to the status of genius. His compositions, in contrast to the less aggressive work of, say, Mozart, included startling passages, abrupt transitions with unexpected dynamic shifts, and, most important, they required vigor and physicality on the part of the performer. Because of the social norms for "feminine bodily comportment," women were discouraged from playing these compositions. With Beethoven's growing popularity, women were pushed out of the ranks of important pianists. Over time, Western ideas about the arts have emphasized the intersection of manliness and artistic genius.

In their study of cultural consecration in popular music, Schmutz and Faupel (2010) demonstrate the continued impact of this ideological intersection. The authors borrow an explicitly religious term, "consecration"—the act of rendering sacred—to convey the processes by which some works and artists are deemed exceptionally valuable. In employing the term, they are applying a bit of irony but essentially mean that critics and other cultural gatekeepers elevate an object of art or artist to a socially revered place. Those gatekeepers, not surprisingly, value specific ideas about gender.

Based on a number of standards, they discovered that only 8 percent of consecrated albums are by women. One of the measures of consecration was the number of times critics referred to the albums and the artists with terms like "works of art," "artist," or "genius." They found that when critics reviewed albums by men, they were much more likely to focus on the originality and singular genius of the creator, whereas even when they provided positive assessments of albums by female artists, they were more likely to stress the influence and guidance of others (males) in the field. This research suggests that the barriers women artists face today are, as in 19th-century Vienna, still affected by ideas of appropriate gender roles rather than intrinsic aesthetic worth.

Objectification, the Body and the Male Gaze

Some feminists argue that Enlightenment thought is at the root of women's subordination. Enlightenment ideas provided a basis for the development of science, technology, and modern political and economic institutions (e.g. Jaggar and Bordo, 1989; Irigaray, 1985; Lloyd, 1984). They claim that the rational, scientific attitude or "gaze" of Enlightenment philosophy and science suggests an opposition between an active, rational, and creative human subject and the natural world, which is either the inert, static and passive object of human will and control or an unruly, irrational force that must be tamed. The literature and ideology of the Enlightenment, they point out, identifies women with nature and men with rational intellect and will. Women are regarded as less than human, objects to be controlled by men. This view of women's "objecthood" finds expression in countless cultural forms, such as the ubiquity of the female nude in Western art (Berger, 1972) and the popularity of styles of dress (like high-heeled shoes, corsets, and tight skirts) that inhibit women's freedom of movement and highlight their physical features. These cultural forms reinforce (and produce) a gender ideology in which women's "natural" role is that of a physical object to be consumed by men.

Other feminists (e.g. Mulvey, 1975; de Lauretis, 1984) make use of Sigmund Freud's (1856–1939) accounts of castration anxiety and fetishization to draw similar conclusions. In these accounts, men, and especially White, privileged men also turn women and other dominated groups into objects of artistic representation, which serve as "fetishes" to neutralize White, male castration anxiety. In other words, White men unconsciously fear that women and other dominated groups will eventually seek revenge for their forced subordination. By symbolically turning these groups into passive objects, this anxiety is temporarily assuaged. Culture, according to this line of thought, reinforces this subject/object dichotomy through forms of representation that consistently objectify, dehumanize, and humiliate women, people of color, working-class people, homosexuals, the disabled, and other groups that fall outside the dominant identity of White, upper-class males.

Pornography (see Steinem, 1977; Dworkin 1989; Bordo, 2003) is the most obvious example of this type of objectification. In pornographic films and literature aimed at heterosexual men, women's bodies, in particular their sexual organs, their poses, and smiles signal constant availability and sexual enthusiasm. Pornography presents women's bodies as vehicles upon which men can impose their sexual fantasies without concern for the desires, feelings, or humanity of the women portrayed. Men who consume pornography, some feminists argue, transfer this dehumanizing attitude to real women, whistling at them in the street or making unwanted sexual remarks or advances based on the assumption that their own sexual desire is all that is necessary to justify an encounter. Pornography also, according to this argument, normalizes the practice of isolating sexualized body parts from human beings. When men refer to a woman as "a piece of ass" or "pair of legs", or when they stare at breasts during a job interview (Frye, 1983), the attitude of objectification has migrated from the realm of fantasy to reality and has consequences for women and for men.

While the objectification of the desired object is arguably unavoidable in pornography, the reduction of women to a passive object of male consumption and action remains a prevailing theme in Western painting (Berger, 2008), film (Mulvey, 1975), and popular media (Aubrey, 2006). Yet, the female nude, a prominent theme in Western painting and sculpture, is distinguished from pornography through the ideology of "pure" aesthetic judgment. According to traditional art historians and philosophers, the viewer of the nude is simply appreciating the aesthetic representation of beautiful form (Clark, 1956). Feminist critics argue that the aesthetic gaze also objectifies women, though in a different way which is negative for women (see in Jones, 2003).

Theorists explain the male gaze, and the objectification of women as both a strategy to reinforce, and a consequence of, male domination. Man exists as an active presence, a surveyor of the world, according to Berger (2008). Women, as human beings, are also surveyors of the world. At the same time, they are aware that they are constantly being surveyed—that their value and survival is assured only if they are appreciated as desirable objects by men. Women are always looking at and evaluating themselves and other women as objects. As Berger says "men look at women. Women watch themselves being looked at" (Berger, 2008: 47). An early generation of feminists rejected high heels, push-up bras and cosmetics in a symbolic refusal of this "double-identity." Today, despite signs of the continued objectification of women such as the phenomenal growth of cosmetic surgery, beauty salons and spas, diet fads and the popularity of high heels, many women are able to maintain positions of power, prestige, and autonomy while at the same time treating themselves as objects of visual consumption. Also, as Bordo (1999) has pointed out, in part because of the influence of gay fashion designers and a more general social acceptance of homosexuality, men have increasingly become the objects of both the male and female gaze in advertising and popular culture.

Artists across a range of mediums have directly responded to various strands of feminist analysis. By the end of the 1970s, artwork, activism, and theorizing aimed at expressing the **essential** nature of women and their experience (such as Chicago's work) gave way to more coolly intellectual styles that explored, often through the incorporation of complicated philosophical and psychoanalytic texts, how gender is constituted in and through social practices (Pollock, 1988). In an early example, the British artist and theorist Mary Kelly (1941–) created a six-section, 135-frame work entitled *Post-Partum Document* (1973–1979), which describes events in her relationship with her son from birth to age five and includes items such as stained diapers, scribbling, and her own written comments. Kelly's intention in this piece is to indicate the socially constructed nature of femininity and motherhood. Other artists are interested in how commercial culture constructs femininity as the object of the male gaze. Barbara Kruger (1945–) deploys the visual vocabulary of graphics and advertising to critique gender and representation. One well known example contains the text "Your body is a battleground" on top of a black and white photograph of a woman's face, one half of which is in reverse negative.

Another strand of feminist art draws heavily on avant-garde developments in performance art and dance, often incorporating text, video, and film and speaks directly to questions of power, subjectivity, and the female experience. In 1972, for example, Faith Wilding performed a piece called *Waiting* in which she recited, in a dead-pan manner, events for which women wait: "... to wear a bra, to go to a party, to be asked for a dance, for pimples to go away, for Mr. Right, for an orgasm, etc." (in Sayer, 1989: 96).

A year earlier in 1971, Eleanor Antin (1935–) began her "theatre of the self." In her first installment, *Representational Painting*, she comments ironically on female narcissism and the gaze by applying makeup using a video monitor as mirror. Later, she points to the social construction and malleability of identity by casting herself as four different surrogate selves: a ballerina, a king, a hobo and a Black movie star. In 1976, Carolee Schneeman (1939–) pushed the limits of body art even further with her *Interior Scroll*, in which she extracts a scroll from her vagina from which she reads. The text was inspired by a male filmmaker who refused to look at Schneemann's films, because "much as he found her personally charming. He simply could not abide the "Personal clutter/the persistence of feelings..." (in Schneeman, 1982). Her work is a rejection of his assumptions that the messiness of feelings and emotion—both associated with female experience—don't belong in the world of art.

Postmodernism and Queer Theory After the Second Wave

> Actually, there is no such thing as a homosexual person, any more than there is such a thing as a heterosexual person. The words are adjectives describing sexual acts, not people. Those sexual acts are entirely natural; if they were not, no one would perform them.
>
> Gore Vidal, "Sex is Politics," United States: Essays, 1952–1992

From Beauvoir to Foucault—Becoming Gender

Since the 1990s both feminism and the arts have responded to a related set of philosophical and political ideas associated with **postmodernism**, post-structuralism, and **deconstruction** (see Nichelson, 1990). These ideas challenge how people think about identity, subjectivity, gender, and sexuality. In 1949, the French writer Simone de Beauvoir (1908–1986) published her highly influential book *The Second Sex*, in which she explored the socially and historically constructed nature of subjectivity. Her work explains how women are socialized to unconsciously play an important role in their own subordination. She makes a strong argument" one is not born a woman, one becomes one"— about the social construction of gender. In other words, gender is created through a series of social processes and institutions. In creating gender as a social category, these same processes also produce women's subordination.

Some 20 years later, another French thinker, Michel Foucault (1926–1984), described the origins of modern sexuality in his *History of Sexuality* (1978) and argued against the idea, popular during his time, that capitalist societies repressed sexuality to make workers more compliant. While he rejected the link between sexual repression and compliant workers, he was concerned with the connection between identities and power. He asserts that modern sexuality and the ways that we think about, discuss, and define ourselves sexually were produced by **discourses**, "organized and organizing bodies of knowledge, with rules and regulations that govern particular....ways of thinking and acting" (Storey, 2009: 101), that accompanied the modern sciences of criminology, education, medicine, psychiatry, demography, and social work. Far from sexuality being repressed in Victorian times, these new sciences were evidence that a heightened degree of discussion, dissection, categorization, and investigation of sexuality unknown in earlier periods was taking place. In the 18th and 19th centuries, through innovative practices of population control, medicine, law enforcement, public education, and so forth, categories of sexual behavior were created and were linked to categories of "being." It was during this period, for example, that instead of *practicing* sodomy (a behavior or desire that might be relatively independent of one's identity, like preferring chocolate ice cream to vanilla), one *became* "a homosexual." We wouldn't identify ourselves as "homosexual," "heterosexual," or "bisexual" if those categories weren't already created through the discourse of sexuality, which frames and produces a way of viewing the world and people. Foucault's point is that identity, including sexual identity, should not be viewed as an ever-present category but as an "effect" of power and the discourses through which power operates.

Butler and Beyond

The American philosopher Judith Butler (1956–), whose work has been foundational for contemporary theorizing about the arts, draws on Beauvoir, Foucault, and others to assert even more radical ideas about sex, gender and identity. Butler agrees with Beauvoir (and most sociologists) that gender is socially constructed, a product of culture, but she argues so is sex. She claims that even the supposedly natural male/female sex distinction is cultural. Grouping people according to their genitals reflects an ideology which is seeks to make gender distinctions and heterosexuality seem "natural". Neither gender nor sex (nor sexual desire) is pre-given in the individual. They are, instead, "performative" (see Austin, 1975). They exist as a result of some kind of action— such as the doctor's exclamation of "it's a boy!" upon delivering a baby, the parents' purchase of pink clothing for a newborn infant, buying tickets to a sports event for "guys night out," or a man's insistence on paying for dinner on his first date with a woman. According to Butler, however, this does not mean that we really have choices about performing gender. Sex and gender performances are *always* mandatory. People who don't establish, through performance, socially assigned sex and gender categories, disappear as persons on the social stage. How would you tell a friend about an encounter with a teacher, parent or stranger without knowing which gendered pronoun to deploy? And which locker room could you use at the gym, if you were undecided about your sex? And, like other forms of identity, the successful performance of gender involves masking that it is performance (Butler, 1990).

The performance of gendered identity, however, is never a seamless achievement. Indeed, the successful iteration of sex and gender identity inevitably takes place through violent acts of exclusion because the discourses that establish these norms operate through the denial and disavowal of their opposite. To perform masculine identity successfully, the performer must expunge all the qualities associated with femininity (the reverse, of course, is true for feminine identity). Women must remove hair from their legs and under their arms because body hair is associated with masculinity, and men who are slight of build work out in the gym and wear padded suits to hide their "feminine" body types. Likewise, to perform heterosexuality, homosexuality must also always be performatively disavowed (this is why young males sometimes perform what is meant to be an insulting parody of stereotypical homosexual behavior; they are performing their own heterosexuality for their friends (see Pascoe, 2011)). That we try so hard to exclude certain behaviors from our gender performance insures that we will sometimes make mistakes or even intentionally subvert our gender performance. It is through such "slippages" that the constructed nature of identity is revealed: the Trockadero Ballet company uses the conscious subversion of gender norms to great comic effect.

Queer theorists have incorporated Butler's insights to question ideas of fixed sexual categories like gay or straight, arguing that these categories serve only to normalize some practices while casting others as deviant. Eve Kosofsky Sedgwick alerts readers to possible "queer readings" or queer nuances in a variety of texts (films, novels, etc.), which most people have assumed are unambiguously heterosexual in their orientation. For example, she traces Henry James' (a writer not usually associated with homosexuality) use of certain kinds of language to references to anal sex and other homoerotic practices. Sedgwick (1993) points out how James carefully choses ambiguous language to avoid the harsh glare of censorious publishers.

Art World Reverberations

While most artists don't literally quote Foucault, Butler, or queer theory, these ideas have had a profound impact on the way that art is practiced and interpreted by critics. The photographer Cindy Sherman (1954–), for example, has been hailed by critics for her successful aesthetic deployment of theatrical performativity, taking the self as that which is perpetually re-enacted (e.g. Auslander, 2006; Jones, 2002). She first began to attract the attention of critics with her show of "Untitled Film Stills" (see photo 5.12). In these 8" x 10" black and white photographs, Sherman dressed up as stereotyped female figures—career girl, model, star, and actress—from 1950s' B-movies. In 1989 she again photographed herself in a series based on Old Master paintings, in which she dressed up in historical costume but attached prosthetic devices such as breasts, noses, and bald-pates to her body. On the surface, the performative aspects of identity that Sherman's work highlights bear a resemblance to the feminist body art I described earlier. Her work differs significantly in its hyper-parodic and slickly staged qualities from the work of an earlier generation of performance artists. Eleanor Antin, Carolee Schneeman, and other performance artists from that earlier generation seem to be wrestling with the idea of an authentic or essential experience of the self that one could uncover by peeling off layers of gender

Photo 5.12 **Untitled Film Still #6, Cindy Sherman, 1977.** (Permission granted from Sean Kelly)

stereotypes and expectations. Sherman's body of work suggests that the self is a series of reinventions based on references to pre-existing models of gender from art and popular culture. Popular culture figures like Madonna, Lady Gaga, Prince, and David Bowie have also consciously played with the performative aspects of gender and sexuality, styling and restyling their image using a multiplicity of gender performances. And, increasingly, celebrities like Chastity Bono and Ru Paul have publicly performed the fluid, changeable nature of gender and sex.

Reflecting on Gender Today

Compared with the 1960s, when second-wave feminism first emerged, many more female composers, choreographers, visual artists, conductors, and film and theater directors receive public recognition and commercial success today. At the same time, women continue to be underrepresented in these fields, and, while commercial films, television shows, video games, cartoons and children's books more often challenge gender stereotypes by presenting powerful and active female characters than they did in the past, women and girls are still frequently relegated to the position of beautiful side-kick, or "eye-candy." Research shows that audiences for popular culture are still divided by gender, but women and girls are more likely to also appreciate "guy" culture, while men and boys consistently show distaste for "chick flicks" and other products aimed primarily toward a female audience (e.g. Oliver et al., 1998).

And, despite all the research and theorizing that has taken place concerning the complex mechanisms through which women have been marginalized in the arts, art world gatekeepers still seem to associate aesthetic quality with masculinity.

So, while women's social position has changed significantly over the past century, in all societies men and women's lives and experience remain deeply affected by gender. And our ideas about gender continue to influence art worlds in terms of art production, interpretation, consumption, reputation, and a whole host of other dimensions. Part of the history and consequences of gendered relations is the resistance to gender inequality, in its myriad and complex forms, waged by various branches of feminist activism and thought. While many young women (and men) associate feminism with their parents or even grandparents' social world, the real-life struggles and new ways of thinking about the social world waged by feminists also shapes the way that we produce and experience all cultural forms, including the arts, today. While not all of your studies of art worlds need to focus on gender, you should at least understand how gender frames the questions you might ask and the art worlds you choose to investigate.

Discussion Questions

1. How have ideas from second-wave feminism influenced contemporary art or art worlds?
2. How have women's position in the arts been tied to gender norms during the historical periods discussed in the chapter? How are women's positions in the arts tied to gender norms, social expectations, or the structure of the family today?
3. How has feminism affected the type of art that is produced and the way that art is discussed and valued by people that you know? How might you find out? What kinds of questions would you ask?
4. Do men and women experience the arts differently? Why? What studies support this view?
5. Feminist artists often self-consciously refer to gender and gender inequality in their work. We have discussed some examples here. Give examples from popular culture in which questions of gender are openly addressed. How do these works (and their audiences) differ from or resemble the examples we have discussed?

6

RACE AND THE ARTS

Photo 6.1 **2009 Inaugural Parade. Michelle and Barack Obama join Joe and Jill Biden watch the parade from the viewing stand in front of the White House, Washington, D.C., Carol Highsmith, 2009.** (Library of Congress, Prints & Photographs Division)

While the results of US presidential elections are big news every election year, Barack Hussein Obama's election in 2008 was greeted with an especially boisterous fanfare throughout the world. It was the first time US voters had chosen a "Black," or "African American" president of the United States of America. The first sentence of a *New York Times* article published on Election Day captured the national enthusiasm:

> Barack Hussein Obama was elected the 44th president of the United States on Tuesday, sweeping away the last racial barrier in American politics with ease as the country chose him as its first Black chief executive.

Ngourney (2008)

While it would be nice if we could take this interpretation of Obama's election and its significance at face value, questions of race and racism are far from neatly resolved today. I use quotation marks around the words "Black" and "African American" to draw attention to the messiness of these terms. These designations are often clumsy or not quite accurate, which becomes especially clear when they are used to describe President Obama. While Obama's father was indeed a dark complexioned African, his mother was, by most standards, White. His description as "Black" by mainstream media and the elaboration by the media that Blackness has historically been an impediment to political success speaks volumes about race in America. Obama's designation as "African American" is also problematic. Though Obama's ethnic heritage is certainly both "African" and "American" the term "African American" is usually used as a racial and cultural reference to Americans of African descent whose ancestors have shared a unique historical trajectory in the United States that they pass down to their children. Obama's African father, on the other hand, spent most of his life in his homeland of Kenya and had little contact with him after his divorce from Obama's mother in 1964. Obama spent much of his formative years with his White, Anglo Saxon grandparents, in Honolulu, Hawaii and, by his own recollection, was not really connected to any African American community until he moved to Chicago to take a job as a community organizer in 1985, at the age of 24 (Obama, 2004).

I bring up Obama's life history and the manner in which his ethnic and racial heritage has been framed by the media not to rekindle debates surrounding the legitimacy of Obama's claims to Blackness or membership in the African American community. I mention these details because they serve as a vivid illustration of the importance, and ambiguity, of racial classifications and racial stratification in our society. Because race continues to play such an important role in the structure of social, political, and cultural institutions and in the construction and reproduction of identity, we need to have a sociological and historical understanding of race to study art worlds.

As with class and gender, the arts have been central to the construction of racial categories and racial identity. In fact, you will notice that many of the ideas that I discussed in relation to class and gender reappear when we talk about race. This is not surprising since the subordination of women and people of color has had a parallel path in Western societies since the Enlightenment, if not earlier. Important Enlightenment philosophers like Kant and Georg W. F. Hegel (1770–1831) suggested that women and non-Europeans were intellectually and culturally inferior to European men (in Bell, 1983; Valls, 2005). Norms of masculinity and European identity developed in relation to stereotypes about both femininity and race. In the United States, the concept of "whiteness" as a racial identity only became meaningful against the background of slavery, genocide against native peoples, and discrimination against people with dark skin (see Roediger, 1991, 2008).

Racism and racial and ethnic inequalities exist in all Western societies (and most non-Western ones as well). Each society, however, has a unique history and way of thinking about racial and ethnic categories. After the first millennium, slavery in Europe was a minor institution and until the 16th century largely free of racial justification. Nothing comparable to the African American experience exists in Europe. On the other hand, European countries have a long history of **colonialism** and **imperialism** in regions of Africa, the Middle East, India, Asia, and the Caribbean, which exploited and imposed European culture on the usually darker complexioned colonized populations (see Gilroy, 1993).

What is Race?

While differences between individuals in terms of chromosomes, genitals, skin color, hair type, etc. exist, people are grouped according to those differences and those differences acquire meaning and consequences only through social processes (Steinberg, 2001). Sociologists mostly agree that race is socially constructed. To put it simply, scientists cannot find definitive identifying genetic or biological markers that correspond neatly with the categories that we use to describe racial or ethnic groups. They can use genetic markers to trace back what parts of the world your ancestors come from or determine the presence or absence of genes that determine if you will have epicanthic folds (the eyelids most common among, but not exclusive to, East Asians) or how much melanin (a substance which controls the absorption of UV rays from the sun and is associated with skin pigmentation) our cells are likely to produce, but these markers don't accurately predict the racial group to which someone will belong in any given society. This point is illustrated in the 1989 film *Do the Right Thing*, directed by the African American film maker, Spike Lee. In one scene, Pino, the son of the Italian American, Sal, who owns the pizzeria where much of the film's action takes place, and Mookie, the African American delivery boy played by Lee, engage in an intense argument about the relative merits of Blacks vs. Italians. At one point in the argument, Mookie suggests that Pino would like to be Black and points out that his kinky black hair and dark complexion indicate that there is a thin line, if any, between Pino and members of the group that he despises. Indeed, as Mookie suggests, East Asians, who we don't consider "Black" or Southern Italians, whom we generally classify as White sometimes have darker skin than those whom we have categorized as African American (see Morning, 2011). Even less will these biological markers give us any information about cultural traditions, behavior or any of the other things that we associate with racial groupings. Race and racial categories are instead created and maintained through social processes and social interaction that sociologists call racialization. Race may not be caused by biology, but the

Photo 6.2 **Do the Right Thing, MCA/Universal Pictures, 1989.** (MCA/Universal Pictures/Photofest © Universal)

effects of racial classification systems and especially racial discrimination are real in terms of health, wealth, power, and culture (Roberts, 2011).

Racialization, Imperialism, Colonialism and European Identity

> Send forth the best ye breed–
> Go bind your sons to exile
> To serve your captives' need;
> To wait in heavy harness,
> On fluttered folk and wild–
> Your new-caught, sullen peoples,
> Half-devil and half-child.
>
> "The White Man's Burden: The United States and The Philippine Islands" (1899), Rudyard Kipling

You may have noticed that this book uses examples of art and the history of art and theories of art from the Western World—the United States, and Europe. This is not because important works of art and ideas about that art do not exist in other parts of the world. It is because my orientation and what I know the most about reflects my own cultural history. I only know about the history of arts and culture of non-Western cultures because of courses I have taken in school or specialized museums I have visited. On the other hand, people from non-Western societies with similar years of education and interest in the arts will no doubt know much about Western culture in addition to knowing about the culture of their country. They will probably be able to read and write at least one European language and will be fluent in the literary, philosophical, and most likely the visual arts tradition of the European country where that language is spoken. If they are trained in a musical instrument they will probably be familiar both with Western and Eastern, Middle-Eastern, or African musical traditions and forms. Few children in the United States or Europe receive training in non-Western music. This is because of the role that imperialism and colonialism have played in the development of European society, culture, and economy.

Imperialism, that is, the economic and cultural domination of the peoples and resources of one geographical territory by another, has been around as long as ancient history. The Roman Empire, the Assyrian Empire, Ancient Egypt, and the Chinese Empire all provide early examples of the ruling powers of one region taking control over other regions. Once in control, the dominating country, through military occupation and sometimes deals made with local elites, pillaged local resources, enslaved people, and imposed with varying degrees of success their language, culture, and religion on the local population. During the 16th century the Netherlands, France, Spain, Great Britain, Portugal and other countries with strong urban centers and easy access to waterways formed settlements in the West Indies, Africa, the Americas, and elsewhere from which they could control trade and extract resources from their new colonies (see, e.g. Amin, 1977; Frank and Gils; 1993).

Sometimes these new territories were populated by civilizations with their own histories of imperial warfare, and sometimes they were populated by loosely connected, indigenous peoples who had had little or no contact with other cultures for thousands of years. Imperialism and colonization facilitated cultural exchange and had a profound impact on the economic, political and cultural development of dominant and dominated regions. Scholars have studied the hybrid, or **creole,** cultures that have developed in countries like Cuba, Jamaica, and Trinidad (see Ashcroft, B., Griffiths, G., and Tiffin, H. 2006). More recently, scholars have pointed out the hybrid nature of European culture and especially European modernity (see e.g. Paolini et al., 1999). As we will see, European culture owes its dynamism in part to the influence of non-Western art forms and to the ways that Europeans imagined non-Western peoples and cultures.

Modern technologies of travel and warfare, the growth of industrial capitalism, and the consolidation of the European nation-state brought about an unprecedented degree of imperialist activity leading to what some historians call "the age of empire" (Hobsbawm, 1987) in the 19th through the mid-20th centuries. In this period and earlier the global north–France, Great Britain, the United States, and other European countries—gained control over vast swaths

Photo 6.3 **St. Lucia in the West Indies taken possession of by Admiral Barrington Monsieur de Micoud and the inhabitants having capitulated the 30th of December, 1778, being the day after Count d'Estaign left the island much disconcerted, 1783.** (Library of Congress, Prints & Photographs Division)

of the "global south"—including India, the Caribbean, Latin America, Africa, Vietnam, the Philippines, the Pacific Islands, and elsewhere.

In Chapter Five, we discussed Victorian views of women in culture and the arts. Identified with nature and sexuality rather than culture and self-control, women, it was believed, needed the guidance, restraint and protection of men and patriarchal institutions, which were reinforced through literary and visual representations of women. Similarly, colonized people and the descendants of African people were denied a voice in Western culture and the arts. Western literature, like the passage of the Kipling poem quoted above, often represented the "natives" of India and Africa as childlike, simple and naïve. Their music, dance, and adornment may be charming, thought many Europeans, but colonized people lacked the rational temperance and control of Western culture and thus were closer to nature and to animals. It may not always be pleasant, but it was the "White man's burden"—as the English writer Kipling (1865–1936) quoted above wrote in response to the American takeover of the Philippines—to lift non-Europeans out of savagery and barbarism.

In addition, Europeans created a romantic, sensual, but other times threatening image of non-Western peoples against which to forge their own identity as Europeans. The scholar Edward Said referred to the stereotyping assumptions made by Europeans about the characteristics of Middle Eastern and East Asian peoples as **Orientalism**. What it means to be a civilized French or Englishman was defined and articulated through the construction (by Europeans) of a primitive, non-Western "other," which had little to do with the way the people being represented experience their own culture and history (Said, 1978).

Thus, representations of non-Western people by European artists during the 19th and 20th centuries were important in the creation of a European identity and in the creation of the idea of the native (see Nochlin in Pindar, 2002).

Non European Arts and Modernism

The discovery of non-Western art forms by European artists and the meaning attached to those forms had a profound impact on modernism. Modernism embraced the ideals of progress, rationality, science, and technology central to the Enlightenment. But many modernist artists and theorists were critical of the social fragmentation, loss of authenticity and excessive rationalism of modern

Photo 6.4 **Le Bain Turc, Jean Auguste Dominique Ingres, 1862.** (Gift of the Société des Amis du Louvre, with the contribution of Maurice Fenaille, 1911)

Photo 6.5 **Man with an Adze, Paul Gauguin, 1891.** (Snark/Art Resource, NY)

society. As an antidote, some artists drew on the culture of traditional or pre-Industrial European cultures (see, Jessup, 2001). Others were inspired by the masks, totems and other ritual artifacts that anthropologists and explorers brought back to Europe (see Bindman et al., 2010; Zolberg in Cherbo and Zolberg, 1997).

Photo 6.6 **Male Figure (Moai Tangata), Rapa Nui people, Early 19th Century.** (Image copyright © The Metropolitan Museum of Art. (Source: Art Resource, NY)

Photo 6.7 **Standing Nude, Pablo Picasso, 1908.** (© 2013 Estate of Pablo Picasso/Artists Rights Society (ARS), New York)

When French artists like Van Gogh and Gauguin viewed painting and sculpture of non-Western peoples at the 1889 Universal Exposition in Paris, this work appealed to their romantic nostalgia for an idealized time before the evils of industrialization and modern society had spread in Europe (Zolberg in Cherbo and Zolberg, 1997).

Slightly later, in 1906, the French artist Pablo Picasso discovered African tribal art in the Paris Ethnographic museum and was attracted to the simplified, stylized forms. Though Picasso may have known little about the meaning of these objects for the people who created them, they helped lead him and other artists to their experiments with cubism (see photo 5.7).

The Surrealists were also interested in the ethnographic accounts of anthropologists because these accounts described "exotic" and unfamiliar forms of ritual and social practices. The American experimental filmmaker, Maya Deren (1917–1961), for example, used footage of Haitian dances in her films. Earlier modernists like Gauguin saw in the art of Africa and Oceana a naïve and gentle simplicity. Later, Expressionists, Surrealists, and Cubists saw a "raw, emotional expressivity revealing the natural and elemental roots of human nature (Goldwater, 1986)." European interpretations and reception of non-Western arts were tied more strongly to the culture of modern Europe than to the art objects themselves.

Racialization and the Arts in the Americas

The cultures of the New World were formed from the complex brew of Europeans, Native Americans, and African Americans, and the experience of

Photo 6.8 **Capoeira or the Dance of War, Johann Moritz Rugendas, 1825.**

African Americans and the legacy of slavery has been central to the development of distinct, New World cultures. For this reason, sociologists of art and culture need to be especially attentive to the role of race when studying the art worlds of the Americas.

Slavery in the Americas

Slavery, which began in the English colonies in the early 1600s and lasted as an institution until the ratification of the 13th Amendment in 1865, constrained the role of African Americans in U.S. culture. By the same token, the experience of slavery and its aftermath provided a context in which new forms of uniquely American culture developed. Slaves combined their shared pan-African musical, performance and storytelling traditions with elements of European folk culture and indigenous culture to produce new forms of hybrid culture (see Blasingame, 1979; Rucker, 2006). In addition to providing aesthetic and spiritual comfort, songs, stories, dance forms, and poetry served as important mediums of communication and resistance during slavery (Levine, 1977; Herskovits, 1958) in the United States and the Caribbean. Capoeira, for example (see photo 6.8), was developed by African slaves in Brazil as a form of cultural expression combining music, dance, ritual, storytelling and martial arts (Almeida, 1986). When it was outlawed in the 19th century, practitioners started to emphasize the dance and musical qualities of this martial art, in effect disguising a style of fighting as a complex, difficult to master, acrobatic form of cultural expression.

RACE AND THE ARTS 115

Photo 6.9 **Al. W. Martin's mammoth production, Uncle Tom's cabin, U.S. Printing Co., 1899.**
(Library of Congress, Prints & Photographs Division)

Photo 6.10 **Richards & Pringle's Famous Georgia Minstrels, U.S. Lithograph Co., 1903.**
(Library of Congress, Prints & Photographs Division)

Since slaves were forbidden to learn to read and write in many American states, (some nonetheless did become literate), official accounts of slave life were mostly produced by White authors, including the novel *Uncle Tom's Cabin*, written by the abolitionist Harriet Beecher Stowe in 1852. *Uncle Tom's Cabin* was an indictment of slavery, but it also reinforced popular stereotypes about Black men and women (Reynolds, 2011).

While African Americans and Afro-Caribbeans created new, hybrid forms of music, dance, word-play, and crafts from the cultural resources of their past and present, Minstrel shows of the 19th century introduced White audiences to racist caricatures and stereotypes which continue to appear in popular culture even today. Minstrel shows (Lott, 1993), a form of popular performance that included music, dance, and slapstick humor were performed by White performers in blackface as early as the 1820s (Mahar, 1999).

Gradually, they developed a series of stock characters, including the "old darky," the "mammy," the "wench," and the "dandy." These characters both drew on and helped to form White stereotypes of naïve and shiftless Blacks enjoying plantation life. They helped to cement a shared White identity among their working-class audiences, many of whom experienced discrimination in the United States based on their Irish and Scottish ethnicities (Lott, 1993; Ignatiev, 1995). By the 1840s and 1850s, African Americans began forming minstrel groups of their own and performing for White and Black audiences (Toll, 1974). Although they sometimes subtly made fun of racism and of Whites, these groups deployed the same stereotypes as their White counterparts.

Photo 6.11 **Kara Walker Untitled, 2002.** (Untitled © 2002 Kara Walker)

Many important Black entertainers got their start performing with minstrel groups and this form helped create a mass audience for Black musical styles and dance, and the slapstick and verbal humor of minstrel has influenced the course of American films, theater, and stand-up comedy (Strausbaugh, 2006). Nonetheless, minstrel shows created enduring racist stereotypes. Indeed, contemporary critics point out that for African American artists to succeed in an entertainment industry that is dominated by Whites, they must appeal to racist fantasies about Black hyper-sexuality, buffoonery, laziness, or dandyism (notice how similar these are to the cultural images associated with women) (see hooks, 1992). At the same time, many contemporary African American artists, like the visual artist Kara Walker (see photo 6.11), the photographer Carrie Mae Weems or the filmmaker Spike Lee use these stereotypes to render probing critiques of racism. Their work highlights the role of racist imagery in shaping White identity and diffusing White fear of Blacks in the United States both past and present.

Blatantly racist stereotypes like those characteristic of minstrelsy are rarely uncritically invoked by mainstream culture today. Some critics, however, argue that post-industrial economic conditions (Wilson, 1978) have helped to create a sector of chronically poor, urban African Americans, who have become the butt of ugly stereotypes in a subtler manner.

Identity, Politics, Performance

The arts shape and express group and self-identity, and are a powerful medium through which questions of identity are explored and group boundaries are erected and negotiated (Lamont, 1992). The arts, and cultural practices in general, take on a particular power and resonance in the context of discrimination and inequality as stigmatized groups enlist the arts as "equalization strategies" (see Lamont and Bail, 2008). As Canadian sociologist Michèle Lamont, explains, these strategies are sometimes "universalistic" in that they seek to emphasize the common humanity between members of stigmatized and dominant groups. Actress Anette Benning won an Oscar for her portrayal of a lesbian mother of two teens in the hit film *The Kids Are Alright*. Benning and her partner, played by Juliane Moore, are depicted as experiencing the same types of issues as straight parents. At other times, members of stigmatized groups explore questions about identity through the use of "particularistic" strategies, in that they draw on experience or perspectives of particular relevance to their group (Lamont, 1992). Feminist artists did this when they highlighted issues unique to the female body in their work. Kara Walker draws on the experience of slavery in a similar manner. Artists from non-majority ethnic or racial groups also bring the reality of cross-cultural, hybrid, multicultural experience to their work, as they struggle with sometimes contrasting cultural forms and traditions. We will examine a few

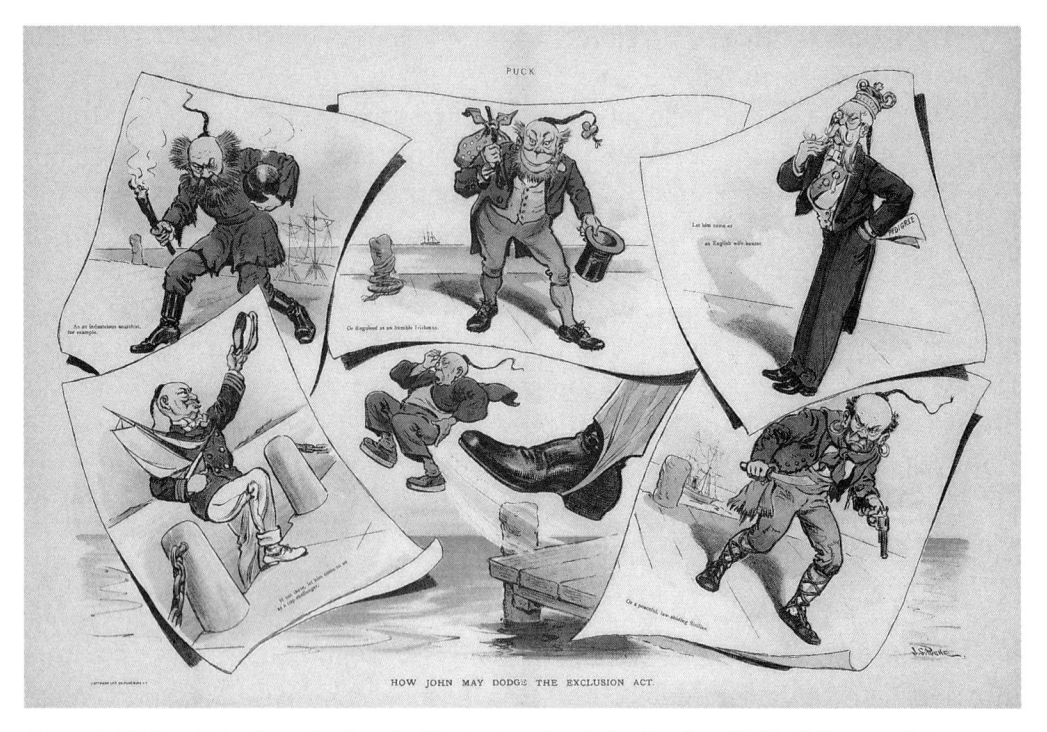

Photo 6.12 **How John May Dodge the Exclusion Act, John Pughe, 1905.** (Library of Congress, Prints & Photographs Division)

case studies in which art world members have negotiated the contradictions of racial and ethnic identity in European and American societies.

Blackness in Paris

> my negritude is not a stone
> nor a deafness flung against the clamor of the day
> my negritude is not a white speck of dead water
> on the dead eye of the earth
> my negritude is neither tower nor cathedral
> it plunges into the red flesh of the soil
> it plunges into the blazing flesh of the sky
> my negritude riddles with holes
> the dense affliction of its worthy patience
>
> From *Notebook of a Return to the Native Land* (1939), Aimé Césaire

By the 1920s in Paris, African arts and African American culture were all the rage among intellectuals and artists, sparking a movement called "Negrophilia" (Archer, 2000). But the influence of African and other non-Western arts on modernism in

Europe was by no means a one-way street. Colonialism and imperialism also brought waves of immigration of colonial subjects to Europe. By the 1920s there were sizable African and Caribbean communities in Paris, which included artists, writers and scholars who had been educated in French Universities. Some of them combined forces to form a French literary movement called **Negritude**. Writers and poets, like Aimé Césaire (1913–2008) who had emigrated from the Caribbean and Africa, sought to cultivate their own voices and experience as Black writers in opposition to French colonialism and racism. Their writing, like their trans-continental histories, represented their own unique blends of European and Diasporan influences. Like African American writers and scholars of the period, they articulated their opposition to assimilation and called for a pan-African collective Black identity. (see Ashcroft et al., 2002).

Harlem Renaissance

> I bathed in the Euphrates when dawns were young.
> I built my hut near the Congo and it lulled me to sleep.
> I looked upon the Nile and raised the pyramids above it.
> I heard the singing of the Mississippi when Abe Lincoln
> went down to New Orleans, and I've seen its muddy bosom turn
> all golden in the sunset.
> I've known rivers:
> Ancient, dusky rivers.
> My soul has grown deep like the rivers.
>
> "The Negro Speaks of Rivers" (1921) Langston Hughes

Even after the Civil War, the legacy of slavery and racism continued to define life in the American South. Between 1910 and 1930 some 2 million Blacks migrated from the rural South to northern industrial cities like Chicago and New York (Lemann, 1991) to escape racism and find work in the growing industrial sectors of the northeast and Midwest. New York City's Harlem became a center of cultural life and a symbol of a better future to its swelling African American population. It was there that powerful new ideas began to take hold among a generation of Black artists and intellectuals associated with the **Harlem Renaissance**.

Alain Locke (1885–1954), an influential African American philosopher coined the term "new negro" to describe the position of urban Blacks in response to the failures of Reconstruction and the racial violence of the Jim Crow South (see Locke, ed. 1997). Along with other intellectuals, notably the sociologist W. E. B, Dubois (1868–1963), Locke, believed that Blacks could succeed in the United States only by developing an independent and self-sustaining cultural, intellectual and artistic life rooted in Black culture and experience instead of trying to assimilate to White, European cultural norms and values. Marcus Garvey (1887–1940), another important figure of the period, began to formulate the influential ideology of Black Nationalism, which advocated an eventual return to Africa for Africans who had been scattered throughout the Americas and Europe through slavery and colonization. In one form or another, these thinkers articulated the beginnings of a kind of "Black essentialism" similar to the gender essentialism described in the last chapter.

A group of Harlem writers including Langston Hughes (1902–1967) coalesced around the ideas of the New Negro Movement. They explored various dimensions of Black identity and experience in the United Sates and incorporated language from everyday Black speech and imagery from African American and African folk culture into their work. These writers were interested in what Dubois described as the problem of "double-consciousness" (Du Bois, 1961). Black people, Dubois explained, faced the predicament of understanding themselves on their own terms as African Americans, "always looking at one's self through the eyes of others, of measuring one's soul by the tape of a world that looks on in amused contempt and pity" (Du Bois, 1961: 3; see also Gilroy, 1993).

Visual artists of the Harlem Renaissance like Jacob Lawrence (1917–2000) and Romare Bearden (1911–1988), and the sculptor Augusta Savage (1892–1962)

Photo 6.13 **The Train, Romare Bearden, 1975.** (© Romare Bearden Foundation/Licensed by VAGA, NY, NY Digital Image © The Museum of Modern Art/Licensed by SCALA/Art Resource, NY)

combined influences from European Modernism with references to African American and African folk culture and focused on themes related to the history and experiences of African Americans. Artists and writers of the Harlem Renaissance consciously explored the meaning of African American identity and experience in their work, while combining developments in European modernism with forms of cultural expression characteristic of African American and African history and culture.

Jazz

Harlem of the 1920s and 1930s was also home to the flowering of jazz. Greats like Louis Armstrong (1901–1971), Fats Waller (1904–1943), and Jelly Roll Morton (1890–1941) played to White and Black audiences in the speakeasies that flourished during prohibition. By the 1930s, musicians like Duke Ellington (1899–1974) and Count Basie (1904–1984) began to develop the big band sound of swing music, and brought Black music into the American mainstream (where, according to some critics (Kofsky, 1998), the music industry exploited the contributions of Black musicians and composers and encouraged bland versions of the genre). The subject of the influence of African musical forms in the United States is too vast to cover here, but jazz deserves special attention because of the plethora of debates that it has generated among scholars and artists. On the one hand, jazz music has migrated from the category of popular Black entertainment to that of high art (Lopes, 2002). Indeed, jazz is sometimes called the "America's classical music"

Photo 6.14 **Louis Armstrong, 1953.**

(Taylor and Reed, 2013). At the same time, jazz music has been at the center of heated debates about the relationship between race and culture.

In 1963 Amiri Baraka (1934–) (at the time his name was LeRoi Jones) published *Blues People* where he argues that the transformation of the Black psyche in America from African to African American is directly reflected in blues and jazz music. Ultimately, he proposes the controversial thesis that jazz represents the essential nature of the experience of African Americans in the United States and really only belongs to African Americans. According to Baraka, while some intellectual or bohemian Americans might identify with the outsider status of jazz musicians, the efforts of Whites to produce jazz has, at best, stripped the music of its unique expressive capacities. Furthermore, he argues, White jazz musicians have gained wealth and popularity by imitating the contributions of Black Jazz innovators (see Kofsky, 1970). Today, the idea that members of any social group, be they women, African Americans, Whites, lesbians, or anyone else possess some sort of shared, undiluted essence is contested. Nonetheless, Baraka's claim that important dimensions of African American experience can be better understood through attention to forms of music central to African American culture remains pertinent.

Black Power and the Arts

The radicalism and social upheaval of the 1960s also affected African American artists, intellectuals, and activists. Despite the gains made by the Civil Rights movement, segregation and racial inequality persisted in the United States. The assassination of Martin Luther King in 1968, the continued political power of White segregationists in the South, urban renewal projects that decimated and isolated Black urban communities in the North, unfair mortgage lending policies, and the loss of jobs to deindustrialization led some African Americans to challenge the notion that racial inequality could simply be "fixed" by lifting the legal barriers that had blocked African Americans from social mobility (see Painter, 2007). Like feminists who argued that patriarchy and the devaluation of women were central to the structure and culture of Western society, Stokely Carmichael (Kwame Ture 1941–1998) and Charles V. Hamilton (1929–), founders of the **Black Power** movement, believed that racism was a fundamental component of the American social system. The ideology of White supremacy, they believed, lay at the heart of U.S. imperialism and the soulless materialism of American culture. Like the founders of the New Negro movement, they argued that Black people, instead of trying to gain acceptance into White institutions and culture, should reject White values and perceptions. African Americans should develop their own cultural, political, and economic resources and communities. Instead of working with White activists as they had during the Civil Rights movement, Blacks should form their own separate political groups.

Photo 6.15 **The Black Panther, Emory Douglas, 1970.** (© 2013 Emory Douglas/Artists Rights Society (ARS), New York)

Photo 6.16 **"June 27, 1970," (We are from 25 to 30 Million Strong...), Emory Dougas, 1970.** (© 2013 Emory Douglas/Artists Rights Society (ARS), New York)

Founders of the Black Panther Party, Huey P. Newton (1942–1989) and Bobby Seale (1936–), went so far as to advocate armed resistance to White authority, and conflicts between Black Panther members and police ended more than once in gunfire and death (Bush, 2001;Van Deburg, 1992).

In addition to its macho version of Black masculinity (Painter, 2007: 121), the Black Power movement, including the Black Panthers, worked to provide much needed services to the Black community like day-care programs and medical clinics. This movement, with its insistence on Black pride and empowerment had a profound impact on Black cultural production. Amiri Baraka set up theaters and schools for young Black artists. Artists working together with community members created murals depicting important figures and events in African American history in inner city neighborhoods. Baraka and other Black Nationalists advocated a return to the African roots of Black culture and studied Swahili and African musical and folk arts and history. Many, like Malcolm X (1925–1965), joined the Nation of Islam, an African American reconstruction of Islam founded in the 1930s. They believed that by identifying with African culture and internalizing the notion that "Black is Beautiful," African Americans could combat the posture of inferiority they had been forced to adopt in the face of dominant White culture. African American visual artists took on themes of race, racism, and self-empowerment. In "Flag for the Moon, Die Nigger" (1969), for example, the artist Faith Ringold's (1930–) painting of an American Flag with the word "Die" appearing behind the stars and the word "Nigger" subtly replacing the stripes comments on the significant role of racism in American history. A similar image by David Hammons (1943–), "Injustice Case" (1970) depicts the artist, bound and gagged, trapped inside a frame of the American flag (see Painter, 2007: 334).

In addition to his writings on music, Amiri Baraka was also instrumental in promoting a new kind of poetry that used Black vernacular forms of English and expressed the values, lives, and experiences of the community. This poetry was not intended for literary critics or professional White poets and their audiences. Spoken poetry (as it was termed) was meant instead as a public expression of the beauty and the harsh realities of ghetto life. This style of poetry, or "spoken word" was often performed in free public spaces in Black communities to the accompaniment of freestyle- or free-jazz. It is one of the sources of inspiration for the poetry slams and rap music of later decades. At the same time that spoken poetry was taking to the streets, a number of Black publishing houses sprang up and Black writers were now able to distribute work that would have been difficult to sell to mainstream publishers.

Afro-centric Identity and the Black Middle Class

As the Black middle class expanded after the 1960s so did the market for work which reflected the experience of Black people in the United States. Middle- and upper-class Blacks sought to express and reflect upon their racial identity by supporting and displaying the work of artists who captured the Black experience (Halley, 1993). As Eric Hanks, owner of a California gallery specializing in African American arts, points out:

Black art speaks to the black experience and that is what sets it apart.... The work has to have meaning.

> Drakes, Sean. 2008 Artistic expression: perspectives on collecting African American art. *The Free Library* (September, 1),

Thus, owning art work that speaks to a shared African American past is part of the way that Black collectors perform, shape and explore their identity as separate and distinct from other Americans with whom they may share a similar class status. Many of these collectors, coming of age in the 1960s and 1970s, were most likely touched by the ideas of the Black Power movement. The American sociologist Patricia Banks (2010: 272–289) conducted a study in which she interviewed over 88 Black, middle-class art collectors to explain why they collected the work of Black artists. She found that many collected Black art specifically to support Black artists, who had historically been excluded from the art market and from adequate representation. In this sense they were drawing on W. E. B. Du Bois' (1903) much earlier plea to highly educated Blacks to use their talents to "save" the race.

What Banks found, however, most consistently in her interviews was that Black collectors collected Black art in an ongoing effort to cement and articulate their Black identity. These collectors wanted to maintain their Afro-American identity even if their economic fate diverged from that of many other African Americans, a disproportionate number of whom continue to live in poverty. For these collectors, collecting visual arts is a display of what the American sociologist Herbert Gans (1979) calls **symbolic ethnicity.** According to Gans, third or fourth generation members of ethnic groups, who have by and large assimilated to the dominant culture, look for intermittent and easy ways to maintain their ethnic identity by consuming very visible symbolic dimensions of culture, like participating in St. Patrick's day parades, throwing elaborate Bar Mitzvah parties, or sending their children to Greek language school on Saturdays. They maintain a sense of shared group identity while still participating fully in American life. Gans was thinking about immigrant groups like Jews, Irish, and Italians when he wrote this essay in 1979. These groups have by and large overcome the stigma of otherness that characterized their experience when they first came to the United States. For them, ethnic identification can be chosen but is not required. The persistence of racial discrimination in the United States means people of African descent do not have the option of "blending in." Gans' insights explain the popularity of Black art for Black collectors, but they need to be supplemented with an understanding of the differences between the way that race (which is almost always conceived in terms of dark and light skin color) and ethnicity play out in the United States.

Exhibition and Display

The public museum also makes visible the public it claims to serve. It produces the public as a visible entity by literally providing it a defining frame and giving it something to do.

Kirstenblatt-Gimlett in Karp et al. (1991)

> Museums are important venues in which a culture can identify itself and present itself publicly. Museums solidify culture—endow it with a tangibility in a way few other things do... Museums have always featured displays of power.
>
> Dubin (1999)

The two quotes above, both from social scientists who study art worlds, address the significance of public display and the institutions through which art and culture are exhibited and presented to publics. The American anthropologist Kirstenblatt-Gimlett points out the role of the museum in creating and forming publics, or groups of people who might be strangers but share an orientation toward culture with one another. Through the display of art and artifacts, museums construct a perspective and invite audiences to understand themselves as members of a particular group to whom that perspective is meaningful and directed. Through the consumption of an exhibition, class, race, gender, national, and ethnic identities are formed and reinforced and publics are created.

With the second quote, American sociologist Steve Dubin explains that the displays of culture and the museum formation of publics are not politically or socially neutral. In fact, museum exhibitions also illustrate, enact, and reinforce relations of power. Members of more powerful groups are able to use the museum venue to display their power and enforce their version of culture. Museums have also provided sites through which controversies and significant shifts in public thinking about race and ethnicity have played out (see, e.g. Coombes, 1988).

People on Display

Have you ever tried to photograph a stranger you found interesting? Did she respond with anger or anxiety? Wish *not* to be captured by your camera? Displaying, representing, or describing someone else for an audience involves an assertion of power. The person or people who are displayed or described move from living, conscious beings moving through space and time to static representations who cannot speak for themselves. People are often rendered powerless through display. Thus, it is not surprising that your unwilling subject did not want an image of himself or herself, which they could not control, explain or alter floating around in an unknown context. Indeed, when representations of people, (or those people themselves) or the objects that belong to them are ripped from the cultural context or their origin and displayed in Western-style museums under the direction of anthropologists, curators, or entrepreneurs for the visual consumption of Western audiences, power has been enacted. Those in charge of installing and explaining these objects and people have the power to define those people to their audiences.

As we have seen, with imperialism, Europeans in the late-19th century had new access to non-Western cultures through the artifacts, accounts, and images brought back (and sometimes stolen) to Europe by anthropologists, explorers, and merchants (see essays in Hight, 2002). Images, artifacts, and even people themselves (or their remains) were brought to Europe and to the United States and displayed before audiences who were eager to learn about other people and cultures but, nonetheless, in accordance with the racial ideologies of the day, regarded those others as less human than themselves (Blanchard et al., 2008).

Europeans and Americans understood these objects and representations of non-White, non-Western peoples through the lens of an ideology formed by the belief in a rigid hierarchy that placed Western civilization at the top of a pseudo-evolutionary pyramid of world civilizations. At the same time, the display of these objects and the peoples who created them shaped and reinforced this ideology. In addition to displaying material objects taken from non-Western cultures, and replicas of people, the display of live human beings in anthropological and ethnographic dioramas was not uncommon in the 19th century. Live Bushmen, for example, were installed in London's Egyptian Hall in 1847 in an exhibit about Africa, where, against a painted background, they nursed their children, ate, slept, and cooked under the gaze of onlookers. In another bizarre example, a woman of Hottentot origins who later became known as "Sarah Bartmann" was brought (perhaps kidnapped or enslaved, see Dubin,

Photo 6.17 **Love and beauty—Sartjee the Hottentot Venus, Christopher Crupper Rumford, 1811.** (Library of Congress, Prints & Photographs Division)

2006: 89) from Cape Town, South Africa, to Europe in 1810, where she was displayed in a skintight costume at sideshows and fairs in England, Ireland, and Scotland. There, she was "subjected to audience members gawking, poking, prodding and hurtling catcalls". After she died, her remains were put on view at the Musée de l'Homme, the famous French anthropological museum, until at least the mid-1970s. Bartmann's body fascinated European audiences because of the large deposits of fat around the hips and buttocks, an environmental adaptation characteristic of the peoples of some African regions, but unusual among Europeans. Bartmann's viewers, during her life and after her death, were especially interested in her genitalia, which Europeans thought would be more developed than their own. In addition, based upon a misunderstanding of evolutionary theory, European audiences thought that Hottentots represented a "missing link" between humans and apes.

By the 1970s, a shifting political climate caused scholars and museum staff to engage in extended re-evaluations of the ethnocentric, racist, ideas that had been created in the name of educating the public. Since then, many museum displays have been revamped and rethought. Human models, or even wax replicas have fallen out of favor, and local representatives of cultures on display are often consulted when exhibitions are mounted (Dubin, 2006: 57). Increasing consciousness on the part of museum personnel and publics about the way that museums have been complicit in, and indeed actively sought to construct, discourses and representations that support racism, stereotyping and dehumanization have led to a much more cautious attitude concerning the display of non-Western peoples. At the same time, ethnographic display of non-White or non-Western cultures still provides a source of entertainment for more privileged audiences at museums, fairs, folkloric enactments and other instances of what some scholars call "staged authenticity" (e.g. Mascardo, 1986).

Art and Objects

While the case may be more obvious with displays that involve human beings or their facsimiles, the exhibition and display of material objects is another way that racial and cultural hierarchies are created and reinforced. Powerful institutions and people have the power to assign legitimacy to certain objects over others. When objects are displayed in prestigious, well respected venues, or collected and valued by powerful, important people, these objects, along with the people who produced them are granted a certain status. In the Western context, as we have discussed, autonomous, singular works of art, whose creator is known, are sometimes granted a very special status which exceeds that of even the most valuable decorative, traditional or popular objects. Where, how and if objects are displayed conveys important ideas about the meaning and value of those objects to society.

African and Oceanic arts maintained the status of ethnographic object, as distinct from "true" art in the early 20th century, but they were nonetheless granted certain legitimacy in Europe because of the interest that Picasso and other important artists and collectors had in this work (see Zolberg, 1997 in Cherbo and Zolberg: 53–73).

Throughout the ensuing decades of the 20th century, many exhibitions of African and other "primitive" arts were launched in major museums throughout Europe and the United States and these institutions created new departments devoted to the study and display of so-called primitive arts (Zolberg, 1997: 54). African art objects have also been of special interest to African American collectors and museum board members and other members of the African American elite. These art objects rose in prestige (and market value) throughout the 20th century and have since been regarded by many of their champions as equal to Western art objects as judged by Western standards of aesthetic and formal values (see Goldwater, 1986).

Thus, African art has, to a certain extent, migrated from the category of ethnographic object to that of art in the Western imagination. Some White American artists, writers, and collectors lobbied on behalf of American Indian art and saw it as a basis on which a truly American (as opposed to European) artistic and cultural identity could be forged (see Mullin in Marcus and Meyer, 1995) and Native American arts have influenced the arts and visual culture in the United States and have commanded strong market and exhibition values. This elevation of native and African objects from the category of ethnographic specimen to legitimate art form represents a greater valuation of those cultures in the eyes of the West.

This kind of reappraisal, however, also suggests **ethnocentrism** or belief that one's own culture is superior to others. Applying conventional Western terms of aesthetic valorization to non-Western arts that have a meaning, function, and history connected to particular, non-Western social groups might enhance the value of these objects to Western collectors, historians, and other arts consumers. At the same time, by revaluing these objects through Western terms, Westerners are still asserting a form of domination over and devaluation of the people who created this work and for whom it was created.

While African, Oceanic, Latin American and Native American arts are highly valued in the United States, the national identity of Americans was formed in part through ideas of "whiteness" promoted through non-profit arts institutions founded by elite Anglo-Saxon Whites. Before the middle of the 19th century, sociologist Paul DiMaggio explains, European-style painting and sculpture was exhibited in the United States alongside "such curiosities as bearded women, mutant animals and popular entertainment" (DiMaggio, 1991). In the late 19th century, New England elites, who were primarily of Anglo Saxon origin, began to feel threatened by the increasing political power and cultural presence of working-class Irish Catholics, who immigrated to Boston to work in the growing manufacturing sector. These immigrants were less educated than the Anglo elites, and contested their power. By creating non-profit arts institutions like the Boston Symphony Orchestra and the Museum of Fine Arts, Anglo elites separated high arts from popular culture. Through educational programs, outreach, and free or subsidized admission to these institutions, elites were able to promote and elevate high, European culture to a mass audience, while at the same time maintaining control and ownership of this culture (DiMaggio, 1991). Out of the diverse and complex assortment of cultural forms available to Americans, White, European art forms became prestigious emblems of American culture. It was this sort of culture, owned and controlled by Anglo elites, to which other immigrant groups were supposed to assimilate if they hoped to prove themselves as legitimate Americans.

Busting It Open: Multiculturalism and Contemporary Display

Displays of art and culture in the United-States, like those featured in major museums and prestigious concert halls and performance spaces, have generally favored arts associated with the White, European tradition. The United States has, however, since its inception, been a multi-cultural and multi-racial society, and along with the rest of the world has become increasingly so. Since the 1970s, this multiculturalism has played out visibly in culture and the arts, as members of marginalized groups have fought for a stake in cultural institutions, access to art markets, and the right to define the terms of their own representation. Battles on the terrain of culture and representation grew out of the anti-authoritarian politics of the 1960s and 1970s, when young people protested US involvement in Vietnam (Wells, 1994). The war in Vietnam, for many of these youth, was not only typical of United States military bullying but also represented an attack on people of color, not so different from the racism that African Americans and other minorities continued to experience at home. In minority communities leaders built arts-based institutions that drew on the shared history and vibrancy of their communities and gave artists, curators, educators and community members who were excluded from White-dominated institutions the opportunity to claim cultural resources. From the early 1960s through the 1980s a number of institutions devoted to the promotion of minority arts sprang up across the United States, including the Studio Museum of Harlem (founded in 1968), The Museum of Mexican Art, which opened in a Mexican, working-class neighborhood in Chicago in 1987, and El Museo Del Barrio, which opened within a mile of New York's Spanish Harlem in 1970.

By the 1980s, the idea that healthy, democratic societies needed to foster cultural diversity and criticisms of the White, male, European bias of Western culture had become consistent themes of discussion at universities, in mainstream cultural institutions, and at least among portions of the public (see e.g. Benhabib, 2002; Bernstein, 1994). Colleges began to include books by African American or Caribbean authors in literature classes, elite theater companies began to stage work by minority playwrights like August Wilson, Miguel Piñero, and Jessica Haggedorn, whose work directly reflected the experience, linguistic styles, and heritage of groups that had experienced discrimination and marginalization in the United States. Large, well-funded museums like the Houston Museum of Art, which featured a show of Hispanic artists in 1987, sought to build bridges with underrepresented communities (see Karp, 1991). In fact, the themes of identity and multiculturalism came to be almost synonymous with art and culture in the 1980s. In 1990, three major New York institutions—the Museum of Contemporary Hispanic Art, the New Museum of Contemporary Art, and the Studio Museum in Harlem—launched a collaborative retrospective of 1980s art called "The Decade Show: Frameworks of Identity in the 1980s." This show, the New Museum website explains:

> brought together more than 200 works by ninety-four artists of Hispanic, Asian, African-American, Native American, and European heritage. The exhibition was issues oriented, rather than a stylistic overview, focusing on the important concerns of the 1980s as they relate to the idea of identity.
>
> http://www.newmuseum.org/exhibitions/226

This ambitious show provoked some criticism, but most of the attention was positive. The *New York Times* art critic Roberta Smith, for example, wrote that:

> This show's message is: when dealing with issues of oppression and difference, let's hear from the oppressed and different....

The success of the multi-culturalist agenda created a heated backlash by the late 1980s. Some critics claimed that so much inclusion watered down the canon and made any notion of universal artistic standards meaningless (e.g. Bloom, 1987). Others thought that focusing on plural "identities" and differences in various group's experience of the world led to an increasing inability of contemporary citizens to find common ground. Some conservative politicians used the growing presence of minority perspectives in arts, education and cultural institutions to fan the fears of White voters that they were losing their position of power in society (e.g. Corliss, 1998). Other critics complained that multiculturalism had become mainstream and had been coopted by an advertising and culture industry eager to raid the pockets of previously marginalized consumer groups, jumping on representations of inner-city youth of color to sell Nikes, and, in the case of media conglomerates like Viacom, creating television networks like BET (Black Entertainment Television) or MTV through which they could help marketing companies advertise more directly to specific "lifestyle" groups. As Jeff Chang notes, by the 1990s "[d]iversity [was] as ubiquitous as Disney". (in Grantmakers and the Arts Reader http://www.giarts.org/article/multiculturalism).

Does Race Still Matter?

After reflecting on some themes from the history of race and racism, and the relationship of this history to the arts in the United States and elsewhere, we might want to return again to the introductory paragraphs of this chapter. As of 2008, race still did matter—at least it mattered enough that Barack Obama's racial identity was pronounced on the *New York Times'* front page story covering his election. And it continues to matter today, as, at least in the United-States, we have seen continuing and in some cases widening gaps between Blacks and Hispanics, on the one hand, and Whites and Asians, on the other, in terms of educational attainment, arts participation, income and wealth, employment, rates of incarceration, and a host of other measures of associated with health and well-being. (e.g. Williams, 1999; Downy and Hawkins, 2008; Goldsmith, 2009; Welch and Kim, 2010).

At the same time, overt displays of racism are frowned upon. The uncritical use of stereotypes, like those associated with minstrelsy, or the kinds of de jure (legal) segregation that artists of color endured during the Jim Crow era is rare today. Nonetheless, artists of color of color continue to be sorely underrepresented in the worlds of film, classical music, ballet, and visual art. Prestigious arts institutions, however, feature the work of artists of color, and art worlds address themes of racism and cultural representation with increasing depth and subtlety. So, in answer to the question "does race still matter?" we must reply that, yes, it still does matter but in ways different and perhaps more complex than 50 years ago.

Discussion Questions

1. List differences and similarities between the way that Women and African Americans have experienced discrimination in the United States.
2. How did imperialism and colonialism affect the arts in Europe? How did the arts of non-Western cultures influence European artists? How did representations of non-European, non-White peoples in European culture form a sense of cultural and racial identity for Europeans?
3. Consider this passage from the chapter: "The arts, and cultural practices in general, take on a particular power and resonance in the context of

discrimination and inequality, where dominant groups and stigmatized ethno/racial groups sometimes enlist the arts as "equalization strategies." These strategies are sometimes "universalistic" in that they seek to emphasize the common humanity between members of stigmatized and dominant groups. They sometimes employ particularistic strategies, in that they draw on experience or perspectives that are thought to be "unique" to specific groups (Lamont and Fournier, 1992). Can you think of an example of art or cultural practice which utilizes either "universalistics" or "unique" equalization strategies?

4. At first, African art was displayed as anthropological curiosity to Western audiences. Later, European and American artists and collectors started to promote African art, pointing to its aesthetic and formal value. Some scholars have argued that this "revaluation" represents a form of domination of Western culture over non-Western cultures. Why would they make this argument? Explain. Do you agree or disagree?
5. How was the encounter between Western and non-Western cultures different in the Americas than in Europe?
6. What does "essentialism" mean in the context of race and the arts? Give some examples of art worlds or art works that have drawn on the idea of racial or ethnic essentialism.
7. What is minstrelsy? How did it develop? How has it influenced American culture?
8. In what ways have museums had an important role to play in creating public representations of race and ethnicity? Visit a museum or exhibition devoted to representing members of a "non-White" group. Report on your findings.

7
ART, POLITICS, AND THE ECONOMY

Photo 7.1 **Study of Perspective - Tiananmen 1995- b/w print.** (Photo credit: Ai Weiwei.)

The Chinese artist Ai Weiwei has been exhibited in countless museums and art exhibitions worldwide, and he enjoys a huge following of art-world insiders and ordinary Chinese citizens. His status in his own country is so great that he was asked to help design the stadium for the 2008 Beijing Olympics. Despite Ai Weiwei's success and prestige inside and outside of China, he has been hounded, harassed, beaten, and jailed by the Chinese Government for his dissident activities. After working on the design for the Olympic Stadium in 2008, he denounced the Olympics as an elaborate public relations routine enacted by the Chinese Government to present a happy face to the world and whitewash persistent human rights violations and clampdowns on basic freedoms in China.

After the earthquake in Sichuan province in China in 2008, he launched a citizen action campaign to uncover the names of schoolchildren who had been killed there. He sought to expose both the Government's attempts to bury the extent of the tragedy and the Government's culpability for the shoddy buildings that housed the schoolchildren. When the Chinese police began surveying and harassing Ai Weiwei, he videotaped their actions and distributed these videos via the Internet and his blog, twittering the details of his cat and mouse game with authorities (Barboza, 2009).

In 2009, the Haus Der Kunst art museum in Munich launched an exhibition of Ai Weiwei's work which included a wall of 9,000 children's backpacks in memory of the victims of the Sichuan earthquake and Chinese characters spelled the sentence "She lived happily for seven years in this world." After the opening, Ai Weiwei was rushed to a hospital for treatment of a head injury he sustained when beaten by Chinese police before leaving the country. While waiting to recover, he photographed himself in his hospital gown, attached to an IV, his middle finger in the air, and sent the photo to the Chinese Government. In January 2011, after his new Shanghai studio was bulldozed by the Chinese Government he called the resulting rubble a powerful symbol and a work of art in itself. (In 2011, http://www.timeout.com/london/art/ai-weiwei-interview).

Ai Weiwei's career and artwork illustrate some of the ways that political and economic systems shape the arts and the role that the arts play in supporting,

Photo 7.2 **Sichuan Earthquake Photos, 2008-, black-and-white photographs.** (Photo credit: Ai Weiwei)

promoting, and challenging political and economic institutions. In all societies, political and economic systems play key roles in the distribution not only of material but also of symbolic resources, such as prestige, security, and so on. To produce and distribute works of art, art-world members need access to art materials and exhibition and performance sites. They also need publicity, food, living spaces for artists, and compensation for the work done by various "supporting personnel" (see Chapter One). The availability of these resources depends on the economic and political organization of society. In capitalist societies, these resources are distributed largely through the market. Art worlds are thus enabled and constrained by their access to the capital (money) with which to purchase the goods and services required to make art. As China's economy transitioned from state socialism to free-market capitalism, more artists had a shot at selling their work on a global market and acquiring resources to keep making and exhibiting work. A thriving commercial art scene helped transform the Dashanzi neighborhood in Beijing from an abandoned industrial site to a revenue-generating tourist destination (Currier, 2008).

On the other hand, even in a market economy, governments play an important role by distributing resources in the form of grants, stipends, exhibition space, and awards. For this reason governments exert pressure on art worlds and artists. With government support, however, comes constraint. When artists make art that criticizes the government or outrages voters who might support elected officials, government support is sometimes withheld. Thus, artists and arts institutions may shape their goals (or at least their funding proposals) to have a better chance for government aid. When government support for the arts shrinks, as it has in the United States since the 1980s, many arts institutions go under. As a result, many people who might have wanted to pursue careers in the arts instead have to devote most of their time to doing other kinds of work to support themselves.

In addition to supporting arts and arts institutions, governments like the Chinese Communist Party sometimes actively suppress art and artists who are critical of them. Even in the United States, where the First Amendment guarantees freedom of expression, state and federal censorship laws have been used to limit the funding and distribution of cultural artifacts deemed obscene or offensive by Government authorities (see Post, 1998). Often, government intervention is unnecessary because arts groups engage in self-censorship when they think the stakes are too high (see e.g. Lewis, 2000).

Finally, art is a powerful medium of communication. Artists and arts groups have often harnessed the communicative, symbolic aspect of art to launch oppositional critiques of society and especially of powerful economic and political institutions. For Ai Weiwei, opposition to the Government and exposing Government abuses are so central to his art that he sometimes blurs the distinction between art and political activism. The arts, as we will see, have played this role on many occasions throughout modern history.

Systems of Distribution

Housing, health care, food, leisure time, status, and political power are not produced and distributed chaotically or randomly. All societies have institutions, arrangements, and systems for the production and distribution of material and symbolic goods, services, and resources. These arrangements (otherwise known as economies) are not usually equitable, and they often fall short of providing sufficient resources to all members of society, but they nonetheless exist outside of any individual's control. While many people think of the economy purely in financial terms, economic arrangements always also imply political (government) arrangements. Even in free market economies, governments determine monetary and legal policies that directly affect financial organizations, workers, and consumers.

Capitalism

Capitalism and socialism, or some combination of the two, have been the dominant economic systems of the modern era. Although scholars argue about definitions, capitalism is usually understood as an economic system in which the technology, land, and labor by which goods and resources are produced are owned *privately* by individual entrepreneurs or shareholders. Employees are hired, and goods and services are provided to society's members for a profit, which individual owners use to enhance their lifestyle and to reinvest in their enterprises. The price of consumer items is controlled by a number of factors, including supply and demand, and individuals' access to goods and resources depends on their own market position or how much money they have (see Chapter Four).

Socialism

Capitalism is based on the belief that human beings are fundamentally self-interested and individualistic. Economies, therefore, are the most successful when they are organized around principles that encourage individual profit-maximization (e.g. DeRosa, 2001). **Socialism** is based on the belief that people produce goods and resources together and that these resources should be thought of as social, rather than individual, products. Property, technology, and everything else needed to produce things that people need should be owned in common; and any extra resources (or wealth) that result from the production and distribution process should either be shared by all of the people who produce those things or should go back into shared, collective projects. According to this perspective, human beings are fundamentally social, and thus the economy works best when it is organized around social rather than individualistic principles.

Karl Marx, the "father" of modern socialism (see Chapters Two, Three, and Four) thought that eventually there would be little need for a state or centralized government in socialist societies (Lenin, 1943). In the short term, however, he thought that the state would act as a proxy for collective ownership of resources. Industries like agriculture, manufacturing, communication and so on would be run and controlled by the government, which would in turn ensure that everyone's material needs were met. Marx believed that the government should also provide abundant public goods like education, health care, support for the arts and culture, childcare, job training, and so forth.

Mixed Economies and the Welfare State

From the early 20th century until the 1980s, socialism as an ideology and form of economic organization provided a serious challenge to capitalism. Capitalist countries like the United States had to ensure that their economies provided citizens with enough resources and opportunities for material advancement so that socialism did not seem like an enticing alternative. Governments of capitalist countries also found ways to discourage or prohibit the activities of socialist and communist political groups, which were trying to encourage workers to overthrow—or at least to challenge—capitalism (Harvey, 1990; Sassoon, 1996). During the **Cold War**, which occurred roughly between the late 1940s and the late 1980s and was spearheaded by the United States and allied NATO nations on the one side and the Soviet Union and its satellite states on the other, the United States expended tremendous cultural, economic, and intellectual resources to produce negative depictions of life in socialist countries (and vice versa). By the 1980s, most of the former Soviet satellite states and China had begun to move toward market-based, privately-owned forms of production and distribution. Today, almost all of the former socialist economies are at least partially capitalist.

While capitalism has prevailed at the beginning of the 21st century, it would be false to say that capitalism is unaffected by socialist ideas. Capitalist democracies like the United States, at least since the 1940s, have incorporated aspects of the welfare state to varying degrees. Before the Great Depression, the United States Government did little to distribute the benefits of economic growth to all citizens. In direct response to the widespread misery caused by the Great Depression, however, the British economist John Maynard Keynes (1883–1946) convinced the president of the United States, Franklin Roosevelt, that the **invisible hand** of the free market needed the guidance of state-imposed regulations and that the state needed to provide a safety net to citizens during the inevitable

ART, POLITICS, AND THE ECONOMY 139

Photo 7.3 The United States also instituted policies designed to foster greater economic equality, to expand public institutions, and to promote the arts and sciences. - WPA women painters, Federal Art Gallery, 50 Beacon St., Boston, 1936–8. (Library of Congress, Prints & Photographs Division)

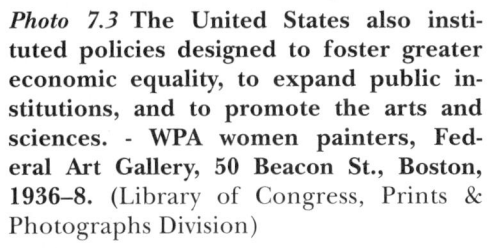

Photo 7.4 The United States also instituted policies designed to foster greater economice quality, to expand public institutions, and to promote the arts and sciences. - Who's who in the zoo. Illustrated natural history prepared by the WPA Federal Writers Project, 1936 or 1937. (Library of Congress, Prints & Photographs Division)

periods of unemployment that occurred with a market-based economy. This welfare state was funded through a system of taxation meant to transfer some of the money of the wealthiest citizens into public services and public insurances, such as Social Security. The principles of state-organized redistribution of resources have been followed more strongly in countries with powerful labor unions. Countries like France, Great Britain, and Norway have provided generous state-funded resources including day care, funding for artists and cultural projects, strong public universities, and universal public health care. Though redistribution of wealth was less comprehensive than in these countries, the United States also instituted policies designed to foster greater economic equality, expand public institutions, and promote the arts and sciences (Clark, 2009; Esping-Andersen,1990).

The New Economy

By the middle of the 1970s, for a range of reasons that economists continue to debate (Harvey 1990, 2005; Stein, 2010; Fabricant, 1972), Western capitalist countries began to experience shrinking rates of profit and productivity, accompanied by high rates of inflation and unemployment. Although rates of inequality had reached unprecedented lows, elites in Western capitalist countries feared that the capitalist economy was unstable under the current conditions. When Margaret Thatcher came to power in Great Britain in 1979, followed by Ronald Reagan two years later in the United States, a new (or rather retooled) idea about the relationship between the state and society began to take hold among elites. This idea, called neoliberalism (a term used by adherents and critics alike), was in part a resuscitation of the "laissez faire" (let it be) approach to the economy developed by the 18th and 19th century thinkers in the liberal tradition. The British philosophers John Locke (1632–1704) and the Scottish political economist Adam Smith (1723–1790) argued that if society allows individuals to pursue their own economic self-interest without too many state regulations and interventions, the market will provide the most benefits for the most people. Consumers' natural desires for good-quality items at a reasonable price, combined with the desire of producers to make a profit, will stimulate healthy competition and ensure that resources that people want will be produced well and efficiently. In addition, they believed that the less government intervenes in the market, the more personal freedoms individuals will experience (Smith, 1979; Friedman, 2012).

New proponents of "laissez faire" approaches, like the American economist Milton Friedman (1912–2006), blamed the policies of John Maynard Keynes and the profligacy of the welfare state for existing economic problems. Political leaders responded to the theories of neoliberal economists by lowering taxes, instituting tax cuts for business and industry, deregulating trade, reducing spending on welfare and public goods, pressuring developing countries to adopt free-market policies, and trying to curtail labor unions (Harvey, 2005). By lowering barriers to corporate profits, they reasoned, economic growth would "trickle down" to less advantaged segments of the population. This economic approach received an additional boost on the global scale with the collapse of the Soviet Communist bloc and China's transition to capitalism in the late 1980s.

While neoliberal policies accompanied periods of economic growth, their long-term effect has been to stimulate unprecedented levels of economic inequality across the globe (Harvey, 2005) and to lower the standard of living of the middle class in Western countries. Despite the global economic meltdown of 2008–2009 and the public bailout of private financial institutions that followed, however, neoliberal ideas continue to dominate our political, cultural, and economic policies. These policies have also influenced artistic and cultural production in numerous ways.

Distribution and Patronage

Prior to the widespread presence of capitalism in the 19th century, artists relied on the patronage of wealthy merchants or royal families or the Church for economic support (see Chapter Two). Since the latter half of the 19th century a combination of markets, governments, and philanthropic institutions have provided economic support and channels of distribution for the arts. In all of the models of distribution discussed above, governments and economies coordinate with each other to distribute resources. Now, we will turn to lenses of the middle range (see Chapter Three) in order to describe some of the more specific organizational forms through which economies and governments support culture and the arts in particular. As you will see, these organizational forms are both enabled and constrained by prevailing political and economic systems.

Large-Scale Commercial Distribution

Most cultural products in capitalist, market-based societies are the product of large-scale, commercial (or for-profit) industries. In addition to covering the expenses of producing art, large, profit-driven concerns (such as commercial publishers, major record labels, and Hollywood film distributors) must be able to generate a profit for the shareholders of the company. All of this is very expensive, so for-profit distribution systems must convince a large (mass) audience to spend money to consume their products. A publishing company like Random House will not be able to cover all of its expenses and make a profit if they only publish the work of avant-garde poets with few readers. They have to publish entertaining and accessible novels or self-help books that will appeal to a wide audience. And, they have to devote considerable resources to advertising, promoting, and marketing their products to ensure strong sales.

This commercial, for-profit mode of distribution has consequences for what is distributed and supported. First of all, it is very difficult for market researchers to determine which cultural products will be popular before money is spent to produce and distribute the product (Alexander, 2003:108–112). There are just too many variables to account for, and audience response is too unpredictable to guarantee the success of a film, television show, or record album before it is made available to real audiences. For this reason, commercial culture industries *overproduce*. They make more products than they will actually devote themselves to reproducing, marketing, and distributing. In this way, they transfer the risks and costs of production onto artists (Romanowski and Denisoff, 1987), who may devote months or years to projects, only to find out that the producer is unwilling to expend enough resources to promote and distribute their work because it did poorly in its initial sales. Commercial industries also tend to keep producing a type of product that has already garnered profit (hence the sequel, prequel, and "return of" seen so often in blockbuster films), and they selectively promote what they think will be most popular.

In addition, commercial industries are unlikely to take on a risky product. Companies like film studios often change an artist's work (Faulkner, 1983; Peterson, 1982; Lewis, 1988) to make it commercially viable to a mass audience. When a writer sells a book to a film producer, the screenplay that is eventually produced often departs in significant ways from the author's original novel. Characters may be made less complicated and more palatable to segments of the intended audience. The movie's ending may differ because film producers don't want to risk disappointing audience expectations. These practices, for obvious reasons, constrain innovation and limit the production of potentially interesting but unfamiliar kinds of art. No matter how you look at it, large-scale commercial distribution systems don't support risky or potentially unpopular or highly controversial work. Artists like Ai Weiwei are unlikely to be part of large-scale, commercial distribution systems.

The Art Dealer Gallery System

The work of Ai Weiwei and other artists whose careers and reputation are grounded in the values of innovation and authenticity is more likely to be distributed through the art dealer gallery system. Art dealers sometimes buy works of art outright from artists, collectors, or other dealers. Or they take an artist's work on consignment and divide the money from the sale with the artist according to a prearranged agreement. Occasionally, dealers will help support an artist with a stipend, in return for the right to sell the work that the artist produces. Like large-scale commercial distributors, art dealers rely on sales to stay in business. On a much smaller scale, the artist-dealer gallery system also relies on profit. Besides generating enough income to pay for their own overhead (gallery space, employees, advertising in art magazine, etc.), gallery owners also need to raise enough money to keep buying and promoting the work of new artists in a competitive market.

This system of distribution, however, differs from mass, commercial distribution in several ways. First, art dealers rely on a much narrower market segment and consequently have a different kind of relationship to artists and consumers (Peterson, 1997; Plattner, 1998; Moulin, 1987; White and White, 1993). Some dealers specialize in selling works of art that have a very stable market value, like **Old Masters** and **Modern Masters,** who are already dead, and **blue-chip artists,** who are still alive but whose reputations are so secure that any work they produce will be valuable. Other dealers take on lots of risk when they agree to spend time representing an artist whose work has not already established its market value. To make up for this risk, dealers ask for a very high commission (usually at least 50 percent) on every sale. In both cases, dealers work with relatively few artists and buyers and must cultivate both with a personal relationship, which relies on trust and shared values.

Collectors place trust in the knowledge and taste of the art dealer and respect both the dealer's close relationship with the artist and the dealer's status in the art world (Velthuis, 2005). In addition, dealers must be able to communicate directly with artists about the intentions of the work, materials, etc. to discuss the work with potential buyers. Dealers also sometimes provide emotional support and encouragement to artists. Because dealers sell to a specialized audience of relative insiders and don't need to mass market, this system provides more room for innovation and autonomy than large-scale commercial systems of distribution. Nonetheless, dealer systems also cater to the market. Artists are often pressured to keep producing the kind of work on which their market value is based (Rothenberg and Fine, 2008). In addition, the relatively small and tightly controlled networks through which dealers meet and select artists to represent restrict opportunities for those artists who lack social connections or institutional pedigree. With this closed system, most artists are unable to exhibit and sell their work, while the lucky few who are selected must anxiously guard their reputations (Karttunen, 1998).

Localized Networks

Artistic innovations are most likely to occur in small, localized networks of distribution, often referred to as scenes. These systems are less dependent on the market for the distribution of cultural goods. They don't need to generate

Photo 7.5 **At the Cedar Bar, John Choen, 1959.** (John Cohen/Hulton Archive/Getty Images)

profit to sustain their members. Artists in these systems often have a day job and don't rely on their art to make a living. The network provides artists support for innovation through non-monetary reward systems: the appreciation of their peers and the enhancement of their reputation (Crane, 1989). Bohemian communities of artists, like the Abstract Expressionists in New York City in the 1940s and 1950s (see photo 7.5) (Crane, 1987; Ashton, 1973), early hip-hop culture, and spoken-word poetry are good examples of localized networks(see e.g. Chepp, 2012; Bennett and Peterson, 2004; Dowd et al., 2004)). In these subcultures, there is a very close connection between audiences and artists; and consumers, critics, and artists, often socialize together in local bars, restaurants, festivals, galleries, and clubs.

Localized networks are often absorbed into dealer systems or large industries, or they gain access to larger cultural organizations. Ai Weiwei, like other Chinese avant-garde artists, spent decades making art that was never exhibited in a commercial gallery or big museum. Only the other members of the underground art community in China knew much about him or his work. Today, his work is in the collections of major museums and high-end galleries. While independent, localized networks support artistic innovation and a sense of community, the small audience and limited material support that such systems provide ensure their fragility in a market society.

Nonprofit Systems of Distribution

Most museums, opera houses, symphony orchestras, dance, and theater companies are nonprofit institutions. Unlike commercial systems of distribution, nonprofit institutions do not generate economic profit and are not directly subject to market pressures. They need to raise funds from various sources, but they don't need to generate revenue in excess of their expenses. Nonprofits solicit individuals and corporations for donations, and because they work for the public good, they can apply for grants and government funds. Nonprofit institutions support the arts in a variety of ways including providing salaries or grants to artists; educational programs; studio, exhibition and performance spaces; community outreach; and libraries and archives.

Like most institutions in American society, nonprofits are highly stratified. Boards of directors govern them, and at elite institutions many of their members are from the economic elite (Osterow, 1995, 2004). To serve on a board of directors, members need to know something about the arts, but they also need to have connections with potential corporate and individual donors. Although nonprofits don't need to generate mass audiences, critics argue that nonprofits are inherently more conservative than localized networks because they need to raise funds (Toepler et al., 2002). Elite nonprofits have to choose repertoire and exhibitions that will interest wealthy donors as well as a sizable audience and subscribers, who are less open to innovation than small face-to-face networks. Smaller nonprofits accommodate more innovation than larger ones because they have fewer mouths to feed (DiMaggio and Sternberg, 1985).

Nonprofits are not market-driven, but their public mission to support artists and the arts is often compromised by the realities of the market. They must spend significant resources in their search for new ways to generate revenue from commercial enterprises like gift shops and restaurants, and they must engage in constant fundraising activities to woo private and corporate donors. Nonprofit cultural institutions provide advertising and prestige for these donors in the form of high-profile events featuring corporate logos, named museum wings, and so forth (see Alexander, 1990, 1996). When government support becomes scarce, as it did in the 1980s in the United States, nonprofits become even more beholden to the interests of wealthy donors and corporate sponsors (Chin-Tao Wu, 2002).

Governments and the Arts

Unlike in the socialist societies of Cuba and the former Soviet Union, governments in modern capitalist societies rarely directly control the distribution, evaluation, and funding of art. Governments, however, can provide significant funds to arts organizations and sometimes to artists themselves. Local and regional governments also sometimes support the arts as part of development projects to revitalize neighborhoods or cultivate regional tourism. In

Photo 7.6 **Zapatistas [formerly Mexican Soldiers] Alfredo Ramos Martínez 1932.**

the systems of arts distribution and patronage that we have discussed so far, the role of the government is indirect. When governments act directly as patrons to the arts (providing grants to artists and arts institutions; building exhibition and performance spaces; commissioning memorials, public sculptures and instillations; and supporting state operas, ballets, theaters, museums, and arts academies), a number of issues and controversies come to the fore.

Nationalism

Art and culture had an important role to play in the evolution of large, centralized, bureaucratically organized and territorially bound nation states in the 18th and 19th centuries (see Chapters Two and Six). The idea of a shared national identity linking people who do not have face-to-face interactions and who may not even have shared a common language or set of cultural traditions has to be manufactured and nurtured by new sovereign states and nationalist movements (Anderson, 1991; Gellner, 1997; Hobsbawm et al., 1983). To invoke a sense of nationalism and shared destiny (important if you want citizens to pay taxes and fight in wars), nation states cultivate a shared culture and identity among people who are unlikely ever to meet one another (Anderson, 1991).

National literacy campaigns, monuments and tombs, parades, national celebrations and other official forms of symbolic display are all important for the formation of a common national culture. In European countries like France, England, and Spain establishing state control of the arts encouraged the development of national identity and imperial power (see Chapter Two). National ballets, operas, theaters, and so forth contributed to a post-revolutionary national identity in socialist countries like the Soviet Union, China, and Cuba. At the same time, state control also means that the arts have to fit in with the goals of the state. Artists have to represent a common history and culture in a way that glorifies the state and its rulers, as in the case of the French Academy discussed in Chapter Two, or they have to contribute to the creation of a special national mythology (e.g. Vieth, 1995).

While state interests are often in line with preserving local and regional traditions, or emphasizing the role of national artists in classical traditions, states can also use arts institutions actively to craft new kinds of culture that promote new ideological goals or political regimes. New governments sometimes try to suppress or eradicate cultural expressions of the past. After the revolution in China in 1949, the Government of the new People's Republic of China sought to refute the imperial, dynastic, and feudal past while glorifying the revolution and workers and peasants of the new society.

ART, POLITICS, AND THE ECONOMY

> The problem facing the workers, peasants and soldiers is this: they are now engaged in a bitter and bloody struggle with the enemy but are illiterate and uneducated as a result of long years of rule by the feudal and bourgeois classes, and therefore they are eagerly demanding enlightenment, education and works of literature and art which meet their urgent needs and which are easy to absorb, in order to heighten their enthusiasm in struggle and confidence in victory, strengthen their unity and fight the enemy with one heart and one mind. For them the prime need is not "more flowers on the brocade" but "fuel in snowy weather".
>
> "Talks at the yenan forum on literature and art
> *May 1942*" (date) Mao Zedong

Officials debated the role that imperial Chinese art traditions and traditional folk art would play in the new society. During China's Cultural Revolution, factions of the government engaged in a vicious campaign to punish artists or scholars whose work referred approvingly to the pre-revolutionary past. Professors were beaten, artworks destroyed, and intellectuals exiled to the countryside to work alongside peasants. Artists who weren't consigned to labor in the countryside were forced to create propagandistic posters, sculptures, and paintings in the style of Soviet **Socialist Realism**. Now, with the turn to a market

Photo 7.7 **Greet the 1970s with the new victories of revolution and production, Shanghai renmin meishu chubanshe, 1970.** (IISH Stefan R. Landsberger Collection, International Institute of Social History (Amsterdam) http://chineseposters.net)

economy, the Chinese Government has worked to restore religious sites as part of its national heritage and has been more tolerant of artistic variety and innovation (Vine, 2008:11).

Sometimes governments employ the arts to engage in direct propaganda campaigns aimed at manipulating public emotions and beliefs. Propagandistic art from a variety of societies shares common themes and stylistic tendencies. Indeed, authoritarian governments have been notoriously hostile to abstract, modernist styles of art and expressionism. According to Hungarian socialist critic Georg Lukács, writing in defense of realism in 1938 (see Chapter Ten for full discussion), abstract, modernist works of art are not only difficult to inject with obvious content but also represent the bourgeois values of individualism, alienation, and moral deterioration. Modern, Western democratic ideals concerning the autonomy of art and freedom of expression (see Chapter Two), however, are fundamentally in conflict with government edicts mandating the style and content of works of art.

For reasons of national interest governments sometimes support art that is less obvious in its ideological intent. As I suggested earlier, China wanted to shed its old-fashioned image as it entered the global capitalist system in the 1980s and 1990s. An important claim made by proponents of free market systems is that the conditions that support free enterprise support other kinds of freedoms as well, including the freedom to make art. In this sense, art that is anti-government or art that doesn't directly express mainstream views indicates that the society in which it is produced fosters not only economic but also social freedom. Such art can thus function as an important public relations tool for governments on the international stage.

Although the success of Abstract Expressionism can be attributed to many factors (see Crane, 1987), some scholars argue that it succeeded in part because it was promoted by the U.S. Government in a variety of overt and covert ways as part of the Government's Cold War efforts. Art historians Eva Cockcroft and Max Kosloz, (see Frascnia, 1985), provide evidence that the United States Government, the CIA, and institutions such as the Museum of Modern Art collaborated to promote Abstract Expressionism in Europe and elsewhere in an effort to cultivate a positive image of the United States after World War II. Though it is likely that some scholars overstate the case, Abstract Expressionism did serve as a handy poster child for the superiority of American individualism and cultural freedom, especially compared to the stilted and state-orchestrated socialist realism art that was coming from the Soviet Union.

The Cold War was, in large part, a war of ideas. Thus, the ways that ideas were represented in words, images, and other cultural products were part of the arsenal that each side used to advance its competing vision of the world. The Soviet Union tended toward heavy-handed propaganda to promote the ideals of collectivism and the dignity of workers. The United States, in contrast, disseminated images depicting material plenty and individual freedom. While Abstract Expressionism may not have depicted the advantages of life in America through recognizable imagery (in the manner of Norman Rockwell's 1943 painting of a Thanksgiving dinner), at least it did not *criticize* American society in an obvious way. In fact, the emphasis on individual style and expression found in the work of Abstract Expressionist painters implicitly suggests that they belonged to a society that valued individual expression above all else.

Censorship of the Arts

In the most extreme cases of imposition of state power on culture, governments can restrict, ban, censor, destroy, or otherwise control public access to works of art deemed threatening to social order, morality, or the authority of the state. When Hitler (1889–1945) took power in Germany, he removed all modern art from museums, including works by masters such as Pablo Picasso, Emil Nolde (1867–1956), Marc Chagall (1887–1985), and Henri Matisse. In Hitler's view, modernism, and especially its association with Jewish artists, had a degrading effect on culture. The only artistic forms that a true Aryan artist should follow, he thought, were the classical styles of ancient Greek and Roman art, which were proper for depicting the purity of the Nordic race and the ideals of the Nazi state. More recently, a number of countries with large Muslim populations banned the book *The Satanic Verses* (1988) by the writer Salman Rushdie (1947–). Rushdie, himself a Muslim raised in India, outraged devout Muslim leaders because of language and imagery in his combination of fantasy and autobiography (Dubin, 1992: 85).

Individual works of art may be censored by governments. Alternatively, artists whose work is considered dangerous or in violation of state interest (as in the case of Ai Weiwei in China) can be jailed, harassed, blacklisted, or otherwise punished or prevented from creating their work. In this way, the careers of many artists were destroyed during the early 1950s by **McCarthyism** in the United States. In the United States, anti-communist paranoia was fanned by the government, and citizens were encouraged to discover and rout out possible Soviet agents and sympathizers operating clandestinely in their midst. There are many wonderful examples of this theme played out in Hollywood movies of the period, such as *The Red Menace* (1949) and *Invasion of the Body Snatchers* (1956). This paranoia was exemplified by the attacks of Senator Joseph McCarthy (1908–1957) and his supporters on countless individuals whom they accused of being Communist sympathizers (Schrecker, 1998). These individuals were forced to testify about their activities and the activities of their colleagues before a special House committee formed to prosecute and punish "un-American" activity. Once artists were accused by this committee, it was almost impossible for them to find employment or sell their work. While artists and intellectuals watched as the careers and lives of colleagues persecuted by McCarthy's "witch-hunts" were destroyed, many chose to censor their own work (Schrecker, 1998).

Obscenity Laws

Governments also use obscenity laws to ban the distribution and sales of controversial works of art. For example, *Lady Chatterley's Lover*, a novel by the British writer D. H Lawrence, which explores a British aristocrat's steamy extramarital affair with the gamekeeper, was written in the 1920s, but a full, unexpurgated edition was not published in England until 1960. This delay was not only because of its graphic (for the time) descriptions of erotic feelings and experience (especially shocking because these were expressed from the perspective of a woman) but also because the story transgressed important social taboos about the separation of social classes. To publish the book, the publisher had to engage in a protracted legal battle during which he had to defend the book's artistic merits against obscenity charges.

In the United States, artistic expression is protected under the First Amendment, which provides that the government cannot make laws abridging the freedom of speech. An important exception to this right, however, is speech or expression that is defined as "abhorrent to the morality of the time." Of course, times change and what we consider abhorrent varies from place to place, especially in a country as large as the United States. For this reason, obscenity charges are notoriously open to extended public debate. When Supreme Court Justice Potter Stewart was asked to be precise about what constitutes obscenity, he famously explained, "I shall not today attempt further to define the kinds of material I understand to be embraced [by obscenity laws]…[b]ut I know it when I see it…" (see O'mara, 1964)

In 1973, a three-tiered test to determine what was merely erotic, and thus protected by the First Amendment, and what was obscene, and therefore not protected, was developed. Based on this test, whether or not a work was labeled obscene depended on:

(a) whether the average person, applying contemporary community standards would find that the work, taken as a whole, appeals to the prurient interest,
(b) whether the work depicts or describes, in a patently offensive way, sexual conduct specifically defined by the applicable state,
(c) whether the work, taken as a whole, lacks serious literary, artistic, political, or scientific value (in Bayasee, 1995).

As you can see, the criteria listed above still leave room for interpretation and debate. Not surprisingly, issues concerning obscenity and infringement of the

First Amendment have come up repeatedly in public controversies about the arts in the United States.

Governments and Controversies

In the United States and in other democratic, capitalist countries today, governments rarely directly oversee arts projects and funding. Instead, organizations like the National Endowment for the Arts (NEA), which began in 1965 (Binkiewicz, 2004), and local artists' councils like New York Foundation for the Arts (NYFA) fund individual artists and arts organizations through competitive direct grants and stipends. Specialists in the field choose grant recipients. While art projects are supported with public moneys, these projects are chosen based at least in part on aesthetic views of art world insiders. These views sometimes contrast with the tastes, habits, and values of the public they are meant to serve.

In 1981, for example, the American sculptor Richard Serra (1939–) installed a public sculpture in New York City's Federal Plaza. Serra's *Tilted Arc*, a 120-foot long and 12-foot high curving wall of steel, cost the federal Government more than $200,000 in public funds. Art critics lauded this sculpture, and Serra had a stellar art-world reputation. Nonetheless, many people, including workers in the Federal Plaza, hated the sculpture because it dominated the space of the plaza, forcing users to walk all the way around the sculpture to get to the other side. The sculpture also cast a long shadow on the open space. In response to a persistent public outcry, unsuccessfully countered by an ardent defense of the sculpture by the art world establishment, Serra's sculpture was removed from the plaza in 1989 (see Senie, 2000).

Photo 7.8 **Downtown Arc, Frank Martin, 1981.** (Frank Martin/Hulton Archive/Getty Images)

Photo 7.9 **Statue of the Three Servicemen. - Vietnam Veterans Memorial, West Potomac Park, Washington, District of Columbia, DC.** (Library of Congress, Prints & Photographs Division)

Photo 7.10 **View from the top of the wall, looking toward the Lincoln Memorial. - Vietnam Veterans Memorial, West Potomac Park, Washington, District of Columbia, DC.** (Library of Congress, Prints & Photographs Division)

Similar, but perhaps even more emotional, controversies also take place around funding for public memorials, like the Vietnam Veterans Memorial Wall, designed by the artist Maya Lin (1959–) and erected in Washington, D.C. in 1982. This memorial, which consists of a series of granite slabs on which are listed the names of all the US soldiers killed or missing in action in Vietnam, represents a stark modernist aesthetic. Veterans' organizations and others complained that the memorial was alienating and inappropriate; they wanted a more realistic, heroic depiction of fallen soldiers. Eventually a compromise was reached with the installation adjacent of an American flag and a more traditional bronze group of soldiers to the Wall (Wagner-Pacifica and Swartz, 1991).

In controversies like the ones involving the work of Richard Serra and Maya Lin, questions concerning aesthetic values and the use of public space come to the fore. In both cases, members of the public objected to what they felt was an imposition of modernist aesthetic values (to which they did not relate).

Controversies about public funding for the arts also sometimes touch directly on questions of norms and morality. In the 1990s, a series of controversies broke out between cultural liberals and conservatives regarding National Endowment for the Arts (NEA) funding of artists whose work conservatives deemed provocative or obscene. The NEA experienced an explosive growth in its budget from the late 1960s through the late 1970s (Dubin, 1992: 280). Its mission of

Photo 7.11 **AIDS quilt, Washington, D.C., Carol Highsmith.** (Libary of Congress, Prints & Photographs Division)

supporting the arts has always been marred by a conflict between populism (catering to public taste) and the support of sometimes esoteric artistic innovation. In addition, the NEA has consistently been unpopular with political conservatives, who favor less spending on public resources.

In the 1970s and 1980s, new social movements arose, including gay and lesbian movements, fighting for both equality and the right to free expression. Many artists of this period dealt directly in their work with issues of sexual politics and sexual expression, often intentionally violating the sentiment of large segments of the public by depicting taboo sexual acts or desecrating religious symbols. By the 1990s gay and lesbian artists and activists, like the group ACT UP (AIDS Coalition to Unleash Power), also used the arts and public displays to draw attention to the AIDS crisis and the lack of Government funding allocated to AIDS research.

At the same time that sexual politics was taking center stage in the United States and elsewhere, a new cultural conservatism was taking hold among other sectors of the public. This backlash was partly against the successes of the women's rights and civil rights movements of the preceding decades (see Faludi, 1991). This increased conservatism occurred at the same time as President Ronald Reagan's calls to slash the budget as part of his economic plan to revitalize the U.S. economy in the early 1980s. These two factors created conditions for what American sociologist Steve Dubin (1992) refers to as a "perfect storm" regarding the work of NEA recipients in the 1980s. Politicians like Senator Jesse Helms (1921–2008), appealing to the sentiments of conservative voters, made

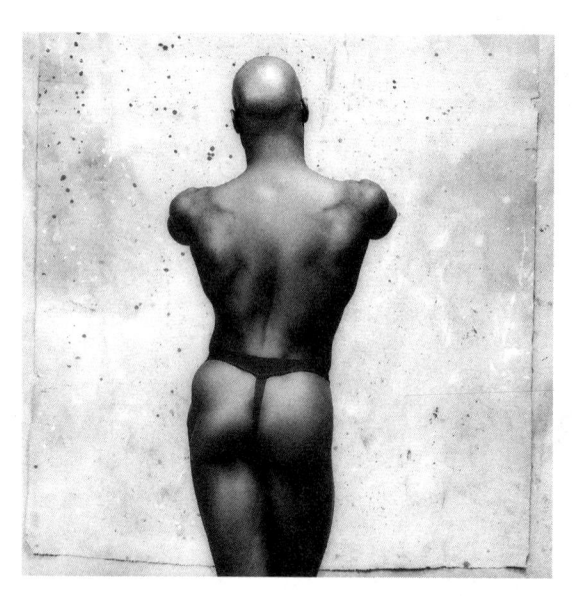

Photo 7.12 **Ken Moody, Robert Maplethorpe, 1983.** (Ken Moody, 1983 © Copyright The Robert Mapplethorpe Foundation. Courtesy Art + Commerce)

emotional speeches condemning the NEA for supporting artists like Andres Serranno (1950–), who created the famous image "Piss Christ," a photo of a plastic crucifix floating in a vial of urine. Helms also condemned institutions that exhibited artists whose work conservatives deemed immoral and offensive. In 1989, a coalition of conservative groups managed through tireless maneuvering and lobbying to block a planned exhibition of the photographer Robert Mapplethorpe (1946–1989) at the federally-funded Corcoran Gallery of Art in Washington, DC. Much of Mapplethorpe's work consists of formally elegant black and white studio photographs.

Some of his images, however, depict male nudes or semi-nudes in erotic poses and with classic S and M (sadist and masochist) props. When Museum Director Christina-Orr Cahill finally bowed under the pressure of prominent conservative politicians and Christian groups and cancelled the show, the museum was picketed by artists, civil liberties groups, gay rights organizations, and others who criticized her for caving in.

A year later, the conservative-appointed chair of the NEA, John Frohnmayer, vetoed grants to a group of performance artists (the NEA Four) after their proposals had successfully passed through the peer review process. Frohnmayer objected to the subject matter of the artists' work, which, he maintained, violated public standards of decency. Indeed, Congress passed a law in 1990 that required organizations such as the National Endowment for the Arts (NEA) and National Associations of Artists Organizations to abide by general decency standards for the "diverse beliefs and values of the American public." The NEA

Photo 7.13 **Card Players (Kartenspieler), Otto Dix, 1920.** (© 2013 Artists Rights Society (ARS), New York/VG Bild-Kunst, Bonn)

Four artists sued the NEA, and in 1993 they were awarded amounts equal to the grant money they had been denied. Eventually, their case made it to the United States Supreme Court, where the decision of the earlier court was upheld (Freeman, 1999). In 1998, however, the NEA, under pressure from Congress, stopped funding individual artists.

Politics and Criticism

Art movements and artists often use the arts to voice social criticism and to move people to political action. We have already discussed examples of this in relation to feminism (Chapter Five), the Black Power movement (Chapter Six), and the politics of AIDS (p. 123). Sometimes artists express their discontent using direct means, deploying imagery and motifs meant to draw explicit attention to social injustices. Sometimes the arts are a vehicle for social criticism in less direct ways.

Varieties of Direct Critique

Direct critique in the visual arts can take different forms. Artists sometimes combine satire, realism and expressionism to represent and criticize society. After World War I, German artists like Otto Dix (1891–1969) and members of the *Neue Sachlichkeit* (New Objectivity) movement responded to the brutality of the war and the economic inequities of the Weimar Republic (the democratic Government that replaced the imperial form of government in Germany in 1919). Dix portrayed greedy capitalists, brutal generals, and disfigured war

Photo 7.14 **Migrant Mother, Dorothea Lange, 1936.** (Libary of Congress, Prints & Photographs Division)

veterans in his paintings, drawings, and prints. He worked in a representational, sometimes cartoonish style, depicting the lurid details of his subject matter (see photo 7.13).

Sometimes artists seek to remind their audience about social injustice in a direct and descriptive manner. In *The Grapes of Wrath* (1939), the American novelist John Steinbeck (1902–1968), writing in clear and gripping language, describes the plight of migrant workers and other victims of the Great Depression. Visual artists, especially photographers, also bring issues of social injustice to their audiences in direct ways. Consider, for example, the American photographer Dorothea Lange (1895–1965), who created moving portraits of the victims of the Great Depression; the Brazilian photographer Sebastião Salgado (1944–), who photographed the horrific conditions of Brazil's gold mine workers; and the American Nina Berman (1960–), who photographed soldiers wounded in Iraq.

Theater and performance arts are also powerful vehicles for waging direct protests against social conditions. In Weimar Germany (1919–1930) theater director Erwin Piscator (1893–1966) and playwright Bertolt Brecht (1898–1956) directly influenced by the ideas of Marx and the Russian Revolution, developed techniques to encourage audiences to think critically about economic inequality and capitalists exploitation of the working class (see Chapters Three and Four). Brecht's plays are not exactly realistic. In fact, he often intentionally disrupts the narrative flow of the story by having actors directly address the audience or by bringing explanatory placards onto the stage. Instead of creating a convincing alternate reality onstage in the manner of classical dramatists, Brecht wants to remind audiences to pay close attention to the reality of their own social conditions rather than getting caught up in the fictional reality of theater.

Performing artists have taken their work to the streets and other public spaces to stage direct political action. These activist artists are often collectivist (working in groups rather than individually). Instead of relying on institutional sites like museums, galleries, or traditional theaters to reach audiences, they seek audiences who are not art-world insiders (see Sholette, 1998). Contemporary performance art has a modern precedent in the Berlin Dada movement, which began around 1918. Dada artists wanted to voice their sympathies for communism and their opposition to the atrocities of the war. Instead of creating depictions of social ills, they wrote political manifestos, staged public demonstrations, and engaged in other forms of **agitation propaganda** (or **agit prop**, a term used by Soviet artists).

> Dada wants nothing, Dada grows.... Dadaism is nothing but an expression of the times. Dada is one with the times, it is a child of the present epoch which one may curse, but cannot deny. Dada has taken the mechanisation, the sterility, the rigidity and the tempo of these times into its broad lap, and in the last analysis it is nothing else and in no way different from them.... Dada is daring per se, Dada exposes itself to the risk of its own death. Dada puts itself at the heart of things. ... Dada is the scream of brakes and the bellowing of the brokers at the Chicago Stock Exchange. Vive Dada!
>
> From *Dada Manifesto* (1918 in Manheim, 1992)

Later, in the early 1960s, a French collective called the Situationist International, drawing on the work of their founder, French Marxist Guy Debord, sought to create "situations" through which people living in an urban environment could counteract the degrading impact that **commodification** and alienation (see Chapter Three) had on everyday life. Like Dada and Surrealist artists, Situationists believed that art should not be severed from politics and that life should be unified with art. Although the group's actual membership was small, Situationist ideas helped to fuel the student uprisings that began in France and spread throughout Europe in May of 1968. Students occupied university buildings and painted slogans on public walls (Jackson, 2011, Feenberg and Freedman, 2001).

Ideas about the relationship between art, collectivism, everyday life, and politics that drove the Situationists have influenced other groups since then. Throughout the 1970s and 1980s a number of activist arts groups joined labor and community organizations and other political groups to protest important social issues (see Shollette, 1998). These activist groups included Artists for Nuclear Disarmament, Artists Against Nuclear Madness, and Political Art Documentation/Distribution.

During the AIDS crisis in the 1990s, the American art collective Gran Fury, a group of artist/provocateurs, described themselves as the "unofficial propaganda ministry" of the group ACT UP. They helped to organize theatrical actions, like "die-ins," at ACT UP protests against the lack of government funding for AIDS research. They created flyers, logos, and posters to inform the public about the AIDS crisis (Dubin, 1992). More recently, large-scale political demonstrations like those protesting the World Trade Organization meetings in Seattle, Bologna, and elsewhere, and the recent Occupy movements in New York City's Wall Street and around the United States have taken place. These were accompanied by myriad performances, music and visual arts directly aimed at illuminating the negative impact of global economic policies on the environment and on the world's poor. Such staged public performances make use of techniques of civil disobedience outlined by Mahatma Gandhi, Dr. Martin Luther King, Jr., and others, whereby protesters deliberately (usually nonviolently) break laws to gain public attention concerning their cause.

Indirect Critique, Autonomous Art, Counterculture

In Chapter Three, we discussed the work of German critical theorists Theodor Adorno and Herbert Marcuse, who linked aesthetic experience to freedom (see Marcuse, 1978). They argued that in modern society, art and aesthetic experience are generally still **autonomous** (or at least semi-autonomous) from the economically driven, means/ends goals of the larger social system. For Adorno, who had been trained as a composer, art provides an opportunity for individual expression in a world that increasingly demands conformity to the short-term logic of consumption, alienating labor, and authoritarian power (see Chapter Three). According to Adorno, really autonomous art also protests against the bad state of reality by presenting a different reality (see Adorno in Bloch et al., 1999). Adorno was not very sympathetic to art that explicitly depicted suffering or social injustice. He also thought that art created to serve political causes was much like advertising or propaganda because it didn't harness the real potential of art to act as a model for freedom.

In fact, Adorno favored very difficult and abstract modern art as examples of works of art that succeeded in opposing society. He believed that these works demonstrated their success precisely because they *were* difficult to understand without special training or knowledge. Because of their opacity, this kind of art was able to veil its critical dimensions in its complicated formal language. Artists associated with the Dada and Surrealist movements also opposed society in an indirect way. They deliberately interrupted conventional ways of thinking in their work, drawing instead on the fragmented, suggestive, and opaque logic of the sort we experience in dreams, when the unconscious is freed from the grip of everyday reality. These artists juxtaposed objects that had no obvious relationship to one another. The French poet Comte de Lautréamont (1846–1870), whom the Surrealists revered, described such juxtaposing as, "Beautiful as the chance encounter on a dissecting table of a sewing machine and an umbrella". Like Brecht, these artists sought to disrupt the everyday flow of social life and shock people out of their routine way of thinking and acting. In doing so, they wanted to liberate unconscious and creative impulses that were stifled by the rigid rationalism of modern society.

The youth movements of the 1960s and 1970s generated a number of indirect forms of aesthetic protest. Many young people from this generation, strongly opposed to the United States interventions in Vietnam and elsewhere, joined political organization like SDS (Students for a Democratic Society) and devoted their energies to bringing about radical economic and social change through direct political action. Others responded to their dissatisfaction with society by forming a "counterculture" (see Aronowitz, 1992; Gitlin, 2011). In opposition to mainstream norms and values of individualism, consumerism, sexual repression, monogamy, the nuclear family, and so forth, these young people experimented with psychedelic drugs, Eastern religions, and new forms of communal life. They also developed new forms of artistic and cultural expression, providing a fertile ground especially for the development of rock music, as exemplified by bands like the Grateful Dead and Jefferson Airplane and performers like Jimi Hendrix and Janis Joplin. These musicians provided more than just entertainment for the new counterculture. Music performances in fields and concert halls were collaborative events during which audience members and musicians camped out, shared food (and sexual partners), smoked pot, dropped acid, and danced.

Many artists during this period launched an implicit critique of social hierarchies by rejecting the distinctions between audience and artist and the related distinction between artistic activity and everyday life. The American sculptor and painter Allan Kaprow (1927–2006) began to organize "happenings" (see Rodenbeck, 2011).

> The line between art and life should be kept as fluid, and perhaps indistinct, as possible.
>
> Allan Kaprow, 1993

Like contemporary "flash mobs," these happenings were unscripted and were more about the experiences of (and interactions between) the people who happened to show up. The events were collective and not under the intentional control of an "artist." The American artist Red Grooms (1937–) describes a happening, "Walking Man," that he participated in, 1959:

> The curtains were opened by me, playing a fireman wearing a simple costume of white pants and T-shirt with a poncho-like cloak and a Smokey Stoverish fireman's helmet. Bill, the "star" in a tall hat and black overcoat, walked back and forth across the stage with great wooden gestures. Yvonne sat on the floor by a suspended fire engine. She was a blind woman with tin-foil covered glasses and cup. Sylvia played a radio and pulled on hanging junk. For the finale, I hid behind a false door and shouted pop code words. Then the cast did a wild run around and it ended.
>
> Stein, (1985)

Other artists expressed a critique of consumer capitalism and the increasing social emphasis on consumption as a sign of success. According to this new generation of artists, individualism and material success were bought at the expense of community and creative expression. Artists reflected their anti-materialism by making art that could not be easily bought and sold or displayed in one's home as a status symbol. They favored ephemeral materials, spontaneity, and non-traditional venues for the production of, and exhibition of, artworks. One famous example is the American artist Robert Smithson's (1938–1973) "earthwork" *Spiral Jetty* (1970). The artist created this piece in the Great Salt Lake in Utah by placing black basalt rocks in the water in the shape of a spiral, creating a 1,500-foot coil in the water. With this work, Smithson sought to avoid commercialism and the market. In the long run, works like Smithson's managed to reject the market in a direct way.

Art, Government, and the Economy Today

The systems of distribution of art discussed early in this chapter still exist today. However, decreased state funding for public resources has affected both government and market distribution of the arts. Since the economic restructuring brought in with the Reagan/Thatcher eras in the 1980s in the United States, the United Kingdom, and elsewhere (Harvey, 2005), local and federal governments have cut spending on most public resources, including funding to artists and cultural organizations. These cuts have led more artists and arts organizations to rely on the market and on private donations to survive. Many arts organizations, especially ones that are less able to generate large audiences, have had to scale back or go under. The loss of these more specialized, nonprofit arts organizations has limited the support available for experimental, cutting-edge developments. Cuts in public funding have also limited the resources available to arts education programs, which are crucial to cultivating a new generation of artists and art consumers (Iyengar et al., 2009).

At the same time, art and culture are economic engines in the post-industrial urban economy, which is fueled by tourism, commerce, and creative industries (Smith 1996; Lloyd, 2006; Deutsch et al., 1984), giving the arts a more central and visible economic position. To lure tourists, businesses, and residents, cities have to provide the kind of cultural amenities (including theater, music, festivals, museums, and so forth) that appeal to the educated upper classes (Florida, 2002). Thus, developers and urban planners are able to steer some public resources toward the arts and culture, as long as they can justify arts spending in terms of economic benefits. For this reason, big, expensive public arts projects and cultural festivals enliven many large cities today.

In addition, art has come to function as an increasingly important symbolic and financial asset for the wealthy. During the 1980s, New York City, the center of the art economy, experienced the greatest art boom in history (Szanto in Halle, 2003: 404). This boom began in 1980 with the first-ever sale of a painting by a living artist for $1 million and was stoked by the unprecedented accumulation of wealth made possible by Japan's economic boom and the trickle-down economic strategies initiated in the Reagan era. These factors contributed to the rise of art investment as a form of financial speculation for a new generation of economic elites. Today, despite some ebb and flow, the international art market has established itself as a resilient resource not only for the acquisition of status and cultural capital but also for investment and speculation. According to the Dutch economist Olaf Velthuis (2008), the turnover rate at contemporary art auctions more than tripled between 2002 and 2006. The recent boom has been further fueled by new collectors, members of the elite class who have benefited from the introduction of free-market economic policies, from developing countries like Mexico, Brazil, Russia, and, more recently, the Middle East and Asia. In addition, money from hedge-fund billionaires such as Steven A. Cohen, Daniel Loeb, and Kenneth Griffin has also been flowing into the market (Velthuis, 2008).

The art world and market have indeed expanded. In the contemporary art world, however, winners take all (Rothenberg, 2012). While the small number of artists who have achieved superstar status command incomes that match their prices, the vast majority of artists suffer the burdens of economic insecurity and a rising cost of living. The robust art market also constrains its winners. Current art stars, whose work often sells in hundreds of thousands of dollars before they have reached the age of 30, must create a more or less predictable and recognizable product if they wish to stay in the game.

Thus, the changed relationship between arts, governments, and the market has created a greater role for the market in support of the arts. In terms of art's role in voicing dissent, market success does not necessarily squash political critique. In fact, in many cases art that is directly critical (of, for example, environmental harm perpetrated by the government, hyperconsumption, and nationalism) is displayed in high-end commercial galleries and in spaces that are supported through public/private partnerships (Rothenberg, 2012). And while the countercultural movements of the 1960s and 1970s and the political activism and sexual politics that fueled much of the art of the 1980s and 1990s has faded, a number of artists and arts groups continue to thrive at the margins or completely outside of mainstream art worlds. In addition, the Internet and digital technologies have made new forms of political participation possible and have generated new modes of social protest in the form of hacktivism, culture jamming, and so on (see Chapter Eight).

Since the end of the Cold War, governments of major powers are less likely to support art in order to explicitly craft national identity. The arts have become global, as we will discuss in the next chapter, and it is a sign of international status to acknowledge this globalism and to embrace multiculturalism. On the other hand, some nations still take an active role in crafting a deliberate national identity, and state-supported arts highlight national and regional cultures. And there are still conflicts about the way to express national identity and national memory, as the heated debates that have accompanied the plans to rebuild the World Trade Center site after the attacks of 9/11 clearly demonstrate (see Marcuse, 2002).

Direct censorship continues to be a rarity in capitalist democracies. Artists whose work is deemed politically or morally threatening may be denied access to the market or public funding, but they are rarely forbidden by the law or prosecuted by the state for producing such work. This, of course, is not the case in societies like Iran or North Korea, where strong authoritarian regimes harass and jail artists and intellectuals and shut down blogs and Internet sites.

Discussion Questions

1. Give examples of works of art from each of the three systems of distribution. How does this artwork either confirm of contradict the pattern described in this chapter?.
2. Do some research on a controversy over public funding to the arts. What kinds of positions/opinions were given for and against funding the project?
3. Why do nation-states care about supporting the arts? Give an example of a work of art, a monument, or a piece of architecture that you think helps to convey a sense of national identity in your country. Explain how it does this.
4. What do you think of the three-tiered test to determine obscenity described above? Think of a particular example (a song, television show, novel, film or anything else) where it might be helpful to apply this test.
5. Should governments support the arts? Explain why or why not. How should government resources be allocated? What kinds of processes would be fair for deciding which art and artists receive funding?
6. Describe how artists use their work to protest economic and political systems. What are some differences between direct and indirect approaches? Do some research on an artist or a movement not discussed in this chapter, and explain why you think their strategies were direct or indirect.
7. What factors have affected the balance between the market and the government with regards to arts funding and distribution in the United States? How has this shift affected the arts?

8

TECHNOLOGY AND GLOBALIZATION

Photo 8.1 **Tye Family, John Clang, 2012.** (© John Clang. Photo Courtesy Pékin Fine Arts)

If you are like many people who live in industrialized, wealthy parts of the world, you probably began your day by turning on your computer, tablet, or smartphone and checking your email and your social networking sites. You may have responded to a text or "poke" from a relative living in a distant city or checked out some pictures that a friend studying abroad shared through Instagram. Later that evening, you may have submitted a class assignment on Blackboard, ordered food from the Thai restaurant down the block, and watched some videos of your favorite band performing somewhere on the other side of the world on YouTube. Before going to bed, you might have Skyped your girlfriend who lives in a nearby city. At some point during the day, you might have waited in frustration on the phone for a technical support person in India or Ireland to help you with a computer or smartphone issue.

If any of this sounds familiar, then your life has been touched by two interrelated phenomena: the accelerated pace of globalization and the development of new communication technologies. These parallel forces have profoundly transformed the way that we work, play, socialize, and understand the world in both positive and negative ways. The way that art and culture are produced, consumed, and understood has changed as well. The photograph at the beginning of this chapter, part of a series called *Being There* by the Singaporean photographer John Clang (1973–), captures these changes. Using Skype, Clang creates family portraits of families who, like many of us today, are physically separated often by thousands of miles.

Globalization

Globalization refers to the processes through which geographically dispersed nations, peoples, cultures, and economies become integrated. Some observers focus on the economic dimensions of globalization, emphasizing the degree to which corporations, markets, and chains of production have become **deterritorialized** (Stiglitz, 2006; Cohn, 2008) that is, no longer tied exclusively to a particular geographic location. Today, geographic boundaries no longer act as a barrier to economic trade, manufacturing, or competition. Multinational corporations seek workers and consumers across national borders, linking together the economies of the globe and opening all corners of the world to capitalist economic development. Industries that were once tied to specific countries or even cities (Detroit's automobile industry, for example) now rely on global networks of production and consumption.

Other observers emphasize the cultural aspects of globalization. They stress the social and cultural impact of global interconnectedness, noting that in today's world cultural practices and identity are no longer exclusively or even primarily bound to a spatially conceived place or nation (Tomlin, 1999; Appadurai, 1996). Cultural practices have become **hybridized** as people come into daily contact, through the Internet and face-to-face, with members of increasingly mobile global populations. In the process, people everywhere become more aware of the diversity of cultural resources from which they can draw. Local cultures shift, change, or sometimes even become more deeply entrenched in response to global influences.

So, is globalization anything new? Why are commentators so quick to point out the significance of globalization to contemporary society? Karl Marx's *Communist Manifesto* informs us that already by the 19th century, "[m]odern industry ha[d] established the world market…. over the entire surface of the globe" and that "old-established national industries have been destroyed or are daily being destroyed." Marx also pointed out that this economic globalization had cultural implications.

> In place of the old local and national seclusion and self-sufficiency, we have intercourse in every direction, universal inter-dependence of nations…
>
> The intellectual creations of individual nations become common property. National one-sidedness and narrow-mindedness become more and more impossible, and from the numerous national and local literatures, there arises a world literature.
>
> Karl Marx and Friedrich Engels *Communist Manifesto* (1848)

Writing from more than 150 years ago Marx demonstrates globalization is not new. It has been a persistent feature of the development of capitalism since at least the 15th century, when Christopher Columbus "discovered" the Americas while searching for a shorter trade route to India (O'Rourke and Williamson, 1999). What is significant is the pace with which globalization has accelerated and density of networks it has produced during the past several decades. Trade agreements, which remove barriers to trade and investment between countries, make it much easier to sell and produce goods internationally. These international policy changes allow companies to invest their resources and move their

Photo 8.2 **The first sight of the new world—Columbus discovering America, M.F. Tobin, 1892.**
(Library of Congress, Prints & Photographs Division)

sites of production from industrialized countries, where the cost of labor is relatively high and environmental regulations stringent, to the developing world where production costs are much cheaper. Globalization is also abetted by the formation and growth of a number of international organizations like the World Trade Organization and the International Monetary Fund. These organizations are dominated by wealthy countries and are global in their reach. Critics argue that they use their power to force developing countries to develop free market policies that favor global business concerns, often to the detriment of workers and the environment. These economic policies help to develop technology and expand the middle class in developing countries, but they have, in many cases, worsened life for the poor and led to increased levels of inequality (Stiglitz, 2006).

Globalization has caused massive shifts in the social arrangements of industrializing countries like China, Brazil, India, and Mexico, where new factories, retail outlets, and service centers have set up shop, bringing with them urbanization, an array of consumer goods and Western cultural products, and a new global elite (Harvey, 2003).

At the same time, there have been massive population shifts of low-wage workers, moving from industrializing countries to wealthier parts of the world, where low-wage service and domestic work is plentiful (Ehrenreich and Hochschild, 2003). In short, the rise of trans-national corporations and global financial institutions, the collapse of barriers to trade, offshore production, the rapid industrialization and urbanization of the global South, and the increased mobility of the labor force, have all led to a rate of global exchange and interconnection unimaginable in Marx's day. But, as we will see, the growth of

Photo 8.3 **Birthday Party at McDonalds, New Delhi, India.** (Courtesy of Jennifer Parker)

communications technology has had an equally significant role to play in speeding up the rate of globalization.

Communications Technology

> Not many of those of us who use the apparatus know what devastation it once wreaked in family circles. The sound with which it rang… was an alarm signal that menaced not only my parents' midday nap, but the historical era that underwrote and enveloped this siesta.
>
> Walter Benjamin, 1938 (in Benjamin, 2006)

The telephone, about which the German theorist Walter Benjamin (1892–1940) writes, along with other communication technologies like radio, stereo, still and moving photography, was a product of the Industrial Revolution. This revolution both heralded and fomented unprecedented changes in the way that people communicated with one another over space and time. Not since the invention of the printing press in the 15th century have developments in communications technology had such a profound effect on society. The printing press, like newer forms of communication technologies, allowed people to exchange and share knowledge, ideas, and images with others whom they might never meet. Communication between disparate people paved the way for rapid scientific, artistic, religious, and political developments throughout Europe (Volti, 1996: 215). And as Canadian media theorist Marshall McLuhan points out, new communication technologies don't only generate new kinds of knowledge and experience in terms of content. Communication technologies generate *new modes of apprehension*—ways of experiencing and being in the world. These new modes of seeing, understanding, communicating, and experiencing the world are perhaps even more socially significant than the actual information they communicate.

> The medium is the message. This is merely to say that the personal and social consequences of any medium—that is, of any extension of ourselves—result from the new scale that is introduced into our affairs by each extension of ourselves, or by any new technology.
>
> Marshall McLuhan and Fiore (1967)

The development of the Internet and related digital technologies has caused a revolution in communication in the late-20th and early-21st centuries that has once again profoundly reshaped our relationship to the world, experience, and each other. The mid-20th century saw the development and spread of television and radio, magazines, and the growth of the film and recording industries. These are all basically "top-down" forms of communication or cultural production. Television stations, for example, produce or purchase content, which is then delivered to consumers who can then select from a given number of choices of news, entertainment, or arts programming. Consumers all over the world (potentially) have access to the same information and entertainment, but communication is basically one-way, or linear (Lievrouw, 2011:11). Content is produced by and delivered through expert cultural workers and institutions and distributed by industries that exert control over and reap profit from cultural products. These products are then consumed by audiences, which, outside of the focus groups and surveys conducted by entertainment industry marketing firms, are unable to answer back (except, of course, through purchasing decisions).

In contrast, the Internet introduces a mode of cultural production and consumption designed (much like the telephone) (Lievrouw, 2011: 9) to facilitate instant back and forth communication between countless individuals. These individuals are connected to one another through computers or cellular devices through which they can access the network of the Internet. Through the capillaries of the Internet highway, users can instantly share information and cultural products and respond to information. And with relatively simple and inexpensive software, users can create or appropriate digital image and sound files, which they can share with countless users through file sharing sites and hyperlinks. With the Internet, top-down control and industry centralization is resisted through the nature of its technical configuration.

The Internet was not envisioned at first as a vehicle for mass communication or the production and dissemination of popular culture. However, in 1993 software developers who created the technology that allowed users to access files from anywhere on a world-wide network system (the World Wide Web, WWW) announced that they wouldn't attempt to patent or claim copyright fees for use of this web technology. Soon after, the WWW became a universal repository for information and knowledge to which everyone can potentially be connected (Volte, 1996). By the end of the 1990s MP3 technology, which allows users to transform music tracks into files that are small enough to share on the Internet, and peer-to-peer file sharing had dug an almost 10 billion dollar hole in sales of recorded music (Oberholzer-Gee, 2007). Just to indicate the rapid growth in Internet use, consider the following: In 1993 there were 663 web sites, but by 2000, that number rose to 7.4 million. By 2008 1.46 billion people were "netizens," a full 21.9 percent of world's population (Volte, 1995: 244). In 2010, 350.9 million personal computers (and PCs are only one of the many devices now available through which to access the Internet) were shipped to customers world-wide. These numbers, of course, don't reveal the persistence of the digital divide that separates those people in less developed parts of the world with fewer resources from the wealthy residents of the global North (and those in the global North who have been left behind digitally). These inequalities become clear when we look at statistics indicating that, for example, 96.9 percent of the population of Norway uses the Internet compared with 5 percent of the population of Bangladesh, or that 68.1 percent of North Americans are logged on compared to 7 percent of the population of Africa (http://www.internetworldstats.com [accessed, 06/19/2013]). Unequal distribution aside, new communication technologies have reshaped the lives of a good percentage of the world's population. And as any older adult with children or grandchildren who have grown up with computer and Internet access (digital natives) can testify, like the telephone in Benjamin's time, the Internet has transformed social and cultural life immeasurably.

Connecting the Two

Together, globalization and communication technology have succeeded in shrinking the world for 21st-century inhabitants not by diminishing its mass, but through what the urban geographer David Harvey calls "the shrinking—or compression—of time and space"(Harvey, 1990). This development has parallels to the Industrial Revolution with the introduction of high-speed transportation and the development of sophisticated new communications media. Steam-ships, railroads, trucks, and later airplanes brought goods and people around the world. Globalization and communication technologies have worked so efficiently together in part because they have a shared driver: the economy. As Marx explained, capitalist expansion (globalization) is fueled by manufacturers and merchants who scour the globe in search of new markets, labor, and cheaper raw materials (Marx and Engels, 1968). Capitalist competition also provides the engine for technological innovation, including the development of mechanization, automation, and transportation and communications systems. These work in tandem to expand markets, transport workers and goods from one place to another, and increase efficiency and thus an industry's profitability. In turn, through the development of communications and entertainment industries like the film and recording industries and changes in the law, intellectual property itself become a source of profit.

The growth of the middle class during the Industrial Revolution created new and expanding markets for cultural and communications technologies for personal and business use. One example was photography. The first photographic processes were developed by the botanist and amateur scientist William Henry Fox Talbot (1800–1877) who, frustrated by his mediocre drawing skills, sought a way to record landscapes and plant life that he studied (Bull, 2010:6).

Later, scientists, amateur chemists and inventors and practicing visual artists like the French Nicéphore Niépce (1765–1833) and Louis Jacques Daguerre (1787–1851) in the 1830s (Eder, 1945) worked to perfect the photographic process, which, according to legend, provoked the French painter Paul Delaroche (1797–1856) to pronounce that "From today, painting is dead" (in Bull, 2010: 8). Photography was first popularized as portraiture, which soon replaced painting as a cheaper and faster way of immortalizing the images of the growing middle class. In 1884, the American inventor and businessman George Eastman (1854–1932) patented the first film-coated paper that could be rolled around a spindle, inserted into a simple and cheap camera, and then sent off to a commercial developer. A few years later, he invented the Kodak camera, designed specifically for this roll film. These innovations eliminated the need for large and expensive equipment and technical training. In fact, just about anyone could record their experiences through the photographic image (see Lessig, 2004: 32). By patenting the Kodak camera and forming the Eastman Company, which remained highly successful until digital processes unseated film photography in the late 1990s, Eastman demonstrated the profitability of new media.

New communication technologies were important to economic growth during the Industrial Revolution in less direct ways as well. Toward the end of the 19th century, the British photographer Eadweard James Muybridge (1830–1904) developed faster shutter speeds, the use of multiple cameras to create stop-action photographs, and the zoopraxiscope, which allowed stop motion images to be projected on a screen (Solnit, 2003). Through

Photo 8.4 **Plate 313, Heaving 20lb Block.** (Courtesy of Edward Muybridge).

Photo 8.5 **Jackson Coil, 1923.** (Library of Congress, Prints & Photographs Division)

stop motion photography, the human body was, in a sense, turned into a mechanical apparatus (Russell, 1999) whose motion could be analyzed and then scientifically organized for the most efficient results. This technology was useful not only for athletic trainers or physicians but was important for developing the new factory management techniques introduced by the American engineer Frederick Winslow Taylor (1856–1915) in the late-19th

Photo 8.6 **Virginia, Julia Margaret Cameron, 1870.** (Library of Congress, Prints & Photographs Division)

Photo 8.7 **Lady Franklin Bay Expedition members Dr. Octave Pavy and Jens skinning a seal, 1881–4.** (Library of Congress, Prints & Photographs Division)

century (Solnit, 2003:12) and satirized in Charlie Chaplin's 1936 film *Modern Times*.

Photography also captured (and contributed) to the globalization processes of the 19th and early-20th centuries by recording nature, anthropological explorations (as in photo 8.7), archeological digs, and even wars. These early photographs, which captured views of people, times, and places previously unavailable to Western audiences, could be reproduced in multiple series from a single negative. They could then circulate in newspapers, magazines and books among contemporaries and be preserved for later generations (Bull, 2010: 9).

New ways of thinking of speed, space, and time also influenced many of the developments in modern art that we have already discussed in this book. Photography and later film, with their uncanny abilities to capture reality, forced artists working in more traditional mediums like painting and sculpture to find new ways to make their work meaningful (sometimes looking, as in the case of Picasso in Chapter Six, to the art of pre-industrial societies now available to European audiences). The ability of film and photography to capture spontaneous and unexpected perspectives on reality also gave artists working in more traditional visual media ideas for new ways of approaching their subjects (see photo 8.8). The social values of spontaneity and newness placed on technological innovation and scientific invention transferred to the arts, where these same values took precedence over adherence to tradition.

Photo 8.8 Dance Class at the Opéra, Edgar Degas, 1872. (Scala/Art Resource, NY)

Photo 8.9 Nude Descending a Staircase, Marcel Duchamp, 1912. (© Succession Marcel Duchamp/ADAGP, Paris/Artists Rights Society (ARS), New York 2013)

A Global Art World: Diffusion, Convergence or Hybridization

In 1999, an exhibit called "Sensation" at the Brooklyn Museum was the subject of heated public controversy. The then-mayor of New York City, Rudolph Giuliani, threatened to withdraw public funding of the museum after viewing a reproduction from the exhibition catalogue of a painting that he found particularly disturbing (see Dubin, 1999). This painting, The Virgin Mary (1998), by a young British artist of Nigerian descent, was made of paper collage, oil paint, and other materials, including elephant dung, on linen.

It depicted a Black Virgin Mary, surrounded by cut-out images from popular culture and lumps of elephant dung that the artist, Christopher Ofili (1968–), had collected from the London Zoo. Giuliani and other Catholics found the work offensive because of the juxtaposition of feces and the Holy Virgin Mary. The artist, however, himself a Catholic, had chosen to utilize elephant dung in his painting as part of his larger project to explore his African heritage and African cultural traditions in his work. Ofili, who had traveled in Africa and studied Nigerian culture, was drawing on the practical and symbolic meanings of elephant dung for Africans. While Ofili's strategy of combining images and material from very different cultures may have been perplexing to some members of the larger public, he maintained the support of the global art world—a network of artists, collectors, dealers, critics, gatekeepers, and markets connected by the increasingly high-speed technology through which information spreads.

Ofili's work is only one example of this impact of globalization on visual art. Indeed, the kind of painting that we see in galleries and museums represents a fairly small portion of global cultural production. More widely distributed media such as music, film, and literature also reflect globalization. Musical forms from outside the United States and Western Europe, like Afro-Cuban music, African music, Indian movie (Bollywood) music, and Brazilian music became increasingly popular in a global arena throughout the 1980s and 1990s (see Inglis and Robertson in Inglis and Hughson, 2002). At the same time, many commercially successful Western artists began incorporating elements of non-Western traditional and folk music into their work. Much of Paul Simon's (1941–) album "Graceland," released in 1986 and a huge commercial success, was recorded in South Africa and featured the vocal group Ladysmith Black Mambazo and Ghanaian master drummer Okyrema Asante (1949–). These musicians were well-known in Africa but had little name-recognition in Europe and the United States. In the world of literature, scholars and more casual readers discovered the work of writers like the Colombian Gabriel García Márquez (1927–), the Nigerian Chinua Achebe (1930–2013) and the British-Indian Salman Rushdie (1947–). These authors painted vivid pictures of experiences of the developing world and drew on written and oral traditions from non-European cultures. At the same time that non-Western cultural forms gathered a global audience, American-born cultural forms like rap and soap operas were combined with or incorporated into local cultures to form hybrids like French rap and Latin American telenovelas (e.g. Bielby et al., 2005; Androutsopoulos, and Scholz, 2003). These new developments raise several interesting questions for scholars and sociologists of art and culture about issues of globalization.

Homogeneity vs. Heterogeneity

One issue that concerns scholars is the impact of globalization on cultural diversity. Does globalization, as Marx, prophesied lead to **cultural convergence**—the development of a universal, world culture that is somehow more than the sum of its parts? Or, has globalization led to the homogenization of culture on a global level, with the United States exerting a **cultural imperialism** that forces local and national cultural forms to die out in the face of Western, or more specifically American, cultural forms and practices? Have interesting and unique local differences given way to standardized and uniform cultural products? Have bland, sanitized versions of different cultures—like the ones you may have visited at the "world showcase" in Disney's Epcot center—replaced real local differences? Alternatively, has globalization, as the commentator Samuel Huntington (2002) suggested, made the irreconcilable differences between differing cultures and traditions all the more profound? Are cultural clashes, like the ones between Muslim women in France who want to wear their traditional head and face coverings and a staunchly secular state's attempts to ban these veils from public spaces inevitable in the global world? Or, are fears about either cultural convergence or cultural imperialism misplaced? Do we gain much more than we lose with globalization, as new and unique cultural forms emerge from the combination of different global and local cultures? After all, only in a globalized world will you find your favorite Latin-inspired sushi, Manga comics, and a Moroccan techno-punk band performance all in one city.

Examples of the homogenizing effects of cultural imperialism abound. From this perspective, Western societies, and particularly the United States, have the economic power and media access to impose their norms, values, symbols, and practices on other cultures. Scholars have pointed out that the vast majority of the media and entertainment produced for world consumption is owned by a shrinking number of multinational conglomerates (Bagdikian, 2000; Croteau and Hoynes, 2006; McChesney, 1999) and overall dominated by U.S. producers. And, as Ryan Moore (2012) points out the recording industry is presently dominated by the "Big Four"—Universal, Sony, Warner, and EMI—which sell over 80 percent of the music in the United States and over 70 percent worldwide. Critics complain that the increasing control held by a few, multinational media corporations over newspapers, television, and other forms of information and the shift away from national control over media and culture, pose a threat to democracy and citizenship. These multinational conglomerates squeeze out independent, non-commercial, and local media outlets, and as critics claim, frame their news programming to promote the agenda of global capitalism and provide a steady diet of advertising, interspersed with sex, violence, gossip, and other easy to consume fare produced by (or in imitation of) Western cultural industries. With the new free trade agreements discussed above, cultural products of nationally-based industries can't compete against the influx of Hollywood films and other US products (see Yúdice, 2003: 218). In addition, new regulations governing ownership rights for new and diverse kinds of cultural products can be more easily obtained by entertainment and telecommunications conglomerates. Thus, the right to digitize or otherwise reproduce folk arts, music, and other national forms of culture is taken away from local or national communities and given to multinational corporations (Yudice, 2003: 219). The success of an aspect of American commercial culture, what sociologist George Ritzer (2004) has dubbed "McDonaldization," has furthered the reach of cultural imperialism. In his view, the principles of the fast-food restaurant, including efficiency, predictability, calculability and control, now dominate all sectors of American society and are being exported to the rest of the world. Thus, the local café in Athens with its thick coffee and baklava is replaced by a Starbucks or Dunkin' Donuts, and rural villagers in Nigeria replace their colorful, handmade clothing with t-shirts from Old Navy.

These perspectives portray globalization as a more or less homogenizing force, which tends towards the annihilation of local and regional cultural differences in favor of a monolithic culture based on advertising and profit, American-style. Others see a different picture. The anthropologist Arjun Appadurai (1986) for example, argues that global flows of people, information technology, media, and finance produce an almost infinite variety of cultural hybrids. Local cultures can be more, or less, open to imported ideas. They will often reconfigure and reinterpret foreign media and cultural forms to suit their unique needs. Tourists, immigrants and other nomadic or transnational communities blend together elements of their mother culture and their hosts to create new forms of music, cuisine, films, sports fandom, and literature.

Some social scientists use the term "glocalization" (Giulianotti and Robertson, 2006) to refer to the interpenetration of the global and the local, which produces unique outcomes in different geographical spaces. This perspective stresses the complex and unpredictable nature of the reaction of specific regions and communities to globalization. Social scientist interested in glocalization focus on the way that global forces and new technologies are translated and reinterpreted for local uses, including the preservation of local cultures. The New Zealand anthropologist Maree Mill (2009) studies how indigenous artists used video and digital media to engage with Maori philosophy and how Quechua artists in the Peruvian Andes have used video cameras to preserve the oral traditions of their communities and share their traditions with other communities. The shrinking of time and space discussed above has also allowed artists living in countries on the periphery of the global art world to collaborate with one another and with artists from commercial and cultural centers on projects and exhibitions. These collaborations often result in fruitful cross-cultural exchanges and bring the aesthetic sensibilities and experience of non-western cultures into the artistic mainstream. (Escobar, 2000: 11–14.)

This kind of hybridity or cross-fertilization is found in the work of the Iranian artist Shiren Neshat (1957–), who currently lives in New York City. Neshat's audio/video installations have been exhibited throughout the world. Her work combines Persian chanting and other Middle Eastern musical forms, dramatizations of Muslim religious rituals, references to Persian painting, poetry, drama and architecture, and actors dressed in traditional Middle-Eastern clothing. Her evocative, black and white semi-narrative videos are usually filmed in Turkey, Iran, or other locations in the Middle East. Neshat's work is visually compelling, but her images of Muslim rituals and women in traditional head-to-toe body covering elicit feelings of discomfort in the Western viewer. These ambivalent reactions reflect Neshat's own conflicted relationship to her culture, gender ideology and her identity as a transnational (moving in between

Photo 8.10 **Shirin Neshet, Fervor, 2000. Production Still.** (© Copyright Shirin Neshet. Courtesy Gladstone Gallery, New York and Brussels)

more than one geographic and cultural location) artist [http://bombsite.com/issues/73/articles/2332].

Through migration and transnationalism new identities are forged and artists comment on these identities. And, artists' work can foster, in the words of American philosopher Anthony Appiah "conversations across boundaries of identity [which] whether national religious or something else begin with the sort of imaginative engagement you get when you read a novel or watch a movie or attend to a work of art that speaks from some place other than your own." (Appiah in Meskimmon, 2011: 7).

Cultural tourism and the heritage industry represent another response to the encounter between local and global cultures. In these cases, locals create new forms of hybrid culture or revitalize or preserve local traditions for global audiences. Indigenous objects, traditions, and rituals, however, take on new meanings when they are displayed as examples of "authentic" culture for outsiders (Bunten, 2008; Pak, 2013). Sometimes, complicated political and historical questions are glossed over in favor of appealing to the tourist gaze. The Israeli Ministry of Tourism advertises desert safaris with guides who are supposedly from the nomadic, ethnic minority of Bedouins. Tours include a visit inside a traditional Bedouin tent where visitors can experience a theatrical version of traditional Bedouin family life. Later, they are treated to oud (a stringed instrument similar to a guitar) performances and traditional dancing near a bonfire. While these tours generate revenue for Israel and for Bedouins, critics complain that issues of mistreatment of Bedouin peoples and land are silenced. Instead, Bedouin-Israeli relations are presented as harmonious and respectful (Stein, 1998).

Also, as American political theorist Benjamin Barber (2000) and others have noted, Western cultural imperialism has created its own backlash, as non-Western cultures attempt to resist the consumerism, secularism, and individualism of the globalizing West. In this view, some societies and groups will cling to, or revive, tribalism, ethnic particularism, religious orthodoxy, and theocracy in an effort to combat global capitalist culture. These societies are often incompatible with democracy, women's rights, and freedom of speech and try to shield themselves from global influences. Cultural clashes between the Western value placed on freedom of expression and the sacred values of Europe's growing Muslim community have resulted in violent protests. In 2005 and early 2006, after a Danish newspaper and other European publications displayed 12 cartoons caricaturing the Prophet Muhammad, Muslims around the world took to the streets, and there were incidents of arson directed at embassies and churches, fights with police, with injuries and deaths resulting (Kimmelman, 2008).

The examples and perspectives I just discussed shed light on Ofili's work and the controversies it generated. His work illustrates the potential for globalization to breed interesting hybrid forms of culture. By combining Western techniques of oil painting with African interpretations of Christian iconography and adding materials from traditional Nigerian culture he created a work of art that transcends easy ideas of cultural boundaries, but resonates with both Western and African experience. On the other hand, despite the African dimension to this work, it clearly "belongs" to a Western-dominated art market and audience. Because curators exhibited it in a museum, its connection to African tribal culture is greatly attenuated. The controversies the piece generated also illustrate the degree to which the culture of globalism in many cases pits traditional values against the value of the global market.

Urbanism and The Wages of Cosmopolitanism

Ofili's work also raises a second set of issues connected to globalization: the disconnect between ideals of urban cosmopolitanism evoked by globalization and the reality of global inequality. Globalization has made the links between contemporary artists and particular locations fragile and tenuous, and this is especially true of artists who reside in "global cities" such as London, New York, or Tokyo (Sassen, 1991). These cities rely on art and culture to secure and maintain global status. In the new economy, manufacturing no longer serves as an economic engine in major cities throughout the world. To maintain their fiscal health, urban centers need to attract highly mobile global elites who work in the financial, creative and information industries. These elites desire art and culture, and art, artists, and cultural institutions are central to urban economies (see Hackworth, 2002; Florida, 2002; Caves, 2000). Not surprisingly, the vast majority of commercially successful artists, like Shiren Neshat, maintain their primary living and work spaces in the global art market capitals of New York, London or Berlin (Quemin, 2006). At the same time, commercially successful artists are just as likely at any given time to be traveling the global art circuit of art fairs and biennials. Here, they are enclosed in a large but gated art-world bubble where their intellectual, social, and political mindsets are shaped by other art world actors and collectors (see Rothenberg, 2012a,b). Critic Eleanor Hartney explains, "People on the international circuit hardly ever get home. They lose touch with local sources, and it becomes all about nomadic travel. You get your brand together and go from place to place to display it" (in Rothenberg, 2012a,b).

These international events, and a spate of new museums, have popped up in cities as far flung as Liverpool, Havana, Shanghai, and Johannesburg as part of the global competition for tourist dollars and international recognition (Stallabrass, 2004). In theory, they serve to reinforce the liberal values of cosmopolitanism and provide a more inclusive forum for regional artists. The work exhibited in these regional venues, however, rarely reflects the concerns of local populations nor does the venue welcome local attendance. This point was made most dramatically at the 1994 and 1998 Johannesburg biennials. In 1994, South African artists who "presented a troubled view of the nation" were excluded. In 1998, local artists complained that their traditions and concerns were sidelined in favor of artists with a cosmopolitan, post-conceptual orientation that were alien to local audiences (Stallabrass, 2004: 38). Meanwhile, the global cities to which successful artists need to be connected have become increasingly expensive, making it difficult for artists who are not highly marketable to live and work in them.

Artists like Ofili represent a new form of global citizenship in a globalization process that has created a two-tiered flow of migrant labor. On the one hand, there is the forced cosmopolitanism of the third-world migrant, risking deportation or even death, who must leave the comfort of local customs and language in order to feed her family (Ehrenreich and Hochschild, 2004). On the other side of this migratory labor force are elite cosmopolitans. These are the NGO and World Bank workers, the CEOs and representatives of transnational corporations, high-powered academics and, increasingly, the top tier of curators, dealers and artists. These migrants, including artists like Neshat and Ofili, are able to both appreciate cultural differences and "bring a concern for all humanity to the fore" (Calhoun, 2002). Youngmi Lim (2009), on the other hand identifies the ideological blinders of advocates for global citizenship, academics for example, who mistake their own ability to transcend boundaries and consume as cultural omnivores (see Chapter Two) for the world at large. After all, the overwhelming majority of people in the world are tied to local cultures and the nation state.

Technology and the Public Sphere: Issues of Democracy and Control

Mechanical means are today, and using them I can get more art to more people. Art should be for everyone.

Andy Warhol 1966 (in Warhol, 1975).

Jürgen Habermas, writing about the development of secular civil society in 18th century Europe (see Chapter Two), pointed out the importance of the public sphere, physical spaces like pubs, coffee houses, and salons, and communication media like newspapers and journals in facilitating the kind of free and open access to information, opinions, and culture necessary to build a democratic society. Habermas hoped that through the communication generated in the public sphere: a democratic society might be forged. However, he concludes, from the perspective of the mid 20th century, that (Habermas, 1989: 169). Now, he writes, communications industry conglomerates—the commercial enterprises that control communication and entertainment in late capitalist societies—produce material designed solely for profit instead of attempting to foster an informed and literate public. In contemporary culture, we have plenty of media and communication, but little access to the diverse ideas or cultural forms that might lead to critical thinking and democracy (Habermas, 1989). As we discussed above, because of the commercial nature of communication media and the increasing dominance of fewer and fewer big media companies the mainstream media has lost much of its capacity to fuel public debate and represent diverse public opinions (see Bagdikian, 2004). Its main function is to provide popular entertainment and encourage consumption. Habermas' viewpoint is compelling on many levels, but the Internet, digital-based communications technologies, and the growing cultural and economic interconnectedness of the contemporary world raise challenges to his dim view. The Internet, while a powerful tool for marketing commercial products, also presents opportunities for user-generated, noncommercial forms of political discussion and the open circulation of creative work through online platforms like blogs, YouTube, Twitter and so forth. These developments have generated a whole new round of debates on the media and the public sphere (e.g. Dahlberg, 2007). So, do new communications technologies provide new potential for democracy and global dialogue? Or, are they destined to become vehicles for advertising and profit, trivializing communication and information?

The Glass is Half Full (Benjamin to the Rescue)

The best place to begin a discussion of the positive potential of communication technologies is with the work of Walter Benjamin, who, as early as the 1930s, speculated on culture and technologies of mass reproduction. Benjamin argues that news print, photography, film, and other forms of mechanical reproduction could provide more democratic access to culture and politics by changing our ideas about what constitutes art. He argues that new technologies could generate a new way of seeing and understanding the world and would transform society for the better. In his 1936 essay, "The Work of Art in the Age of Mechanical Reproduction" Benjamin explains that mechanical reproduction—including prints, photography, film, techniques of sound recording (he was writing long before the computer age)—destroys the **aura** that surrounded classical and modern art. This aura, itself a remnant of art's connection to religion in traditional societies, refers to the distance that viewers feel from works of art and the sense of awe and un-approachability that classical works of art were meant to inspire. Works that have been mechanically reproduced, on the other hand, are neither unique nor irreplaceable. They do not (or did not in Benjamin's time) hang in museums, churches or official buildings. Rather, they are produced in bulk, can be bought and owned by the average citizen, and can be held close, inspected, and manipulated at the viewer's will. While "auratic" art is inaccessible to most people and, in a sense, acts as a symbol of power and authority, objects that can be mechanically reproduced implicitly challenge traditional culture and society (Benjamin, 1968). One no longer needs to be wealthy or powerful to consume, circulate, or even produce cultural objects.

Photo 8.11 **Portrait of Sergei Eisenstein.**

And furthermore, photography and film allow us to get close and inspect the art objects (and the objects represented by art). These media allow us to see things from multiple viewpoints, opening more ways of apprehending reality to a collective audience. They also allow audiences to put works of art to whatever uses they want. They give control of culture back to people. For Benjamin, the proliferation and circulation of visual and sound objects might have suggested a dilution of each object's value and uniqueness, but it certainly made culture more accessible, democratic, and representative of most people's aesthetic experience. New kinds of technology and the social practices they engender, according to him, actually *create* new relationships between individuals and the symbolic and material world and between people.

Benjamin's views have been very influential for a couple of generations of scholars and artists since his time and even help us to look backward at art that was produced shortly before Benjamin was writing. Dada artists like the German artist John Heartfield (1891–1968) for example combined elements of news media and commercial imagery in collage form to provide commentary on current events and social criticism.

Film makers like the Soviet Sergei Eisenstein (1898–1948) utilized the capacity inherent in film editing to cut and paste various perspectives on one scene and to sequence images in unexpected ways to create new perspectives on reality. The themes of many of his films, like his classic *October* (1928) about the Russian revolution of 1917, documented events that were relevant to ordinary people and in fact featured the faces of non-actors.

Since Andy Warhol and the advent of Pop art in the 1960s, it is common practice for artists to base their work on images and signs derived from commercial media and techniques of mass reproduction and even to use mechanical reproduction to make their own work. Many artists in the 1980s, like Barbara Kruger, Jenny Holzer (1950–), and Cindy Sherman, experimented using images, techniques, and language directly from Hollywood and advertising explicitly to subvert the messages disseminated by these industries. Their work is socially critical, but also appealing to a mass audience because of its popular culture references and its irreverence toward traditional forms of art, and, by implication, traditional culture. These artists create work that affects audiences on a variety of levels (aesthetic, emotive, cognitive) and raises important issues concerning the culture of consumption and the objectification of sexuality.

With Internet and digital technologies, artists, and more casual users of technology have even greater access to audiences and modes of expression. Indeed, with the advent of the Internet, cultural producers don't need to go through gatekeepers like curators, art dealers or music producers to circulate their work. With simple technology they can self-produce and promote and access billions of users on the Internet who can consume, circulate and comment on this work with the click of a button. Thus, cultural producers can create the kind of risky or socially critical work in which big, for-profit industries are reluctant to invest, and market this work to a potential audience of billions of Internet users. And, cultural objects have become truly user friendly in that technology users can borrow, quote, appropriate, recombine, and remix the work of others to create new meanings, interpretations, and experiences. In this sense (legally or not, which is a question to which we will return in the next chapter) all culture belongs to everybody in the world of new media. Internet and digital technologies truly live up to the democratic ideal proposed by Benjamin. In this digital universe of plenty, individual works may have lost their aura and uniqueness, but more people everywhere are able to participate in culture as producers, consumers, and critics. Not only are individuals linked in an almost constant web of communication through new media, but images of, and information about, major events like 9/11 are circulated around the globe within seconds of occurring in real time. Thus, people are connected together in a potentially "global village" of cosmopolitan citizenship and opening up possibilities for political participation (Beck, 2006). Communication technology also, according to some optimists, creates new, borderless communities of people with shared interests in global justice, activism and social change (Hamel, 2001).

In addition, new technologies allow artists to address global audiences concerning issues and perspectives that may otherwise have remained in the confines of subcultures or unknown to a larger global public because of political repression in the countries in which they originated. The recent controversies surrounding the work of the Russian, feminist, punk art collective Pussy Riot is a case in point. This dissident group has created a number of performances in public spaces in Russia to criticize the government of Russian President Vladimir Putin (Schuler, 2013). After one of these events, several of the group's members were arrested and sentenced to jail terms for "hooliganism." Videos of Pussy Riot's work, and later news of their arrest, captured on inexpensive digital cameras and smart phones, were quickly circulated on the Internet through their own website and blog (later banned by the Russian Government), Facebook, and on YouTube, leading to a global outcry of support for the artists. Luminaries like Madonna, Yoko Ono, and Barak Obama as well as countless other supporters have demanded the release of the jailed members of Pussy Riot and have drawn attention to the climate of repression in Russia. Other kinds of crowd sourcing media have had a direct impact on political uprisings and protests in Egypt, Iran, and elsewhere (Howard and Hussain, 2013).

...Or Half Empty?

Critics, however, point out that Internet technologies have not escaped the fate of the earlier forms of new media for which Benjamin held so much hope. They point to a number of deleterious effects on the public sphere engendered by Internet and related technologies. While the Internet can potentially reach a user-base of all of the world's inhabitants, in fact, as I pointed out earlier in the chapter, there is a growing digital divide. This divide leaves educated, White, middle- and upper-class people with a vastly disproportionate access to the Internet and to the related computer skills that facilitate internet use. For this reason, the internet is dominated by the presence of a demographic minority and remains essentially closed off to the majority of the world's population. This increases the divide between the haves and the have-nots in terms of political voice and cultural resources. On the darker side, the Internet has become an important tool for terrorists and hate groups around the globe (Tyler, 2002), who have Internet access and can use the Internet as an anonymous medium through which formerly isolated individuals can find one another.

New technologies present another threat to democracy in that they make increasingly insidious forms of surveillance possible. Through the ubiquitous placement of digital security cameras, tracking devices in our cell phones, high-tech facial and voice recognition software and by monitoring Internet activity, governments and corporations have broadened and deepened their abilities to unobtrusively monitor the activity of citizens. Internet surveillance, combined with the threats—real and inflated—of global terrorism have provided governments with opportunities to clamp down on basic privacy rights that we take for granted in democratic societies. Equally alarming to some critics of the Internet is the capacity of search engines like Google and social networking sites like Facebook to collect and sell data about user habits and purchases to marketing companies. Through the use of "cookies," Google can track user activity and use this information to generate advertising targeted directly to each user. This is why, if you visit, for example, a camping goods website, you may be stuck with pop-up advertisements of tents and camping gear every time you log on to the Internet. Even when you are simply socializing with friends on networking sites like Facebook, your exchanges can be monitored and mined for advertising. While you do have the option to "opt out" of this data tracking, few people bother to do so, and few users are aware that every time they "like" a product or website, they are participating in unpaid marketing efforts. In this way, the spaces in which we socialize and express ourselves are turned into commercial spaces for the promotion of consumption. As some commentators note, the Internet has facilitated a shift in our identities from "citizens" to "consumers" (see e.g. Bennet, 2004).

Identity, Community and Self

Critics argue that in today's society, an ethos of individual consumption has replaced community bonds as a means to satisfying human desires for self-expression and social connection. Zygmund Bauman (2008), a Polish-born, English sociologist points out, the kind of market solutions to social problems proposed by neoliberalism also promote private consumerism as a model for meeting individual needs. Speed dating, Facebook, and text-messaging are disposable fast-fixes, and impermanent solutions to the human problems of insecurity, anxiety, and loneliness that can't really be met through the market and consumption. The American sociologist Richard Sennett (1998) points out that the global economy, with its increased out-sourcing, down-sizing, and use of freelance, flexible labor, flexible organizations, and a geographically pliant workforce has altered the way that we work and has had a profound impact on the identity of workers in global society. Constant job insecurity, the inability to plan for a life-long career and the needs of family and community life, and the need to constantly reinvent and market oneself to remain employable have altered our identities, as we struggle to adapt to our own disposability as workers. The self has become increasingly shallow, fragmented and superficial, as people constantly promote themselves, using all social life to "network" for the next job opportunity instead of developing long-term friendships and commitments (also see Mcgee, 2005). These critics have highlighted the negative social effect of this increasing "individualization" and its affinity with the spread and increasing intensity of **consumer capitalism**.

Technology is a Tool

The artist Natalie Bookchin (1962–) creates video installations from material that she finds on YouTube and other social networking sites. Her work

Photo 8.12 **Now He's out in Public and Everyone Can See, Natalie Bookchin, 2012.** (Courtesy of the Artist, Natalie Bookchin)

addresses some of the questions and contradictions concerning community, identity, and citizenship in the contemporary world raised in this chapter. One of her themes, as she puts it, is the "exalted promises of creating social relationships and making the world more open and connected" granted by the Internet and social networking sites in contrast with the "cacophony of millions of isolated individual voices shouting at and past each other" that in fact characterizes communication on the Internet. In pieces like *Mass Ornament*, created in 2009 from clips of videos of people dancing alone in their rooms in geographically disparate spaces that she found on YouTube, she attempts to reimagine these solitary dancers as a "public body in physical space" through the editing process. In other installations she addresses current events and the muddled public sphere of the Internet more directly. One of these pieces *"Now he's out in public and everyone can see"* first opened on election night, 2012. In this piece she constructs a narrative out of found vlogs in which various speakers articulate their views of four prominent African American public figures (for example Tiger Woods) as well as a number of media scandals involving these figures.

This piece, in her own words, is about race, citizenship, and the media in the United States, and her own longing for a more utopian forum of communication:

> The project seeks to examine…polarizing responses, which dominate our media-driven conversations about race and class, driven and inflamed by fears over demographic changes, by tough economic times, and by reactions to our first African American president. My aim is to create an installation that offers greater depth and a broader critical context to otherwise scatter-shot individual online voices by drawing links and making connections and…between different individual rants, responses, and interpretations.

Bookchin attributes this utopian longing to her subjects as well:

> We have entered another level of alienation when our equivalent of a public forum is a person alone in his or her room speaking to a computer screen. But, my work suggests, we are not alone in our need for public conversation and debate about the circumstances of our lives.
>
> (http://rhizome.org/editorial/2011/mar/9/out-public-natalie-bookchin-conversation-blake-sti/)

Bookchin's work, like that of many other artists, uses the materials and themes of contemporary society to comment on that society and to reflect back to the viewer the dangers, trauma, pain and possibilities presented to us by the world in which we live. Globalization and communications technologies have together helped to shape a world, which for those of us who grew up in the last century is new and confusing but possibly not any newer or more confusing than the world that confronted people in other periods of rapid social and technological change. It is our job as sociologists of art and culture to make the connection between these monumental changes and the works of art that emerge from these moments of change.

Discussion Questions

1. What are the differences between the economic and cultural forms of globalization?
2. What factors have led to the increased pace of globalization over the past few decades?
3. How do globalization and new communications technologies work together to "shrink space and time"? Give two examples.
4. During the Industrial Revolution, the development of communications technologies changed the way people interacted and produced culture. Give an example. Give an example for the digital age as well. How has the Internet and digital technology made your life different than the lives of your grandparents when they were your age?
5. In your own words explain what Marshall McLuhan meant when he said that "the medium is the message." Give an example.
6. Give an example of how the Internet is different from top-down modes of cultural production like television or radio.
7. Has globalization led to more or less diversity within our culture? Provide examples. Explain the terms "glocalization" and "cultural convergence."
8. How, according to Walter Benjamin, did techniques of mass reproduction destroy the "aura" associated with older types of art? Why did he feel that this destruction made art more democratic? How does this relate to McLuhan's claim that "the medium is the message"?
9. What role have social media played in the organization of oppositional social actions or movements in Egypt, Syria, Iran, China, or elsewhere? How have Facebook, Twitter, text messaging, or other forms of Internet communication helped to facilitate political action in one of these countries?

9

ARTISTS AND THEIR WORK

Photo 9.1 **Lust for Life, Vincente Minnelli, 1956.** (MGM/Photofest © MGM)

When we think of important artists in any field, original, creative, quirky, larger than life personalities like Alfred Hitchcock (1899–1980), Kurt Cobain (1967–1994), and Vincent Van Gogh (1853–1890) come to mind. Our mental images of artists are created and sustained through media representations like the Hollywood-style "biopic." Shakespeare, Basquiat, Mozart, Goya, Frida Kahlo, and more popular artists like the singer Diana Ross, the cartoonist R. Crumb, and the punk rocker Sid Vicious have all appeared as central characters in big budget dramatizations of artists' lives. This genre of film tells us much about our society's view of artists and what they do. While these films vary in details, without exception they focus on the psyche and life events of the individual. Whether the artists are presented as disturbed geniuses, neurotic bohemians, or visionary outsiders, the emphasis is on the unique and special qualities of the art producer. The social and historical conditions that make it possible for the artist to produce the work that we admire so much are, at most, presented as a backdrop to the "real" star of the show.

In a scene in the biopic *Pollock* (2000) Lee Krasner, the American painter Jackson Pollock's wife—and a talented painter in her own right—interrupts him while he is painting in order to give him a mini-lecture about the many artists who have influenced his work. She reminds him that even abstract art is indebted to tradition. She also points out that artists create their abstractions from something outside of themselves, namely, nature. Pollock, unmoved by her attempt to convince him that his creative process is connected to anything outside of himself, replies "I am nature."

Many people inside and outside of art worlds still accept the idea of the artist as uniquely talented and view works of art purely as products of individual inspiration. Sociologists, in contrast, think that art works are the products of particular historical, social and cultural events. Indeed, the conception of the artist as a free and spontaneous creator, with special powers and vision who needs to be given free rein is relatively new. And it is specific to modern, Western societies. Its origins can be traced back to the middle- and late-Italian Renaissance, the period from roughly the 15th through the 17th centuries that preceded the Enlightenment. To the degree that this idea is alive and well today, it is continually recreated and sustained through social practices, structures, and institutions.

Sociologists don't usually (or at least, in my view, shouldn't) deny that artists often possess special qualities of perception, sensitivity, intelligence, and talent for handling the medium in which they work. The sociological perspective, however, reveals that artists (and their talent and their work) are produced through historical processes, institutions, and social arrangements. The work they produce, in turn, has meaning to us because of those same processes, institutions, and arrangements.

The Social Construction of the Artist and the Work

I began this book with a discussion on the work of the American sociologist Howard Becker (see Chapter One). He explains why sociologists of art think in terms of art worlds instead of focusing only on "great works of art" or the careers of individual artists. He reminds us that works of art are the product of coordinated social action involving a range of people. These people coordinate their activities in fairly predictable ways within art worlds. This perspective sheds light on the processes through which we come to recognize certain individuals as artists or even great artists. It also helps us to understand how and why we treat their work as unique, special, and different from the cultural production of other kinds of people.

Symbolic Interactionists like Becker are interested in the shared assumptions, or beliefs that orient and give meaning to the actions of people ("actors") in any world, including art worlds. Without some kind of outlook or set of beliefs that we share with the other people who help to create the worlds that we inhabit, the things that we do would make no sense at all. And, the interesting thing about our beliefs is not whether they are true or not but that we accept them as natural or inevitable. We assume that beliefs guide our actions because they *are* true not because we *believe* them to be true. For the honorific title of "artist" and the special connection we assume they have to "great works of art", art world members (and society's members more generally) must share a general and indeed rather circular view, or belief. Everyone involved must believe "that the making of art requires special talents, gifts or abilities which few have" and furthermore, that "… [w]e know who has these gifts by the work that they do because, these shared beliefs hold, the work of art expresses and embodies those special, rare powers. By inspecting the work we see that someone special made it" (Becker, 1982: 14). In other words, how do we know a real artist? He or she creates a real work of art. How do we know when we are dealing with a real work of art? It was created by a real artist.

That we share these beliefs has a number of social consequences. One is that we accord special rights and privileges to people we believe possess those rare

Photo 9.2 **Masterpeice, Roy Lichtenstein, 1962.** (© Estate of Roy Lichtenstein)

gifts and powers. We allow those people to violate certain norms and rules of decorum, which we would not allow others to violate. In another scene in the film *Pollock*, Ed Harris (the actor playing Jackson Pollock), having had too much to drink at a party at collector and art patron Peggy Guggenheim's home, urinates in the fireplace. This action would surely have resulted, for most of us, in ensuring that we receive no further invitations to the hostess's home. Pollock, on the contrary, was not only invited back, but became one the most esteemed artists in her "stable" (this is what gallery owners call the artists that they represent). If anything, Pollock's bizarre behavior only provided more evidence to inhabitants of his art world that he was indeed a special and gifted artist.

Because we believe so strongly in the idea that artists have special gifts that we can discern through studying their works, we need to elaborate mechanisms for sorting out artists from non-artists. For this purpose, we have schools and academies of accreditation and respected institutions to support and distribute art works. We also have a variety of institutions through which accolades, awards, and recognition are distributed. These institutions and academies are staffed with highly trained gate-keepers including art historians, critics, and other esteemed artists. They need to sanctify and approve that works meet the standards imposed by the field and that works are properly attributed to the correct artist. In addition, we rely on the mechanism of the market to sustain our beliefs about artists. In capitalist societies at least, we believe the market will adequately reflect the worth of an object by providing an appropriate price and willing consumers. If a work is expensive and sought after, we infer that it is a great work of art. And reciprocally, if we deem an artist to be great and important, the work produced by that artist will be costlier and harder to obtain (see Velthius, 2005).

Photo 9.3 Art Basel Miami Beach Showcases Work Of Over 2000 Artists, (Courtesy of Laurens, 2008).

Photo 9.4 **The Crosby Garrett Helmet on auction at Christie's, London, on 7 October 2010.** (Photo by Daniel Pett)

All of this social activity (judging, sorting, agreeing, and competing for positions) is necessary to produce artists and their work. The people involved in these activities must tacitly agree that while their actions may be important, the work of art is, in the end, really created only by the artist. Becker refers to the unstated but tacit assumptions behind the actions that create and reinforce

Photo 9.5 **New York City–Sale of the Stewart collection of paintings at auction, at Chickering Hall–"Sixty-six thousand dollars and–sold!" 1887.** (Library of Congress, Prints & Photographs Division)

the status of artists and their work as the theory of reputations. This common-sense theory also holds that the value of the artist is intertwined with the value of his or her work. Becker sums up the main assumptions of this widely-held theory:

> ... [s]pecially gifted people ... create works of exceptional beauty and depth which (3) express profound human emotions and culture values. 4) The work's special qualities testify to its makers' special gifs and the already known gifts of the maker testify to the special qualities of the work.
>
> (Becker, 1982: 350)

Based on this theory, many people might produce what we recognize as art by following conventions, but only unique individuals can create something extraordinary. Art worlds, according to this theory, sort through all that is produced in order to elevate some producers to the status of truly worthy artists whose reputations, over time, continue to confer value on what they produce. Art-world members then "use reputations once made, to organize other activities, treating things and people with distinguished reputations differently from others" (Becker, 1982: 352).

Becker himself does not subscribe to the theory of reputations. In his view, reputations are not based on the creation of very special work, but on the collective activity of art worlds. Again, he points out the importance of supporting personnel: critics who develop theories of art and criteria of quality; historians and scholars who develop a canon of authenticated works; and distribution systems that rely on these judgments to choose what to distribute and how much things are worth (Becker, 1982: 360). A number of factors converge to make a reputation. A large enough volume of work should be produced in one genre or medium to be filtered through the available critics and gatekeepers. Less successful artists, as well as audiences who are trained to respond to the criteria established by gatekeepers are needed to create a context in which the work has meaning. A large enough audience should understand a work in question (Estonian novelists writing in their mother tongue may lack a sufficient reading public).

For Becker, and for other sociologists working in this tradition, what is of interest is not the individual biography or unique abilities of artists, but the social processes through which artists gain and maintain reputations. Ai Weiwei, Vincent Van Gogh, Cindy Sherman, and Ludwig van Beethoven may make fascinating case studies, but what sociologists typically investigate are the institutional frameworks and social processes through which their reputations were secured and their work was made available to a public that understood and appreciated it.

Artists and their Work through the Lens of History

Becker reminds us that this theory of reputations is unique to modern Western history. We know little about the makers (including their names) of most art objects from most cultures throughout most of history. He points out that this preoccupation with singular and specific makers is "characteristic of societies which subscribe to individualism over collectivism" (Manheim in Tanner, 2003: 217). All societies produce special objects, rituals and performances, which reinforce collective identity and shared systems of meaning. But in traditional societies where social solidarity is based on strong identification with a collective identity, such objects and rituals are conceived as products and expressions of this collective identity. In the artistic expression characteristic of traditional societies, "the collective ego of the community is at work" (Manheim in Tanner, 2003: 217). Material objects may be produced by skilled artisans and invested with special meaning by shamans or other holy men, but they don't have a special connection to that person. The notion of the creative artist, to which he or she can claim a unique bond to works of art akin to ownership, only really began to emerge in the West, during the Renaissance,(Hauser, 1992; Moulin, 1978, Elias, 1993; Baxandall, 1988. Also see Chapter Two). This new idea became normalized through accompanying shifts in the institutional arrangements through which cultural workers were recruited and trained (see Moulin, 1983; Menger, 1999).

From the Renaissance to the Enlightenment

> The fundamentally new element in the renaissance conception of art is the discovery of the concept of genius, and the idea that the work of art is the creation of an autocratic personality, that this personality transcends tradition, theory and rules, even the work itself…
>
> (Hauser in Tanner, 2003: 120)

In Chapter Two, we discussed factors that explain how and why the Western idea of the high arts, as a unique and autonomous sphere of human creative expression, emerged from the Renaissance through the Enlightenment. Between the 16th and 18th centuries Europe experienced a weakening of the authority of the Catholic Church, a growth in wealth and prestige of the non-titled entrepreneurial class (or, the bourgeoisie), an expansion of market society, and the rise of humanism and rationalism in philosophy and political thought (Wolff 1989: 27). As we have seen, these factors gave rise not only to new ideas about the arts but also new ideas about the special creative powers of the artist.

The Hungarian art historian Arnold Hauser (1892–1978), who wrote one of the earliest extended works in the sociology of art, provides an interesting account of the transition of the status of painters and sculptors from artisans, or craftsmen, in the Middle Ages to free, intellectual, and highly esteemed workers in Renaissance society. Early Renaissance painters, he explains (Hauser, 1992), like other craftsmen, were trained under a guild system. They apprenticed in workshops learning the skills of their trade from master goldsmiths, stonemasons, and ornamental carvers (Hauser, 1992) and were accorded the same social status as other skilled tradesmen. The altarpieces and religious paintings of artists of the Italian Renaissance such as Giotto (1267–1337), Bellini (1430–1516), and even Leonardo da Vinci (1452–1519) were created on this guild model, in workshops. There, apprentices, working together on shared projects, learned their craft by following the instructions of their teacher. The resulting works, Hauser explains, reflected a mixture of "individual differences, a communal form and the tradition of craftsmanship" (Hauser in Tanner, 2003: 120). Until the end of the 15th century, works of art were largely the product of this type of communal and highly rule-bound enterprise. This is one of the reasons why you will often see paintings from this period labeled in museums as "from the workshop of" instead of assigned to an individual artist. Although the work reflected the style for which the workshop master was known, it was always executed by a number of workers. Individual artists had to work their way through the tight hierarchy of the workshop, under the direction of a master, before they could open their own workshops. The scale of the commissioned works artists needed to produce for the Church and for aristocratic patrons required many assistants. And the people who paid for this work expected a predictable product that followed the tradition and style with which everyone was familiar. Most artists lived comfortably either through a stipend provided by a patron or through piece-meal commissions, but none became wealthy from their occupation. They more resemble unionized technicians or gaffers in the film industry, who earn a comfortable living and work hard, than movie stars or famous film directors.

In the early Renaissance, the creators of sculptures, paintings, murals, carvings and other esteemed objects were highly trained, hard working professionals, valued for their technical skill and their ability to produce high-quality work that conformed to stylistic conventions and the desires of their patrons. With the rise of a merchant-class of wealthy consumers in the 15th century came an increase in market demand for objects through which wealth could be displayed. In addition to the growing merchant class, the market was helped along by the increasing success and sophistication of Italian princes, who wished to

Photo 9.6 **Plaque with the Journey to Emmaus and the Noli Me Tangere, 1115–1120.** (Image © The Metropolitan Museum of Art)

display their own status by commissioning and collecting paintings. As the unified culture of the Middle Ages gave way to the individualism and competition of an urban-based market economy, artists began to emphasize their originality and uniqueness as a "weapon in the competitive struggle" (Hauser, 1992: 24) with other artists for profitable commissions. By the 15th century, increased demand for works of art and court patronage liberated individual artists like the Italian Michelangelo (1475–1564).

The new status of the visual artist was also enhanced through the late Renaissance association of the visual arts with nature, mathematics, and science. These fields flowered during the Renaissance, as Church doctrine was gradually challenged by the burgeoning rationalism of philosophers like René Descartes (1596–1650) and Baruch Spinoza (1632–1677), who argued that the knowledge of truth could only be achieved through reason and mathematical laws and that the source of this knowledge was the human mind. Artists like the Italian Leonardo Da Vinci were increasingly valued because of their ability to imitate nature. Eventually, young artists were no longer required to apprentice under a guild master, and it was easier for young talent to rise. Instead, they studied nature and science (perspective), anatomy, and geometry. Artists looked

Photo 9.7 **Studies for the Libyan Sibyl (recto); Studies for the Libyan Sibyl and a small Sketch for a Seated Figure, Michelangelo Buonarroti, 1510–1511.** (Image © The Metropolitan Museum of Art)

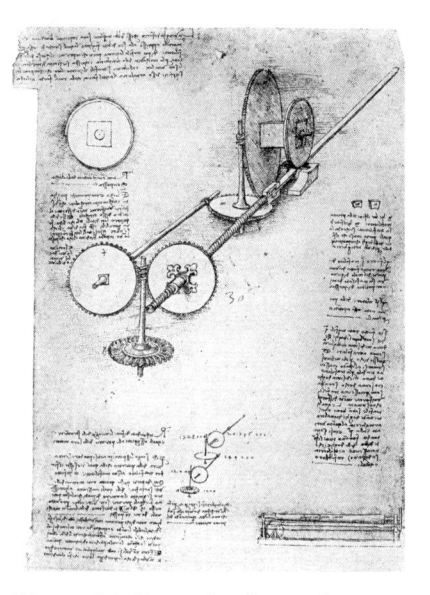

Photo 9.8 **Reproduction of page from notebook of Leonardo da Vinci showing a water-powered, gear-driven machine for manufacturing cannon barrels, Leonardo da Vinci, 1894–1904.** (Library of Congress, Prints & Photographs Division)

to science as a model through which to derive laws, like one-point perspective, through which they could produce a mathematical approximation of human spatial perception. Theoretical and scientific instruction was now just as important as craftsmanship and public academies took the place of workshops. Well-educated Renaissance artists viewed artistic activity as more akin to the invention, exploration, and originality displayed by scientists than the mastery of tradition of the craftsman.

Artists of Mannerist (1520–1600) and Baroque (1600–1750) periods following the Renaissance cultivated increasingly original and recognizable styles. Some, like the Italian painter Caravaggio (1571–1610), famous for his hot temper and public brawls, also cultivated colorful and flamboyant public personas, which added to their image as uniquely talented individuals. In the 16th century, the Italian historian, architect and artist Giorgio Vasari (1511–1574) wrote a series of biographical sketches of some of the important artists of the day. The boxed passage about Michelangelo below captures some of the new ideas that were taking hold about the special nature of artists and their work.

> Michael Angelo's imagination was so perfect that, not being able to express with his hands his great and terrible conceptions, he often abandoned his works and destroyed many of them. I know that a little before his death he burnt a great number of drawings and sketches. It should appear strange to none that Michael Angelo delighted in solitude, being as it were in love with art.
>
> (in Vasari, 1965)

The Enlightenment and Romanticism and the Invention of Genius

You will remember our discussion of the rise of art's autonomy during the Enlightenment from Chapter Two. Ideas about art's autonomy paralleled the development of ideas about the importance (and autonomy) of the human subject itself. These ideas found a receptive audience in the rising moneyed but untitled "bourgeoisie" (see Chapters One, Two, Three, and Four) who were fast gaining power. This group responded favorably to ideas that emphasized individual autonomy over authority and tradition.

Before the philosopher Immanuel Kant (see Chapter Two) could give center stage to the human subject in shaping perceptions, another German writer, Karl Philipp Moritz (1756–1793), proposed that works of art should be thought of as "totalities" (complete in and of themselves) that should be enjoyed for their internal attributes and independent of external relationships they

Photo 9.9 **The Musicians, Caravaggio (Michelangelo Merisi), 1595.** (The Metropolitan Museum of Art, Rogers Fund, 1952 (52.81))

provoke or effects that they generate (Woodmansee, 1994: 11). The idea that art was independent and self-justifying, and not an instrument to some other end, was new. Until Moritz and Kant, the arts were supposed to impart and empower beliefs and truths. Art wasn't art unless it moved the soul and made people feel deep emotion (Woodmansee, 1994: 18). The human mind was built, however, in such a way that it was capable of apprehending this perfection. The aesthetic attitude might be a very human capacity, but to achieve it, one had to forget oneself and perceive the object as complete and perfect.

What kind of person could create art that was perfect in and of itself? Kant answers with a concept familiar to us today, "Genius." Unlike the work of diligent craftsmen who can learn a trade through hard work and skill, the artist (like nature) gives order to the work of art but not a formula or rule that another could follow. Artists were extraordinary individuals able to transcend the everyday worries and desires that plague the rest of us. The German philosopher Arthur Schopenhauer (1788–1860) wrote "genius is the capacity to remain in a state of pure perception, to lose oneself in perception …". (Schopenhauer, 1969: 178). The present, he argued, "can seldom satisfy" men of genius because they have a "restless, zealous nature, that constant search for new objects worthy of contemplation and also that constant longing, hardly ever satisfied, for men of like nature and stature to whom they may open their hearts" (Schopenhauer, 1969:186). Artists who are interested in fame or approval are not true artists.

By the 19th century, Romantic philosophers and poets moved even more toward a focus on the inner life and experience of the artist. The German writers Johann Wolfgang von Goethe (1749–1852), Friedrich Wilhelm Schelling (1775–1854) and Friedrich Schlegel (1772–1829) believed that modern works of art embodied freedom and the human capacity for autonomous sense-making. Writers, poets and composers of this period expressed the intensity of inner, emotional life and the importance of aesthetic experience in personal development. The artist's job was to give expression to a kind of inner necessity and intensity and to highlight subjective emotions and sensations. This sentiment is captured in an excerpt from the poet Rainier Maria Rilke's "Letters to a Young Poet":

> No one can advise or help you … There is only one thing you should do. Go into yourself. … Confess to yourself whether you would have to die if you were forbidden to write. … Then build your life in accordance with this necessity. … Write about what your everyday life offers you, describe your sorrows and desires, the thoughts that pass through your mind and your belief in some kind of beauty.
>
> (Rilke in Cazeau, 2011: 293)

Intellectual historians can trace the birth and development of the conception of the idea of the artist-genius and his (it was usually a he in those days) organic relationship to the product of his work. Sociologists, however, analyze the social processes that account for the success or failure of an idea to take hold and exert continued social influence. The American historian Martha Woodmansee (1994) employs a production of culture approach (see Chapter Three) in her investigation into how and why this new theory of art and artists took hold. She pays particular attention to shifts in the structure of laws and regulations, occupational careers and markets to help explain important shift in the role and social conception of the author in 18th century Germany.

Prior to the 18th century art was about imitation or description of nature and idealization of form for the purpose of pleasing a polite audience. In addition, people did not think of authors and poets as the owners of the product of their labor. Instead, writing was considered a vehicle for communicating ideas that were already part of the public domain. With the emergence of a new middle class demanding reading material a group of writers and intellectuals responded to this critical mass. They sought to broaden the reading public and to develop institutions like libraries and journals to encourage a literary culture in Germany. They urged writers to produce novels and other accessible literary forms that would speak to the hearts (rather than the heads) of popular audiences. They were so successful that by the middle of the 18th century, authors were referring to the "reading craze" that had struck Germany. There was enough demand to support a new class of writers more than happy to cater to popular tastes. "Serious" writers like Goethe and Moritz began to complain that writing had been taken over by lowbrow, light literary forms and that pure artists like themselves were unable to support themselves selling their work. In addition, writers in Germany lacked anything resembling copyright protection. Nefarious publishers could easily pirate work that was already published and keep all of the profit from the sales. Serious writers were thus doubly handicapped (by popular taste and by lack of legal protections) and unable to support themselves with their work. In response to this problem, argues Woodmansee, these writers set about redefining the nature of writing by shifting public definitions of a work of art's value away from entertainment and towards an idea of internal perfection—or "autonomy" that had nothing to do with popular audience perceptions. In addition, serious writers sought to supplant the classical idea that great works are inspired by God with the argument that they are the unique property of special individuals who are solely responsible for and due the rights of ownership and profit from their own creations. By the end of the 18th century, writers like Goethe and Johann Gottlieb Fichte (1762–1814) had successfully advocated for copyright laws that required publishers offer authors written contracts (Woodmansee, 1994).

Birth of the Author in Germany as Seen through Production of Culture Perspective

The Invention of Modern Art and the Autonomous Artis

By the late-19th century, new factors came into play to refine and define the role that artists were to occupy in modernity. The Enlightenment and the modern world that emerged from it substituted the abstract authority of science, rationality, and the market economy for religious and feudal authority (see Chapters Two and Three). Artists and thinkers keenly felt the loss of tradition, community, and spirituality that accompanied this social change. The Romantics emphasized art and aesthetic reason as remedies for the Enlightenment's disenchantment of the social and natural world. They called attention to the creative and spiritual dimensions of the autonomous subjectivity that had been awakened by the Enlightenment over the cold and calculating dimensions of modern life. The German philosopher and art critic Friedrich Wilhelm Nietzsche (1844–1900) suggested that great artists model those characteristics of the exceptional man–creative, virile, unique, and self-commanding in contrast to the passionless, practical, subservient mediocrity of ordinary modern people (Nietzsche, 2013).

Karl Marx suggests that artists' work is a sort of antidote to the soulless labor to which most people are confined in the new capitalist economy. Wage workers are not only exploited in industrial capitalism (see Chapters Three and Four). They are also alienated from the work process. The complex division of labor and mechanization of assembly-line type production "de-skill" the worker and reduce his labor to mindless repetition (Braverman, 1974).

Table 9.1

Facet of Production	Research Question(s)	Effects
Law and Regulation	How did laws and regulations shape development of the author as sole creator and owner of a work of art?	New copyright laws honored the property rights of writers. What was once in the public domain was now treated as individual property. Copyright laws allowed authors to profit from their own work.
Occupational Careers	How were high-status positions created and maintained within the literary field? What were the reward systems?	New aesthetic treatises argued that authors possessed special genius and unique creative capacities. These writings emphasized the author's "purity" over audience reception.
Markets	What groups consumed literature? How did producers create demands for their cultural products and shape tastes?	A growing literate middle class created markets for literature. Influential writers and intellectuals advocated for libraries and publication outlets, while raising the status of writing.

Photo 9.10 **Modern Times, United Artists, Charlie Chaplin.** (United Artists/Photofest © United Artists)

Yet, the rise of market societies that accompanied industrialization had a positive impact on the freedom and control that artists had over their own work (see Chapter Seven). While artists before the Industrial Revolution were expected to innovate, the content and even the style of visual art and music continued to be controlled by the individual patron, whether the Church, royalty, or the wealthy merchant. The lives of artists were thus bound to those of their patrons, with whom they occupied a shared social, moral, and political universe.

In contrast, the modern artist who was to emerge within an urban, bohemian subculture at the end of the 19th century, found him or herself relatively free from direct ties to a patron. The impersonal forces of the market came to replace the more explicit directives of patronage. Artists who were not protected from poverty by family fortunes were left in positions of profound economic instability. In return for material insecurity, however, artists were now able to be innovative risk takers, beholden only to their own vision with its new and flamboyant modern identity.

The French sociologist, Pierre Bourdieu whom we met in earlier chapters, outlines structural conditions that led to new conceptions of "bohemian" artists and art in the mid- to late-19th century (Bourdieu, 1993; 252). With the advent of the Industrial Revolution and the swelling of the middle class, educated youth swarmed to cities to make their fortunes. An unprecedented number were attracted to the world of arts and letters and tried to enter these professions. State-controlled art academies, with their rigid professional standards and entrenched hierarchy, offered only a limited number of positions.

Photo 9.11 This year again ... Venus ... always Venus and nothing but Venus ... as if there were women with such figures! (Cette année encore des Vénus. ... toujours des Vénus!. ... comme s'il y avait des femmes faites commeça!), Honoré Daumier, 1864.

Many ambitious and talented would-be artists were turned away. Sheer demographics, then, contributed to the rise of a group of artists who, rejected by the academy, fought for a position of legitimacy in the field of artistic production. They did this in part by setting up new and radical artistic standards. In the case of painters, young artists juxtaposed the classical, highly-finished history painting and flattering depictions of rulers made by state-sanctioned and trained academic artists (see Chapter Two) against more gestural and experimental paintings, often capturing the fleeting moments and characters of urban life.

Fueled by the pace, dynamism, and relaxed norms of urban life, these artists formed their own independent, creative enclaves. They gradually developed an audience and market for their work outside the official academies. In the world of visual art, independent commercial galleries began to organize alternative exhibitions (Salons des Refuses) for the work of artists who had been rejected by the large-scale exhibitions sponsored (and juried) by the French Government. One game-changing year, the French Government actually sponsored a public exhibition of artists who had been rejected by the academy as a kind of sideshow to the official exhibit, in the words of an imperial decree, to "let the public judge" the legitimacy of complaints made by rejected artists (Boime, 2008). This exhibition featured artists like Manet, who are considered unimpeachable modern masters today, but who were unknown to the general public at the time. While the show generated much derision among critics and the public, the buzz and controversy created by the exhibition ultimately brought attention and legitimacy to new styles of art. Eventually, in part through their ability (like the Enlightenment thinkers we discussed) to create convincing accounts of the special nature of their activities, modern artists and their supporters subverted the control of the academy. Bourdieu points out these new rebellious artists were successful because, drawing on the ideas of the Romantics, they created a subculture—the avant-garde—that valued an alternative set of norms, definitions, and reward systems. In contrast to the state academy's supposedly slavish relationship to political power and the artistic limitations engendered by this connection, they stood for "art for art's sake."

Ironically, artists' adherence to a modern ideal of art for art's sake was made possible by the replacement of state systems of artist support with market systems. When artists rely on state support, they have to stick within the guidelines dictated by academies which themselves are beholden to the political interests of the state. Market systems of support are open and impersonal (see Chapter Seven). Artists, publishers, gallery owners, and critics can argue over and shape the tastes of potential buyers. If the market is large enough, many different types of work can find support, including conventional, crowd-pleasing, and familiar artistic production, mass culture, or more experimental and unfamiliar types of art that appeal to a specialized audience. Ultimately, artists are as beholden to buyers as they are to the state or the church, but, as you can see, there are greater opportunities to experiment and break from tradition. Artists of the late-19th century experienced a new sense of freedom and claimed they were creating art for its own sake and not to satisfy other interests, including monetary interests. Eventually, this idea of art for its own sake was elevated to a standard by which quality and authenticity could be judged. Artists who pandered to the state or to the market in an obvious way were rejected by an elite sector of the art world as vulgar, shoddy, and mediocre.

Bourdieu explains that artists' renunciation of cultural production aimed at economic or political gain should really be understood as a ploy—though not necessarily a conscious one—by which artists could enhance their status and their own work in relation to other kinds of cultural products (Bourdieu, 1993: 114). To maintain value in commercial markets, risky, unconventional works of art needed to differentiate themselves from other products. Artists had to promote an aesthetic standard through which this type of work could legitimate its quality. The legitimacy of the makers of this type of work also had to be proven through these new standards. A reward system had to be instituted through which these artists could receive some kind of acknowledgment and enhanced reputation for their accomplishments. These rewards were not in the form of immediate wealth but instead in the form of "symbolic" capital—that is status, reputation, and regard by peers.

According to these new standards, a work can only succeed to the extent that it proves its autonomy and hence its purity. "Real" artists have to be willing and able to endure a lack of market success for many years to prove their worth and gain the esteem of their colleagues. The position of these artists is sustained through the accumulation of symbolic capital. Artists and their work are valued because they have resisted the pressure to produce commercial work in favor of purity and poverty. This value does not necessarily or immediately translate into economic capital. In the long run, however, the success of these artists still ultimately rests on the existence of an audience and middle-class buyers who will eventually be won over.

Bourdieu (1993), however, points out that the disavowal of economic self-interest so crucial to the identity of these artists conceals an important contradiction: as in any gambling situation, the position of highest risk stands to reap the greatest gain. Production within this restricted field of avant-garde art is risky. Many attempt but few succeed in achieving enough symbolic capital to make it in the long run. For every Van Gogh and Kurt Cobain—artistic mavericks who toughed out obscurity and eventually (maybe after their deaths) became well-known and valuable—there are thousands of other artists who toil away, devoting their life to work which will remain undiscovered long after their deaths and possibly forever. And those adventurous collectors and friends who believed in and supported those artists may find their efforts and money did not yield any financial or symbolic gain. Those willing and able to invest in lesser-known, cutting edge artists (and this includes the artist himself who presumably can garner the economic resources to stay in the game for the long haul) have much to gain, if the cultural endeavor manages to accrue symbolic capital. Theo Van Gogh (1857–1891) provided financial and emotional support to his psychologically unstable brother Vincent, which enabled him to buy art supplies, rent a studio, and devote his time to painting (see Heinrich, 1997). Van Gogh was almost completely commercially unrecognized during his lifetime by anyone but a few fellow artists, but since his death his fame and the value of his work has skyrocketed. While Theo might not have seen much economic return on his investment in Vincent, others certainly did. Vincent Van Gogh—at least posthumously—was well rewarded in status and regard for his earthly sacrifices. (In 1989 his Wheatfield with Cypresses (1889) sold at auction for $57 million.) And the symbolic value gained by Vincent's uncompromising devotion to art, and his renunciation of materialism and wealth, was eventually converted into economic value.

The Institutionalization of the Modern Artist

From a sociological perspective, artists are never "outside" of society, even during periods in history when they form distinctive subcultures or self-identify as rebels or social critics. Nonetheless, during a relatively brief period from the end of the 19th century to the middle of the 20th, artists' paths to professional success and their market positions remained marginal compared to that of other middle-class professional workers. Intriguing and romantic figures, perhaps, but removed from the lifestyle, values, and mores of mainstream society. Most artists did not expect to earn more than a meager income selling their work. Entry into the field did not require a university degree or credentials. Even the most avant-garde, innovative, and radical artists were content to receive attention in only the very limited field of what Pierre Bourdieu (1993) called the "field of restricted cultural production."

By the end of the 1960s in the United States and elsewhere, the social position of artists had changed. Even as they continued to produce new and challenging ways of making and thinking about art, artists were gaining an unprecedented level of social respectability, status, security, and integration into middle-class culture (see Zukin, 1982; Crane, 1987). The "de-marginalization" of artists in the United States had many interrelated causes, including the expansion of the middle class, a robust art market, the increasing professionalization and growth of higher education, expansion of government support for the arts (see Crane, 1987), and the "de-politicization" of avant-garde (see Frascina, 1985) artists. Looking at the careers of two artists whose work falls into the period from the 1940s through the 1950s helps us trace some of these changes.

Jackson Pollock (1912–1956), the subject of the biopic I discussed at the beginning of this chapter, was a member of a group of artists living in New York called Abstract Expressionists. These painters created large, painterly, abstract paintings. Their paintings had few references to recognizable objects and the specific type of gesture, mark, or brushstroke made by the individual artist defined his painting style. Like members of other modern art movements, these artists distanced themselves from mainstream society, forming a fairly close-knit community (what the sociologist Barbara Crane calls "face-to-face networks" (Crane, 1987; 28)). Most of them lived around the Lower East Side in New York City and drank and talked together nightly at the Cedar Street Tavern, the Club, and Studio 35. Though characterized by venomous infighting (Rubenfeld, 1997; Ashton, 1973), this community was held together by a shared moral universe and a belief in abstract art and the importance of high culture. Their interpreters juxtaposed their art to what they saw as an increasingly insidious and degraded mass culture (Greenberg 1939; Macdonald 1960). The American art critic Carter Radcliff links together the outsider status of this group with their sense of a higher calling: "People [artists] in the '40s and '50s lived marginal lives. It was part of their project—almost political—living morally exemplary lives" (Radcliff in Rothenberg, 2012).

Photo 9.12 Life Magazine Centerfold for Autumn Rythym, "Jackson Pollack - Is he the Greatest Living Painter in the United States?"

Nonetheless, despite their self-exile from mainstream culture and that their work was understood by only the most initiated viewers, these painters ended up commanding large sums of money for their work. They even made occasional but noteworthy appearances in popular culture. In fact, in 1949, *Life* magazine featured a glossy spread of Jackson Pollock and his work.

In addition to making inroads in American popular culture, Abstract Expressionist painting triggered the first serious market for contemporary American art in the United States (Robson in Fascnia, 1985). Between 1939 and 1946, the number of galleries in New York quadrupled to 150 and their sales tripled between 1944 and 1945 (Szanto, in Halle 2003. Also see Crane, 1987). In the period of just a few years the romantic, misunderstood artist of modernity had evolved into a popular icon and market success.

If Jackson Pollock achieved notoriety outside the rarified circles of the bohemian art world and helped fuel the first boom cycle in American art, Andy Warhol (1928–1987) is a true exemplar of the artist's new position as celebrity and businessman in post-war U.S. society. Abstract Expressionists like Pollock embraced the basic tenets of Modernism. They shared distaste for consumerism; a belief in the creative, expressive power of the individual artist; the claim that art is, or at least should be autonomous from other spheres of culture, and a general preoccupation with the formal language

Photo 9.13 **Andy Warhol (left) and Tennessee Williams (right) talking on the S.S. France, James Kavallines, 1967.** (Library of Congress, Prints & Photographs Division)

and devices of specific mediums. The same cannot be said of Warhol. In 1964, about five years after Andy Warhol decided to branch out to fine art from his successful career as a commercial artist, the philosopher and art critic Arthur Danto saw an exhibition of Warhol's work at the Stable Gallery on New York's Upper East Side. This show included roughly four hundred sculptures, each of which replicated everyday grocery store brand name items like Heinz Ketchup, Campbell's tomato soup, Kellogg's Corn Flakes, and Brillo soap pads.

> …If only I had stayed with doing the Campbell's soup can, because everybody only does one painting anyway. Doing it whenever you need money is a really good idea, just that one painting over and over again, which is what everybody remembers you for anyway.
>
> (in Michelsen 2002: 120, 124)

These items were not exact replicas of their brand-name inspirations: they were larger than the originals, and made out of cheap wood rather than cardboard. Like the homely products to which they referred, however, they were stacked up in piles and similar enough to one another that variations seemed incidental. This work represented a radical break from modernist ideas.

In contrast to Pollock's painting, Warhol used imagery from pop and consumer culture immediately recognizable to his viewers. And, he unabashedly used techniques drawn from advertising and mass production. In fact, in a nod to industrial manufacturing, he even had other people produce much of his work in a studio that he called "the factory" (see Jones, 1996).

The general tenor of the 1960s, combined with the easy, fun, and decorative nature of Warhol's work transformed the social atmosphere of the art world. During the heyday of Abstract Expressionism, gallery openings and other art-world social events were serious, bohemian affairs, characterized by heavy drinking, smoking, and debate, sometimes leading to fistfights (see Ashton, 1972). These events were attended mostly by artists, critics, and other writers and intellectuals, with occasional select collectors, like Peggy Guggenheim, who came from old money, education, and culture. In the "Warhol sixties" gallery openings evolved into parties, where media celebrities mingled with artists, hangers on and smartly dressed middle-class or nouveau riche collectors like Robert and Ethel Scull (Wolf 1968). These gallery-goers' clothing matched the pictures on the wall, which included Warhol's silk-screened series of celebrity icons (notably Marilyn Monroe, James Dean, and Elvis Presley) and his commissioned "Society Portraits" in which some of the attending public literally viewed images of themselves. Warhol's style as well as the content of these works helped integrate a growing class of newly moneyed entrepreneurs and professionals into the world of art and culture traditionally reserved for more established elites (Jones, 1996, also see Crane, 1987). Not surprisingly, Pop art's accessibility and its association with glamorous celebrities attracted not only collectors but also the larger commercial media to New York's art world and the art market experienced another boom. This economic boom was also unprecedented in its international nature. Warhol's work was not only a hit on the American market but also sold well in Europe (Indiana, 2010).

Unlike earlier times, this new art world did not attempt to neutralize or euphemize the relationship between art and commerce. As we have discussed, modern artists underplayed their need to sell their art to survive. Art dealers soft-pedaled the market transaction necessary to make a sale by conducting such events quietly in the back room of the gallery. By contrast, in 1964, Bianchini Gallery opened an exhibition called "The Supermarket" in which Warhol's Campbell's soup canvases were installed next to a pyramid of the real thing signed by Warhol and sold at the going rate of 20 cents a can. While some critics (see Masuhn, 1989) have claimed that this work was a criticism of post-war society's obsession with consumption, it could just as easily be interpreted as a celebration of such consumption. Andy Warhol's art market success and reputation as a celebrity are indicative of the "de-marginalizing" of artists. During this period, as the American sociologist Andras Szanto points out "questions about merit would increasingly be settled in the marketplace. The bond between art and money had cemented" (Szanto in Halle 2003: 397). And, this bond between art and money, as we discussed in Chapter Seven, was further cemented by the new role, already salient in the 1960s, that art and artists played in the economies of post-industrial cities.

In addition to providing new sources of revenue and contributing to the economy of tourism, the arts and specifically artists had an important role to play in rebranding undesirable neighborhoods and old manufacturing spaces. These spaces, made hip and fashionable by artists whose status had become enhanced provided value-added investment opportunities to real estate developers and city planners who now welcomed artists into their ranks (see Lloyd, 2006; Zukin, 1982; Mele, 1996).

By the 1980s, the price of contemporary art soared and art openings in the Manhattan neighborhood of SoHo became photo opportunities not just for artists and their coteries, but also for the television and film stars, models, media moguls, financiers and designers with whom they socialized. Today, art market news makes front-page headlines, collectors engage in public frenzies of speculation, and artists have become savvy businessmen, actively intervening in the market to control the value of their work (see Velthuis, 2005). Full-scale magazine spreads and reality TV shows have been devoted to publicizing the lifestyle, wardrobes, and homes of wealthy artist-celebrities. In 2008, the artist Julian Schnabel, who rose to fame during the art market boom of the 1980s, added an entire, 50,000 sq. foot palazzo-type building to the top of a factory building in New York City's Greenwich Village. Schnabel called this building, which he had painted in faded reddish pink to resemble Renaissance-era design in Venice, "Palazzo Chupi(see photo 9-14)." This multi-million dollar renovation spurred a string of celebrities to inquire about purchasing remaining floors in that and remaining buildings. According to an article in the magazine *Vanity Fair*:

> Sonny Bono, Johnny Depp, Martha Stewart, Hugh Jackman, and Madonna have all checked out the remaining residences for sale, at prices ranging from $27 million to $32 million. (Schnabel declines to reveal his overall construction costs.) So far two units have sold: a single-floor, for $15.5 million to Credit Suisse executive William J. B. Brady; and the other single-floor to Richard Gere for an undisclosed sum.
>
> Venice on the Hudson by Ingrid Sischy
> [http://www.vanityfair.com/culture/features/2008/03/schnabel200803].

Thus, a lucky group of artists have achieved the status and many of the lifestyle trappings of Hollywood celebrities and super-successful entrepreneurs.

Photo 9.14 **Venice on the Hudson.** (Courtesy of Geoffrey Berliner)

Others serve as a model for the way most professionals work and live in the new economy. Artists have long accepted a high degree of economic insecurity. They understand that they must continuously market themselves and tend to their image to maintain their careers, while other educated professionals could count on some degree of job stability and economic security as long as they played the

Table 9.2

Period	Social Status and Forms of Support	Relationship to Work of Art	Type of Labor
Renaissance	Respected professional; Court and Church patrons.	Worked within established conventions adding a personal touch.	Workshop, still some craftsman dimension.
Enlightenment	Some Court and state patronage, market; beginnings of artists as genius.	Artist as owner of work—flows directly from artist, art is uplifting.	Artist work distinct from other types of labor.
Modernity	Some state patronage, mostly market, artist as outsider, bohemian communities, artist as rebel, artist as neurotic.	Innovation springing directly from artist, unique and original touch, scientific investigation, personal expression.	Unalienated labor in contrast to industrial labor; handwork and gesture important.
Post-modernity	Artist as celebrity, artist as businessman, corporate, state and market support, integrated into elite.	Ownership of property, appropriation of other work—artist as librarian and encyclopedist.	Entertainer, creator of speculative value, creative worker, recombiner of signs, emphasis away from originality.

game right. With the decline of organized labor and the rise of freelance and temporary jobs, other professionals have become more like artists. Even workers outside the creative industries often work freelance, with little job security and must constantly revise their portfolio and cultivate their self-image to remain employed (Boltanski and Chiapello, 2005; Mcgee, 2005; Holmes, 2007). In this sense, the financial insecurity and restlessness long associated with the artist has become a fact of life for most workers and artists have become less unique.

In the transition from Pollock to Warhol a dramatic sea change took place. Pollock was neurotic, often solitary, expressive, and intense in his work. His paintings were tied to his being through the signature gesture with which he applied the paint. They were unmistakably distinct from mass culture. Warhol, despite his flat affect, was a "party animal," at home with celebrities, business people, and artists alike. He expressed a casual attitude toward his work and its authorship, relegating many aspects of the production to assistants—both formal and informal—who hung out in his "factory." In contrast to the gesture of the Abstract Expressionists he relished mass production techniques, and he borrowed both techniques and imagery from mass and popular culture. Far from eschewing the market or celebrity, Warhol actively courted both. In many regards, Warhol is a harbinger of artists like Schnabel, who followed in his footsteps.

Artists and Postmodernism

In Chapters Seven and Eight we focused on some of the economic and technological factors that distinguish the contemporary period of history from what preceded it. These changes have been accompanied by shifts in the nature of culture and, more broadly, the way that people perceive and interact with the world around them. Some commentators use the term "postmodern" to distinguish the contemporary period, from about the middle of the 1960s to the present, from the "modern" period that preceded it. In the postmodern world, many observers argue, boundaries between reality and media are dissolved. The American theorists Douglas Kellner and Steven Best, for example, point out that technology has "brought a flow of sights and sounds into people's homes ... and [has] erased firm distinctions between material reality and artificiality, and produced new modes of experience" (Best and Kellner, 1997:13). According to the French theorist Jean Baudrillard (1929–2007), the real and simulations of reality are experienced without difference today—creating a kind of "hyperreality" (Baudrillard, 1983).

Postmodern culture is characterized, across a range of fields including film, architecture, painting, music, and literature by the use of a pastiche of cultural signs, forms, and references. The American literary scholar, Fredric Jameson explains that as "... aesthetic production ... has become integrated into commodity production generally" "contemporary culture [has become] ... flat and

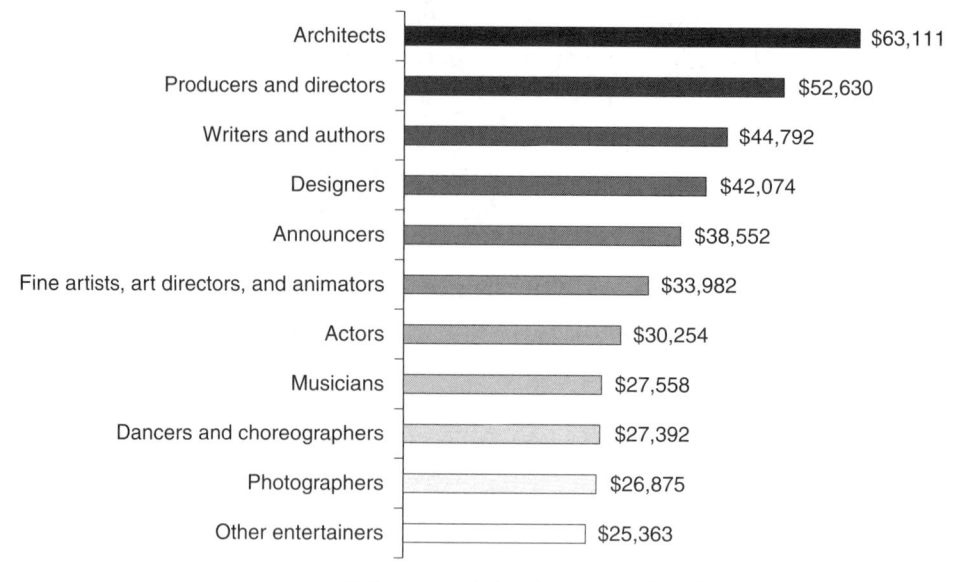

Median Wages and Salaries by Artist Occupation: 2005–2009

Occupation	Median Wage
Architects	$63,111
Producers and directors	$52,630
Writers and authors	$44,792
Designers	$42,074
Announcers	$38,552
Fine artists, art directors, and animators	$33,982
Actors	$30,254
Musicians	$27,558
Dancers and choreographers	$27,392
Photographers	$26,875
Other entertainers	$25,363

Median wage/salaries of artists as a whole: $43,230
Median wage/salary of U.S. labor force: $39,280

Note: Figures are measured in 2009 dollars for full-year, full-time workers.
Source: 2005-2009 ACS PUMS, U.S. Census Bureau, U.S. Department of Commerce

Photo 9.15 (Source: NEA)

superficial, marked by nostalgia and pastiche" (in Bennet et al., 2005: 271; see also Jameson, 1991). Bits and pieces of culture have been decontextualized from their original source and recombined in the postmodern object. Postmodern paintings contain elements from high and low culture; postmodern architecture combines details from a variety of historical periods and locations (like Schnabel's Palazzo Chupi); postmodern music fuses melodies and rhythm tracks from a range of musical styles, decades, and artists. Postmodern culture has moved from the emphasis on originality, unique expression, and gesture of modern art (like Pollock) to an aesthetic of reuse and copy (like Warhol).

Theory and the Death of the Author

Cultural forms and social changes of the Enlightenment and modern periods were accompanied by a spate of philosophical debates and theories intended to explain, promote or criticize these new developments. Not surprisingly, postmodern culture has also generated new debates and theories, many of which have raised important questions about ideas concerning subjectivity and authorship on which previous notions of the artist relied. Cultural critics and theorists in the 1970s, influenced by young, French radicals and the political unrest of the late 1960s, began to question whether Enlightenment rationality and universalism should continue to guide political action and critique (Best and Kellner, 1997: 6). They argue that many of the failures and injustices of the modern era could be linked to Enlightenment assumptions (e.g. Liberalism, Marxism, rationalism) that there is one "universal" human perspective according to which truth can be known and society can be organized. Instead, they maintain, a text, a political system, a work of art, or any other social product can be interpreted from multiple perspectives, none of which is more true or accurate than another. In addition, they reject the idea that individuals possess a stable, autonomous and coherent identity or "self" from which meaning, expression, and intention ushers forth and to which these things can be reliably linked. From this new skepticism, it follows that there is no inevitable connection between an artist and the meaning or intention of the artwork.

The conventional understanding of a text (or by extension a painting, musical composition, and so forth) is that it is the product of an individual and reveals something about the mind of the creator. French literary critic Roland Barthes (1915–1980) argues that, on the contrary, the Author (he uses the capital) is not a generator of meaning. Barthes notes that in pre-modern societies, the shaman or storyteller was a master of narrative code, not a creative or original artist. Since the Enlightenment, he explains, the study of literature has been "….tyrannically centered on the author, his person, his life, his tastes, his passions … the explanation of a work is always sought in the man or woman who produced it ... as if it were always in the end … the voice. And this voice is thought to bear a single message or meaning." (in Cazeaux, 2000: 520).

Barthes counters that all texts are simply spaces, or "occasions" in which fragments of language that are already out there—already part of the culture—coalesce. His argument parallels Becker's claim that works of art cannot be attributed solely to their author. They are rather the product of multiple social processes and social actors who provide meaning, context, technical support, and relevance to the work. Barthes' focus is on the social dimensions of language in particular. Language does not belong to any one individual. Individuals do not invent their own language, but rather recombine already existing sign systems. Thus, the author is not an original font of meaning (Pollock's "nature"). Instead, he or she is more like a librarian, DJ, or encyclopedist, who has a large collection of sources from which to draw and recombine. And, since texts are always drawn from multiple sources and refer to multiple sources, they also contain multiple meanings. Once we consider a text in this way, Barthes points out, there is no point in trying to "decipher" what the author intended to say, or what the artist wanted to express. It turns out that what gives meaning and unity to text is not the author after all, but the reader.

Contemporary artists, many of whom have been influenced by this essay and more generally have self-consciously minimized the role of originality in their work. They freely appropriate or "quote" from well-known work of the past, mixing and matching cultural references, which may have different meanings to different "recipients." Quentin Tarantino's (1963–) recent film *Django Unchained* (2012) provides an example of this sort of pastiche approach. In this revenge fantasy, on the eve of the civil war a bounty hunter purchases a slave, Django, whom he believes will help him find two brutish brothers. As it happens, these brothers are holding Broomhilda, Django's beloved wife, in captivity on their plantation. In return for leading the hunter to his bounty, Django and Broomhilda will receive their freedom. What follows is a gory tale that borrows themes and cinematography from a buffet of film genres including spaghetti westerns, blaxploitation films, gangster films, slapstick comedy, and German opera with a degree of violence familiar to players of super-violent video games like Grand Theft Auto. Of course, not all of the references in the film will be available to all viewers. The ultimate impact and meaning of the film can only be determined by the viewer (or reader) and will invariably oscillate depending on that viewer's social position. (I personally was upset by the fact that Tarantino downplayed the voice and perspective of Broomhilda and the few other female characters in the film). The point is that as a self-conscious, postmodern artist Tarantino is not attempting to convince viewers that he is coming up with an original style or even that he is telling the "true" version of the story. Instead, he wants to show the viewer that he is a master at operating the cultural codes available to him.

Amateurs and Professionals

In addition to shifting the job of the artist from creator to a kind of curator, postmodern culture has also blurred the distinction between artists and audiences. Walter Benjamin's (see Chapter Eight) views were prescient about the impact of the Internet and digital technologies on conventional Western distinctions between artists and consumers. In modern Western societies, there is a clear distinction between whom we consider artists and art consumers. We expect artists to create innovative, distinct, and original works of art, which can then be sold to individuals or institutions. Owners and consumers pay for the privilege of enjoying cultural objects but don't have the skill, expertise, or temperament to create such objects themselves. This distinction more or less holds true for both commercial culture and restricted, high art. In both cases, originality is valued and cultural objects are privately owned, either in the form of copyright privileges, in which case the owner of the copyright can sell the right to reproduce the cultural object, or in terms of the object itself.

With technologies of reproduction, as Benjamin points out, cultural objects lose their uniqueness and become more accessible (in Benjamin, 2006). It is very expensive to buy a one-of-a-kind painting or sculpture, but when a photograph of a painting or sculpture can be reproduced millions of times over in postcard form and sold at a museum gift shop for a dollar, it becomes available to almost everyone. But once it leaves the gift shop, its new owner is free to put it to just about any use he or she pleases. A reproduction of a painting by Monet could become a coaster on someone's coffee table or part of diorama for a 5th grade social studies project. It could be pinned to a bulletin board next to a grocery receipt, or could be a canvas for a complicated doodle. Technologies of reproduction make the circulation of art works more plentiful, but they also take control of the work away from the creator.

With today's technology, "digital natives" can mix, match and recombine cultural products made by other people with relative ease. They can create their own Fan Fiction based on bestsellers, substituting their own endings when they are not happy with the author's or create spin-offs from plots and characters from their favorite books. In fact, producers and writers can consult fans mid-season on discussion boards and Internet sites as TV shows like the long-running "Lost" are in production. Fan input can affect following episodes. In addition to raising questions about authorship, new cultural forms and technologies raise new questions about the status of cultural ownership, originality, and theft.

Originality, Copyright, and Remix Culture

Picasso was rumored to have said "good artists borrow. Great artists steal." After all, aren't we always building in some way on the work of others? Despite Picasso's (rumored) adage, the ubiquity of cultural products that borrow freely from the work of other artists (and the ease with which technology allows such borrowing to take place) has generated a number of controversies concerning copyright and intellectual property laws (see Gaines, 1991; Coombe, 1998; Vaidhyanathan, 2001; Lessig, 2004). Our conventional views of artists' relationship to their work are based on ideas about private property developed during the Enlightenment (Harrison, 2012). Our legal structures link owners to ideas and cultural objects, treating these intellectual and creative products as intellectual property. As sociologists, however, we are bound to find the idea that artists (or their patrons) can claim sole credit—and thus ownership—of culture problematic. Like Picasso, sociologists recognize that ideas and art have a basis in a social community without which they would not exist. Ideas and innovations never really occur in a vacuum. On the other hand, since our society has a core belief in the sanctity of private property and the rights of the individual to own and control (and benefit materially from) this property, where do we draw the line between borrowing ideas in order to contribute to a common culture and theft? And, how have new technologies, creative industries, and social change, affected norms and beliefs about the relationship between the artist and his or her work of art?

Prior to 1980s, there were few (enforced) restrictions on the use and reuse of other artists' material, especially if little revenue was generated by the results. Many genres of popular music, like reggae, club, and rap evolved as urban youth discovered old recordings, which they mixed, mashed and blended to create new and unique musical forms (Navas, 2012). During the 1970s, new technologies also made it very easy for rappers and DJs in the emerging hip hop scene to "sample" or appropriate breaks, melodies, and beats from already existing albums by other artists (Rose, 1994). They integrated the fruits of these plunders into their music without much concern for questions of ownership. They didn't offer to pay the artists whose music they had "borrowed" and rarely even acknowledged that they had done so. And, until 1976, when copyright laws were updated and expanded, existing laws did not provide enough clarity to insure that the creators or owners of intellectual property would prevail in a court of law. In the 1980s, a number of visual artists even began exhibiting actual copies of other artists' work as their own. In a famous example, the American artist Sherrie Levine re-photographed the iconic work of famous photographers like Walker Evans and presented them as their own work. Levine was not trying to pass off someone else's ideas as her own, but was rather asking questions about an artist's claims to originality (http://levine.sscnet.ucla.edu/general/intellectual/againstnew.html). The appropriation of pre-existing images raises questions about the role originality plays in how we evaluate contemporary art and artists.

It has, become increasingly risky, however, from a legal perspective, for artists to "borrow" the work of others without first obtaining expensive permissions from the owners of that work. In 1992, the Second Circuit, the highest US court to hear the case, ruled against the American artist Jeff Koons (1955–) for using photographer Art Rogers's (1948–) postcard of a husband and wife holding a litter of puppies as the source material for the sculpture *String of Puppies, 1988* (see Bushkirk, 2005). According to newspaper reports, Koons had sent the postcard to his fabricators in Italy with written instructions that the "work must be just like [the] photo" (http://www.theartnewspaper.com/articles/No-longer-appropriate/26378).

In 2011 a federal judge ruled against the American artist Richard Prince for copyright infringement. Prince had used photographs from a book about Rastafarians to create collages and paintings made without the photographer's or the book publisher's permission.

Artists working within popular music genres began to run into similar troubles. Early rappers and DJs sampled from other artists in non-commercial contexts like dance parties, but by the 1980s, rappers like Grandmaster Flash were producing and making money on records with sampled material, and the recording industry and individual artists began to take notice. In an early lawsuit, the rap group 2 Live Crew sampled the base, drums and opening lines of American songwriter Roy Orbison's (1936–1988) song "Oh, Pretty Woman" on their 1989 album "As Clean as they want to be." Orbison's publisher sued the group for copyright infringement. 2 Live Crew eventually prevailed in this case by arguing that their version was a "parody" rather than a straight copy, or cover. Thus, it did not violate the doctrine of fair use. This high profile case, however, led to a spate of lawsuits over copyright violations involving big name entertainers such as the Beasty Boys, Kanye West, Ludacris, and Public Enemy (Keller, 2008; Navas, 2012). Today, artists are aware of the financial and legal costs of using other artists' work without securing what are often costly permissions from the owners of the intellectual property. Thus, granting permissions has become big business, and artists without financial backing have to think carefully before incorporating obvious references to the work of others in their products.

The current situation regarding the risks of borrowing intellectual property has fueled criticism. Boosters of appropriation and remix culture are enthusiastic about its potential to generate innovation. They oppose the use of copyright law to restrict creativity, arguing that human beings learn through copy and imitation. Expanded copyright legislation passed in 1976 may have been intended to insure that innovators had some control over their work. Critics argue, though, what has really happened is that big entertainment conglomerates buy rights to innovations from the creators and then use these rights to sell access to this material for exorbitant fees. The end result, they claim, is that there is less room for innovators to explore and build on the work of others. And only the biggest artists profit from this system. Meanwhile, critics argue that ideas, which should be part of the "commons" or public domain, are being held hostage to corporate interests.

Regardless of your views on the subject, an irony remains. Current technologies return intellectual and creative ownership to the type of collective or public domain that they occupied in pre-industrial, traditional societies. These technologies take control away from individual artists conceived as owners of their product. But current copyright legislation makes the use of this material increasingly difficult and reinforces the idea of individual (or corporate) possession of art works. It is worth noting that many artists whom I have interviewed are opposed to copyright legislation, believing that artists as well as non-professionals and art consumers benefit when intellectual property is accessible and circulates most rapidly.

Discussion Questions

1. Watch a Hollywood biopic and pay close attention to how much of the film is devoted to explaining or portraying the social and historical conditions that impacted the artist's work and life. From a sociological perspective, does the film depict the social context in which the artist succeeded? Explain.
2. What are the main components of the "theory of reputations" described by Becker? Explain how this theory has worked to create the reputation of an artist whom you admire. What, according to Becker, is wrong with this theory?
3. List factors that led to the increased prestige and independence that artists began to experience during the Renaissance.
4. What were Romantic conceptions of artistic genius? To what extent do people today hold similar ideas?
5. In what ways did the artist Jackson Pollock embody Romantic ideas about artists? How did Warhol depart from this stereotype?
6. Describe characteristics of postmodern culture. How are postmodern artists different from modern artists?
7. What is Roland Barthes' argument about the unique responsibility artists have for their products and the meaning of these products? How does he argue against this theory? What does he propose instead?
8. Describe how boundaries between what constitutes an audience and what constitutes an audience have been blurred in the postmodern era.
9. To whom should artistic ideas and innovations "belong"? Give examples from earlier periods where artists openly appropriated or used the work of someone else. What impact has copyright legislation had on artists? Do some research on this and report on some of the legal cases.

10

MEANING AND INTERPRETATION

What Does it Mean?

Photo 10.1 **Jannis Kounellis, 2013 exhibition at Cheim & Read, New York.** (Courtesy Cheim & Read, New York)

> Artworks derive from the world of things in their preformed material as in their technique. There is nothing in them that doesn't belong to this world.
>
> (Adorno et al., 1997: 134).

Recently, I brought my students on a field trip to New York City's renowned commercial gallery district, West Chelsea. A student of mine—a man in his mid-forties who had recently emigrated from Nigeria to the United States—contemplated an art installation by the Greek artist Jannis Kounellis (1936–). Surveying a slab of steel on the floor of the art gallery embedded in a mound of what appeared to be used charcoal from a barbeque, in front of several shelves of ordinary glassware, he shook his head and asked me "but what does it mean?" We had stumbled upon this gallery almost accidentally, and I didn't know much about this artist. In the absence of any clues in the form of wall text or even titles that could help me out of my predicament, I shamefacedly moved to the entrance of the gallery, in search of one of the printed press releases that inevitably accompanies such shows. The text, possibly written by a curator or art historian, told us that

> Kounellis's multi-layered, eloquent installations juxtapose earthy substances (i.e. coal, wool, iron, glass, stone) with evocative objects (such as sewing machines), producing theatrical compositions in which "art" collides with the "everyday." In this way, he attempts to deconstruct and re-contextualize artistic and cultural hierarchies, challenging not only the consumerist ideology of the art market but also the viewer's passive gaze.
>
> [http://www.cheimread.com/exhibitions/2013-05-02_jannis-kounellis/?view=pressrelease]

Now, with this and other pieces of contextual background provided by the text, the piece made more sense to my student and me. During our next in-class meeting I engaged the students in a lively discussion about the meaning and social relevance of Kounellis's work, which, even with the background information, provided the opportunity for multiple interpretations.

A couple of weeks previously, I had brought the same class to an exhibition of art works from Tanzania at our college art gallery. Fortunately, this exhibit of sculpture, masks, and other ritual objects was accompanied by plenty of informative wall text and several videos of objects being used in ritual performances. The accompanying material provided a portal for those of us who were outsiders to the culture and from which we could glean information about the art's meaning. My African student, it should be noted, was able to make valuable connections between this art and the art of his own culture. He provided an additional layer of interpretation to the work because many of the forms, conventions, and usages were similar.

Despite the progress we were able to make as a class addressing questions of social meaning and art, the question—"but what does it mean?"—continued to remind me why sociologists of art tend to leave sustained attention to actual works of art out of their studies (see Zolberg, 1990; Wolff 1989). First of all,

Photo 10.2 **Martins Manjibula Jackson Helmet Mask (lipiko) Makonde, c. 2000 Wood, animal fur, animal hide, cloth, pigment. Length: 34.1 cm (13 ½ inches) Collection of the QCC Art Gallery, the City University of New York.** (Courtesy of David Stiffler)

Photo 10.3 **Martins Manjibula Jackson Helmet Mask (lipiko) Makonde, c. 2000 Wood, animal fur, animal hide, cloth, pigment. Length: 34.1 cm (13 ½ inches) Collection of the QCC Art Gallery, the City University of New York.** (Courtesy of Queensborough Community College Art Gallery)

what exactly are we asking when we ask what a work "means"? For something to have meaning it must have a communicative intention. But, surely an object, song, or theatrical performance does not have intentions. For this reason, it makes most sense to sociologists to translate the question as "what does the work mean to the viewer or audience"? With this type of approach, sociologists can focus on what they feel most comfortable with: social groups, interaction, and patterned social behavior. They can use the methods of data collection that are accepted within the field of sociology. They can conduct surveys, interview people, count the number and types of art consumed by various groups, and so on. We have already encountered several examples of this approach in this book. The sociologist David Halle (1993) (see Chapter Three) conducted research on the art preferences and home decoration styles of New York City residents across class, race, and religious groups. Patricia Banks (2010) (see Chapter Six) asked African American collectors of African art why they collected this type of art and what it means to them. These studies tell us about the relationship between variables that describe groups of viewers and their preferences in art, but the actual works of art consumed by these audiences remain peripheral to the research.

Art and architectural historians, musicologists, film scholars, and literature professors, on the other hand, address works of art directly in their research. They have developed complex systems of **iconography** for cataloging and translating the meaning of representational conventions and symbols in art works into descriptive equivalents. Other scholars have emphasized formal or stylistic conventions, explaining and analyzing the use of composition, color, narrative, or rhythmic structure in individual works of art, genres, or **oeuvres** (the body of work of an individual artist) and how these formal elements relate to each other and to the history of art more generally. Others have suggested that works of art are the expressions of the innermost feelings and emotions of individual artists and have sought to discover these in works of art. These approaches, in which individual works of art are described and analyzed in great detail, are in keeping with the belief in the autonomous, free-standing nature of fine art (see Chapters Two and Nine).

Traditionally, literary scholars, art historians, and others from humanistic disciplines focus on works of art, while social scientists focus on the people and societies from which works of art emerge. So why mess with this division of labor? Why should sociologists try and understand why and how individual works of art generate or communicate meaning or what that meaning might be? Well, one reason sociologists might want to include the analysis of actual works of art in their studies is because they provide a multilayered and rich source of information about society. Works of art are what I call "hypersocial" objects. Utilitarian objects, like forks, knives, computers, blankets, and clothing are created by people through social processes for use in social contexts. By studying these things, we can learn for example how labor is divided or about levels of technological development. From the structure and design of these material objects we can learn about the values, norms, and beliefs of social groups. A second type of "man-made" object is also functional, but is intended, *primarily*, as a carrier of complex social meanings that we associate with beauty, the sacred and aesthetic experience. Craft objects like jewelry, book covers, textiles, ritual objects like the monkey mask depicted above, and garments, music, and performance fall in to this category. The aesthetic and formal qualities of these objects are not secondary to their function. It is *because* of these qualities that such objects are meaningful to the people that use them. Members of modern, Western societies also create and consume a third type of material object created *solely* for the purpose of generating meaning: fine arts. This meaning is communicated through their aesthetic and formal properties. If we can agree, along with many social scientists, that one of the key elements of human social life (and that is what we study) consists of our ability to generate meaning through communicating with one another, objects of the second and third categories are *hypersocial*.

Admittedly, in modern and postmodern societies this meaning tends to be, like Kounellis's work, complex and difficult to pin down. In the past artists, patrons, and audiences have agreed on meanings. The opulent jewelry worn by a lady in a 16th-century portrait signifies that she is wealthy. Christians during medieval times understood that a figure depicted with a cruciform halo—a cross within or extending beyond a halo—is meant to represent a member of the Holy Trinity. Drawing this kind of correspondence is much more difficult with, say, a solo by the jazz drummer Max Roach or an installation by Kounellis. The latter objects, however, are also intentional, meaningful, and social, and potentially provide a portal into a deeper understanding of society. Unfortunately, many of the strategies that we can draw from to interpret the social meaning of works of art are difficult to reconcile with empirical (scientific) approaches to sociology. Some of the strategies, though, draw on themes and theories quite familiar to the sociological tradition.

Anthropological Holism

Until recently, sociology has marginalized the study of culture and focused instead on social structures and institutions like stratification, the economy, and politics. These aspects of society were thought to be distinct from culture. Anthropology, on the other hand, has a long-standing interest in culture. Anthropologists have therefore developed many strategies for studying **material culture.** Since art, by almost all definitions of culture (see Williams, 1982: 13) counts as material culture, sociologists of art have much to learn from anthropology's lengthy engagement with "the social life of things" (Appadurai, 1986). Anthropologists usually study societies and culture from a holistic perspective in which no dimension of culture is considered in isolation (Marcus and Myers, 1995: 66). This holistic perspective draws from many of the same ideas as structural functionalism (see Chapter Three), conceiving society as an organic whole whose individual parts contribute to maintaining equilibrium. Material objects, including art objects, then, have a function in assuring the vitality and smooth functioning of the whole social and cultural system. As in the example above, the monkey mask is used in a dance that is part of a Yoruba initiation ritual. Through this ritual, young initiates achieve their position as responsible and mature members of the group, thereby ensuring the continuity of tradition and culture from one generation to the next (Van Wyk, 2013). The meaning of the mask must be understood from the perspective of the social process in which it is embedded (and which it helps to facilitate). Such objects need to be understood in terms of what they do rather than what they are. As British anthropologist Alfred Gell (1945–1997) explains, art objects are "intended to change the world rather than encode symbolic propositions about it" (Gell in Appadurai, 1986). How objects act in the world and with each other constitutes their meaning:

Photo 10.4 **rock concert: bass guitarist playing on stage.** (Shutterstock)

Some anthropologists emphasize the role, or function of art objects in creating and maintaining social order (Leuthold, 2011). The moral and social order of most societies throughout history has been structured, maintained, and reproduced through religious beliefs and institutions. These beliefs are communicated and reinforced aesthetically and thus are embedded experientially (Leuthold, 2011: 199) through the senses. For this reason, music, visual art, and performance are central components of worship in most cultures. Even in secular cultures, like our own, the arts, by affecting us on the level of emotion and

Photo 10.5 **Children's choir of Pentecostal church. Chicago, Illinois, Lee Russell, 1941.** (Library of Congress, Prints & Photographs Division)

sensual perception, produce and reinforce collective sentiments, norms, and values. Gender norms, as we have seen in Chapter Five, for example, are reinforced through ballet performances. Our collective valorization of individuality is sensuously expressed through the extended guitar solo of classic rock music. To understanding the meaning of individual works of art from this perspective we need to place them within the culture more broadly.

Aesthetic and Social Forms

Other social scientists working from a perspective of holism search for correspondences between the characteristic social structure of a society or type of society and the works of art of that society (Manheim in Tanner 2003). These researchers are less focused on the function or role that art objects play in social processes. Instead, they link aesthetic forms and styles with the structural features of a society, features which often lie outside the realm of "**culture**" as it is usually understood. The underlying claim is that some type of homology, resemblance, or pattern between a society's characteristic social forms and aesthetic forms can be identified. The challenge for the researcher is to identify these shared characteristics. One strategy is to group together social formations into structural types and to group art styles into structural types. Individual works of art can then be understood as examples of a certain type of aesthetic form and correlated with the corresponding social form. In the best examples of this strategy, generalizations and unity of artistic style and culture are viewed not as absolute and closed but provide a context for understanding art works in relation to society. Thus, artistic forms can inform us about the norms, beliefs, values and what British cultural theorist Raymond Williams (1921–1988) calls the "structures of feeling" (1958) shared by members of a culture.

The German sociologist Georg Simmel (1858–1918) explained that human beings try to bring order and structure to what could seem like the random and chaotic movements of history, social interaction, and nature. Human beings try to represent and systematize, structure and understand this outside world by organizing it through aesthetic forms. Symmetry, according to Simmel, is one of the most basic formal organizing principles. For this reason simpler, earlier societies are marked by the use of symmetrical patterns of representation. According to Simmel,

> the lower level of the aesthetic drive finds expression in the building of systems which arrange objects into symmetric pictures. Thus, for example, the penance books of the sixth century arrange sins and punishments in systems of mathematical precision and balanced structure.

(in Tanner, 2003: 55)

This type of symmetry is also present along a vertical plane, according to Simmel, especially in both the art and social organization of more advanced forms of despotic or authoritarian forms of society. Because

> symmetrical organizations facilitate the ruling of many from a single point, with the ruler at the top and a symmetrical organization of ruled beneath.... elements in the upward direction of power rapidly decline in number while their amounts of power increase until they meet in the pinnacle which rules equally over the whole.

(in Tanner, 2003: 56.)

The pyramids built for the Egyptian Pharaohs pictured below provide an example of this type of aesthetic expression of social organization.

In modern, liberal societies, according to Simmel, the ideal of symmetry is rejected for another ideal, which allows for a more complex articulation of the individual parts of the art object. In such societies, in line with the value placed on individual rights and self-expression, aesthetic conventions "permit each element to develop independently according to its own conditions. The whole… looks disorganized and irregular. Nevertheless…there is an aesthetic charm even to this lack of symmetry, in this liberation of the individual" (in Tanner, 2003: 58). In modern, complex, individualistic societies, he writes, we associate beauty with the representation of an individual in his or her own right, not as a static element in a symmetrical organization. This tendency is seen, Simmel

Photo 10.6 **Vue de la pyramide de Chéops pendant la rue, Maison Bonfils, 1867–1899.** (Library of Congress, Prints & Photographs Division)

Photo 10.7 Miniature with the Apostles Paul and Peter and the Evangelists John, Luke, Matthew, and Mark, Annon, c. 1070–1100.

Photo 10.8 English: St. Thomas, from Rubens' Twelve Apostles Series. Peter Paul Rubens, 1612.

would argue, not only in representations of people, (compare the Byzantine illustration of the apostles with the portrait of St. Thomas by the Baroque artist Peter Paul Rubens (1577–1640)) but even in "the organization of modern flower gardens, they are no longer bound into bundles but are arranged individually so that every single flower is seen as an individual" (in Tanner, 2003: 58).

Talcott Parsons, whom you might remember from Chapter Three, also argues that there are important correspondences between art forms and types of societies. Parsons grants an important social position to art, which he argues helps to create "relations of attachment" (in Tanner, 2003: 209) between societies members at the levels of feeling and expression. For him artistic evolution from one period to another corresponds to the increasing complexity, technological sophistication, and specialization of tasks and parts of society more generally. Art in complex societies has adapted to this increasing complexity with more abstract and complex forms of aesthetic expression, which "permit the creation of a wider range of more complexly ordered and hence more affectively powerful expressive meanings." For Parsons, the fact that it is more difficult to define the meaning of a Kounellis installation than a 12th-century illuminated manuscript is because Kounellis's work reflects more densely packed and complex meaning.

On the other hand, you shouldn't assume that a one-way or linear direction between social structure and artistic form and stylistic conventions can be found. First of all, several different types of artistic expression can exist simultaneously in one period. As Williams points out, social change does not cause any particular type of artistic response. In fact, the possible artistic responses to any type of social change are multiple, and artistic forms and styles can in turn be causally related to social processes, social structure, and social change. The American sociologist Chandra Mukerji argues that landscaping styles, like the 17th-century styles employed at the royal gardens of Louis XIV at Versailles, were instrumental in helping to construct a new political culture. The design of these gardens emphasized the territorial boundaries of the French Empire central to the new nation state (Mukerji, 1997) through aesthetic means that paralleled military engineering and territorial expansion. The garden design harnessed techniques of survey geometry, forest management, and hydraulic water systems, all of which were central to securing and maintaining French control of vast territories. The gardens functioned as a symbol of national authority and unity, but they also constructed and mobilized this authority through the aesthetic experience of French and foreign visitors to the garden.

Marxist Approaches

From a holistic perspective, researchers try to understand both works of art and the social formations of which they are a part simultaneously. You may have recognized ideas from Durkheim, Weber, and Marx in the discussion

Photo 10.9 View over the palace gardens and the palace at Versailles, around 1860.

above. All of these sociological theorists are important, but the work of Karl Marx has provided an exceptionally fertile starting point for a number of approaches to analyzing works of art. While Marxist approaches differ in many regards, they share an implicit assumption that Marx's description and analysis of society is accurate and true. They also suggest that the meaning of works of art in relation to society is determinate. In other words, using the tools and concepts of Marxist theory, Marxists believe that an objectively correct interpretation of both society and the work of art's relationship to society is possible. For this reason, such approaches are attractive to sociologists who wish to develop a systematic approach to understanding art's meaning. For the same reason, these approaches seem overly reductive and deterministic to other sociologists.

Materialism in review

Marx, if you remember from Chapter Three, has a **materialist** view of culture in which social institutions, ideas, knowledge, politics, the arts, and so on are understood in relation to the material, or economic, base of society. People are organized into classes that correlate to their position in relation to labor and resources. The means for producing material goods are owned privately (see Chapters Four and Seven) by relatively few people, the bourgeoisie, the ruling class of capitalist society. Everyone else (just about) belongs to the working class.

In addition to controlling material resources, the dominant group, or class, also controls the shape taken by the dominant ideas, values and beliefs of a society. They are able to do this because they control the institutions like art schools, newspapers, publishing houses, and universities and research institutes through which ideas are produced and disseminated. According to Marx's view of ideology, people's ideas, experience, and perception of the world reflect their class position. Cultural norms, forms, ideas, and works of art, which are produced and distributed through these institutions, present the world in a one-sided way that benefits the class in power. They reflect the dominant ideology and in doing so obscure what for Marx is the real fact of exploitation. Marx's theory of ideology states that the ideas that people have are going to systematically relate to their material conditions of existence. In capitalist societies like our own, one group of people does not actually have to produce material things. This group can in turn support the production of thoughts, ideas, and works of art that seem to be pure and detached from the material world. But this appearance is only an ideological expression of the division of material and intellectual labor in our society. It also reflects the fact that one class is able to live off of the labor of another class, and is able to use its access to resources and wealth to support pure intellectual and cultural production (see Wolff, 1989: 50).

Central to Marxist theory is the idea of contradictions. Marx believed that societies change or evolve because of contradictions between the level of technological development in a society and the class structure, or social organization, of that society. He believed that feudalism evolved into capitalism because the forces of production (namely technological development) of late feudal society were evolved to the point where wealth and resources could be more efficiently generated than before. The feudal social structure, where a landed aristocracy held on to power and resources and inhibited social and technological change, however, was obstructing overall social development. The new merchant class was better able to make use of technological development for the betterment of all people and so eventually was able to take power from the aristocracy. Marx believed that capitalism also generated contradictions. He argued that technology, mass production and the division of labor made it possible to produce enough resources, efficiently enough, that everyone could live a fairly easy life with considerable free time. Because one group of people, however, holds on to a disproportionate share of social wealth and the means to create this wealth, most people continue to live in misery. Eventually, he thought, working-class people would realize this contradiction and overthrow the capitalists and bring about a new era of social, economic, and political development. Many people debate whether the societies that did attempt this type of transformation left their citizens better off. My point is that capitalist society generates inevitable contradictions, and these contradictions will "appear" in works of art.

Reflection Theories

Marx's thoughts on the relation of ideas and the arts to the material base of society have been subject to countless interpretations and reformulations, but his concepts have all been important to subsequent theorists. Some scholars have extrapolated from Marxist theories more or less schematic programs for interpreting art's meaning, "reading" individual works of art in terms of relations of power and ideology. The British art historian John Berger, for example, argues that oil painting as an art form developed along with private property in the 17th century.

> ...before it was anything else [painting] was a celebration of private property....it derived from the principle that you are what you have.

> (Berger, 1972).

In an analysis of a painting by the 18th-century British painter Thomas Gainsborough (1727–1788) Berger reads the placement of a couple in the

Photo 10.10 **Mr and Mrs Andrews, Thomas Gainsborough, 1750.**

corner of the painting with their land taking up much of the image as an important ideological statement regarding the importance of private property to the landed gentry of the period.

Other Marxist critics interpret the relationship between the material base of society and the form taken by works of art in more subtle ways. From this perspective, works of art will, if properly analyzed, reveal the structure of the historical period from a perspective that coincides with the insights of Marxist theory. An example of this can be found in the words of Marx himself, writing about a novel by his contemporary the French writer Honoré de Balzac (1799–1850):

> In a social order dominated by capitalist production even the non-capitalist producer is gripped by capitalist conceptions. Balzac, who is generally remarkable for his profound grasp of reality, aptly describes in his last novel, *Les Paysans*, how a petty peasant performs many small tasks gratuitously for his usurer, whose goodwill he is eager to retain, and how he fancies that he does not give the latter something for nothing because his own labour does not cost him any cash outlay. As for the usurer, he thus fells two dogs with one stone. He saves the cash outlay for wages and enmeshes the peasant, who is gradually ruined by depriving his own field of labour, deeper and deeper in the spider-web of usury.
>
> [http://www.marxists.org/archive/marx/works/1894-c3/ch01.htm#r7]

Some Marxist critics have taken a more prescriptive approach, arguing that art that does not truthfully or adequately reflect society's material base is not art at all but rather "...is a case of distortion, falsification or superficiality: not art but ideology" (Williams in Tanner, 2003: 81–82). You can see how this type of programmatic approach might favor realistic styles over abstraction or expressionism. It is easier for an artist to transparently depict social relationships and history in a realistic novel, painting or film than it is to represent these things using a "formal" or artistic vocabulary that does not correspond to our normal experience of reality. In the first decades of the 20th century, Hungarian Marxist, Georg Lukács (1885–1971) (1938) argued that writers of modern movements like Surrealism and Expressionism such as James Joyce (1882–1941), Franz Kafka (1883–1924), and Samuel Beckett (1906–1989) present fragmented, overly abstract and idiosyncratic representations of modern life. Such representations distort social reality and privilege the eccentric, self-absorbed perceptions of the alienated individual (the one represented in the text or the artist) instead of accurate representations of social conditions. Formal devices like stream of consciousness narration, non-linear representations of time, and the focus on the inner world of a-social characters, according to Lukács, do not exactly provide a false view of reality. In fact, the modern world really does feel fragmented, alienating, and chaotic. Cultural representations of that world put forth by mainstream institutions are likely to gloss over the real contradictions and inequalities that exist. However, from a Marxist perspective, the appearance of chaos can be explained by underlying historical and social forces. The problem with modernist writers is that they simply present the anxiety and alienation generated by modern life as a fact, without grounding them in a (Marxist) perspective on history that takes into account the possibility of social change. Realistic novels by writers like Balzac or Thomas Mann (1875–1955), on the other hand, provide

> Might manage a sketch. By Mr and Mrs L. M. Bloom. Invent a story for some proverb. Which? Time I used to try jotting down on my cuff what she said dressing. Dislike dressing together. Nicked myself shaving. Biting her nether lip, hooking the placket of her skirt. Timing her. 9.15. Did Roberts pay you yet? 9.20. What had Gretta Conroy on? 9.23. What possessed me to buy this comb? 9.24. I'm swelled after that cabbage. A speck of dust on the patent leather of her boot.
> Rubbing smartly in turn each welt against her stockinged calf. Morning after the bazaar dance when May's band played Ponchielli's dance of the hours. Explain that: morning hours, noon, then evening coming on, then night hours. Washing her teeth. That was the first night. Her head dancing. Her fansticks clicking. Is that Boylan well off? He has

> money. Why? I noticed he had a good rich smell off his breath dancing. No use humming then. Allude to it. Strange kind of music that last night. The mirror was in shadow. She rubbed her handglass briskly on her woollen vest against her full wagging bub. Peering into it. Lines in her eyes. It wouldn't pan out somehow.... James Joyce, *Ulysses*, 1946

the reader with the opportunity to recognize that what seems like disparate and unrelated perceptions are in fact reflections of an underlying social pattern. By using conventional narrative structure and providing rich detailed representations of modern life they illustrate that characters' actions and emotions are tied in a meaningful fashion to their environment and to other people and are actually related through the historical forces and contradictions.

Herbert Marcuse (see Chapter Two), on the other hand, explains that much of the art of bourgeois society is ideological because it presents, beautifies, or resolves social contradictions aesthetically. By delighting and calming the senses (he of course is not talking about modernist works like Joyce's *Ulysses* in the excerpt above) high art presents a false image of the world as a beautiful or at least a bearable place, obscuring social contradictions.

> One of the decisive social tasks of affirmative culture is based on this contradiction between the insufferable mutability of a bad existence and the need for happiness in order to make such existence bearable. Within this existence the resolution can be only illusory. And the possibility of a solution rests precisely on the character of artistic beauty as illusion.
>
> Marcuse, (in Marcuse, 2007: 103)

Mediation

There is no material content...no formal category of an artistic creation, however mysteriously changed and unknown to itself, which did not originate in the empirical reality from which it breaks free.

(Adorno, "Commitment," in Bloch, Jameson, et al., 1999)

It is one thing to claim that society, as understood from a Marxist perspective appears or is reflected somehow in works of art. It is yet another, more difficult task to explain exactly how this takes place and how it can be identified by the critic or other receiver. Clearly, this relationship between what Marxists sometimes call the "base" and "superstructure" is not one way or predictable. One set of class relations can produce any number of different works and styles of art. And art works themselves have an impact on social relations, as we have seen. Different thinkers have come up with a variety of solutions to these questions, most of which involve a discussion of what Raymond Williams calls **mediation** or, how social material gets actively transformed in the art process. According to Williams, we shouldn't expect to see social processes and social relations directly reflected in works of art because these processes have been "intercepted" or translated through the specific artistic media by which they are created. Social processes are also mediated through the perceptions and intentions of artists, who have their own personality, and through the consciousness of people who are consuming the art. Marxists believe everyone is a member of one social class or another, and thus to some degree shares a world view with others in her class. These world views, however, are internally somewhat variable (some members of the bourgeoisie support gay marriage and some are against it) and the world-views of different classes are also always in struggle and conflict with one another. This variation, struggle and conflict finds its way into works of art in unpredictable and contradictory ways, which make it difficult, if not impossible, to explain a work of art in terms of a neat and orderly reflection of dominant ideology, the class position of the artist, and class struggle. And, to make matters more complicated, according to many theorists, social forces don't only make their way into works of art in obvious representational ways. They affect what we think of the formal dimensions of the work of art as well.

> The deep consciousness of the time is achieved only in certain major works and is achieved by them in their form and not in their content.... A certain disposition of human relationships is always present as the deepest consciousness of a particular epoch, and this disposition is homologous with a specific ordering of the elements of the literary work.
>
> [http://newleftreview.org/I/129/raymond-williams-marxism-structuralism-and-literary-analysis]

One Marxist approach to the question of mediation is provided by Theodor Adorno. What Adorno suggests is that the nature of the problems of construction and compositional possibilities that present themselves to artists are themselves social in a very broad sense (Adorno, 1973: 33). An example illustrating

Photo 10.11 St. Jerome in His Study, Albrecht Dürer, 1514.

Photo 10.12 The Knife Grinder (Principle of Glittering), Kazmir Malevich, 1912–1913.

the social dimensions of formal development in art can be found in the device of one point-perspective. One could view the development of one point perspective as simply the solution to the representational problem created by trying to depict three dimensional space on a two dimensional surface. The emergence of this technique, however, can also be viewed as an attempt to wrestle pictorially with the emergence of the subject as the center of knowledge and truth during the Renaissance (see Chapter Two) (see also McLuhan, 1962). During this period, fixed ideas of divine right and unquestioned hierarchies in social relationships were being displaced by the emergence of a new merchant class who valued personal identity, science, individualism, and entrepreneurship. This called for a new form of representation that organized space around the perspective of the rational individual. The emergence of cubism, similarly, may be the result of a crisis of faith regarding subject centered knowledge and the possibility of representing reality from such a perspective (also see Panofsky, 1972). Artists come up with these formal strategies in response to issues that might seem to them as internal to their efforts to make interesting, beautiful, or relevant works of art. However, through these technical devices, social and historical problems, contradictions and forces are expressed.

Adorno is especially interested in the social contradictions that present themselves in the more abstract forms found in modern art. Technologically advanced democratic capitalist societies claim to offer individuals freedom, but in reality real individuality is squashed by the capitalist system, which demands "worker bees"—cogs in a machine of intellectual and material production oriented only toward profitability. Individuality, he argues, cannot be reconciled with the larger society as it was in the earlier, classical stage of capitalism that produced composers such as Beethoven or Wolfgang Amadeus Mozart (1756–1791) (Adorno, 1973). These composers were able to produce compositions using harmonies that stimulated a satisfied emotional response in their audiences. Modernist composers, like Arnold Schoenberg (1874–1951) and Anton Webern (1883–1945), in contrast, experiment with atonality and dissonance, which is a combination of notes that sounds harsh or discordant to the Western ear. These composers may have been compelled to create dissonant music by the formal demands of modern musical composition. What the dissonance really reflects, however, is the alienated, contradictory, and thus discordant position of the individual within modern capitalist society. Modern music forces the listener to "feel" the frustration of her true position in society. And, though modern music may seem incomprehensible or ugly to the public, in fact, he claims, "the dissonances which horrify them attest to their own conditions; for that reason alone do they find them unbearable" (Adorno, 1973: 9). As he puts it, with reference to the plays of the Irish writer Samuel Beckett, which also seem alienating, obscure and difficult to many readers everyone shudders at them, and yet no one can persuade himself that these eccentric plays and novels are not about what everyone knows but no one will admit…they deal with a highly concrete historical reality: the abdication of the subject.

(Adorno in Bloch, 1999: 190)

For Adorno, these works are sources of social information because they accurately reflect present social contradictions instead of glossing over them with a satisfying harmony or providing narrative resolution in the plot.

Furthermore, the obscure and highly abstract form of modern art, Adorno argues, is a response to the increased permeation of commercial industry into the realm of art: for art to maintain its position as a separate, autonomous activity, it had to distinguish itself from the products of the culture industry. For Adorno, products of the culture industry reinforce the ideology of late capitalism (see Chapter Two). These products, with happy endings, clear moral themes, and familiar plot lines present a version of the world in which harmony exists between individual needs and what the system can offer. Think, for example, of popular reality shows like "America's Got Talent." These shows suggest that anyone has a shot at being a star if they work hard enough and have enough talent. In reality, according to Adorno, the objective structure of modern capitalist society does not allow for its members to have their real needs gratified, even if mainstream ideology suggests that all our needs can be met. Difficult, atonal modern music, to return to this example, takes up this contradiction as a formal problem, and rather than affecting reconciliation in the tonal structure, actually leaves unresolved the actual conflict that exists between the objective social structure and the people who make up this social structure. Works of art that are difficult to understand (like the Kounellis above) or seem to assault our perception in unpleasant ways—like much heavy metal and punk music from my youth—is more true to the actual state of society than a Hollywood film in which the plot and meaning seem transparent.

Working with similar ideas, the contemporary American literary scholar Fredric Jameson argues that this division between art and the culture industry has ceased to exist in the contemporary, post-modern world. In this economy, culture, including the arts, has become completely integrated into the world of commodity production. Art no longer has the kind of distance from the world of production that made it possible for the work of artists like Beckett or Schoenberg to reflect critically on society (Jameson, 1991). This situation is reflected in the forms taken by postmodern art, in which surface elements are emphasized and disparate older forms and styles are combined in a pastiche (see Chapter Nine) that loses a critical relationship to society outside of the aesthetic object.

Adorno's approach makes serious demands on the sociologist who wishes to use it to interpret or understand works of art. First of all, we have to accept his pessimistic version of the state of society. Secondly, it requires that the interpreter be versed in the formal aspects of the art work that he or she is analyzing. For this reason, while his ideas provide a sort of methodological "missing link" for identifying the correspondence between the formal elements of art works and society, they are not often used in the sociology of art today.

Hermeneutical and Reception Studies

If works of art correspond to society, and we can identify the nature of this correspondence, then it must be possible to apprehend both society and art in an objectively accurate way, one that is more or less descriptive of the way things "really are." With the approaches described above, we can derive meaning by starting either with society or culture conceived abstractly or with the work of art itself. These approaches correspond with the macro approaches to sociology discussed in Chapter Three. Another set of approaches to interpreting works of art is much closer to micro approaches to sociology like symbolic interactionism (see Chapters One and Three). Sociologists working in these paradigms study social life by paying attention to the way that people interact with one another and exchange symbols to "create" a meaningful reality. Grounded in a tradition of literary scholarship called **hermeneutics**, which means, broadly speaking, the study of interpretation, and for our purposes, the interpretation of artistic objects (Wolff, 1989: 98), such approaches start with the problem of interpretation itself. The practice of hermeneutics concerns itself with interpreting the meaning of texts both within the society and historical period in which these texts are produced (here, I use the word text in a general sense: literature, visual arts, music, and other concrete forms of symbolic communication) and with recovering meaning from one period or society to another.

Scholars have taken a number of positions on how best to approach the task of interpretation and to what degree a "correct" interpretation of a text is possible. Many modern scholars draw on the German philosopher Edmund Husserl's (1859–1938) **phenomenology**, which asks how the human mind (consciousness) creates the outside world through processes of apprehending the world. For Husserl, objects don't exist without a perceiving subject, but consciousness does not exist without external objects to perceive. From this perspective, the "meaning" of Kounellis's work depicted at the beginning of this chapter can be found by trying to recover his emotions, perceptions, and intent. The form, materials, and imagery that Kounellis used in his piece constitute an embodiment of the "deep structures" of his mind and subjective state of being, which the critic can uncover through a rigorous, objective, study of the object. The meaning of the work of art is found by understanding the mind and intention of the artist.

This position on interpretation, which views the author's conscious and unconscious intentions as the most valid source of meaning in a work of art, is clearly un-sociological. It leaves history, social structure, socialization, and all of the things we have been discussing so far untouched. Even if the artist is the source of meaning, don't we need to know about the specific historical and social circumstances of the author's biography and historical period to understand what he or she might have intended? It certainly must be relevant to Kounellis's work that he spent his childhood in Greece during World War II, or that he was living in Italy just as the radical Arte Povera movement was forming or, for that matter, that the contemporary art market is able to support the exhibition of large, cumbersome art instillations that will most likely not be sold to individual collectors. And furthermore, what should you (as the analyst) do about the fact that you most probably did not live through a world war or the early stages of this art movement yourself? You surely bring to Kounellis's work a set of experiences and mode of understanding that cannot match or replicate his. How can you hope to be truly objective in your reconstruction of his state of mind? And what about my African student, who grew up in a small Nigerian village where art objects were bound up with ritual practice and not meant to be evaluated by passive viewers? How likely is it that he, my grandfather, and I will all interpret the work in the same way and that this interpretation will correspond with Kounellis's inner intentions?

The hermeneutic approaches of thinkers like the German philosophers Martin Heidegger (1889–1976) and Hans Georg Gadamer (1900–2002) address just these concerns. For Heidegger, both the object (the work that is analyzed) and the subject (the person doing the analyzing) exist within a social, cultural, and historical context. This context creates certain specific horizons or frames within which the world can be represented and understood (see Heidegger, 1977). To use an example from Chapter Six, both the film *Django Unchained* (the object of analysis) and I (the subject doing the analyzing) exist within the world of American society in the 21st century. To analyze this film as something separate from me that I can know the truth about is impossible because my understanding of the object (and myself) is bound up with history and with time. Me, the film, and the film's creator are actually expressions of a specific historical, spiritual and social formation. In the words of the British literary scholar Terry Eagleton, for Heidegger "[a]rt, like language, is not to be seen as the expression of an individual subject: the subject, or the person is just the place where the truth of the world speaks itself, and it is this truth which the reader of a poem must attentively *hear*" (Eagleton, 1983: 56). If we open ourselves up to works of art, we can gain a deeper understanding of our self and our world, but we will not be able to pin down the meaning of the work in any concrete way.

Gadamer, a student of Heidegger's, takes on the question of how to understand or interpret works that were created in a different historical period. To do this requires some kind of dialogue between past and present. And, this dialogue is possible and even fruitful because the past and present form a continuity. According to Gadamer, we can only understand the past partially and from the viewpoint of the present, but our only hope for knowing the present is to understand the past. Through understanding both the historical context and possible meanings of a past work and also identifying the prejudices and assumptions that come with our own historical period, we can somehow "fuse the horizons" of the past and the present. When we do this, we gain a more profound understanding of ourselves.

For both Heidegger and Gadamer, we don't experience works of art through analytic concepts and categories, which is why we can never pin down their meaning once and for all. Indeed, it is the nature of works of art to be "open in a limitless way to ever new integrations of meaning" (Gadamer, 1976: 98). According to Gadamer "the inexhaustibility that distinguishes the language of art from all translation into concepts rests on an excess of meaning (Gadamer, 1976: 102)." Thus, meaning cannot be objectively given to the work of art. Instead, the meaning is created through the reader or recipient as he or she engages in a dialogue with the work.

This method, or approach, to interpretation works well when concerned with works of art and interpreters who share the same cultural tradition.

Photo 10.13 **David von Michelangelo, 1501–4.**

Photo 10.14 **Woman of Venice VII, Alberto Giacometti, 1956.**

Interpreting a work of art—fusing horizons—is possible when we can identify and in a sense relate to changes within the context of a shared tradition. We have a dialogue with our own projected meanings and modify them. We pose questions to the work of art that relate to our cultural prejudices and history and we open ourselves to the various answers suggested by our encounter with the work. I can have a dialogue with Michelangelo's *David*, created in the early-16th century. I can't get at michelangelo's mind or original intention, but I can bring to *David* my own experience of figurative representation in Western art and its connection to culture because art forms within a cultural history are connected and are self-referential. Even when there is a break with tradition and radically new types of art appear on the scene, this is a break from *something* and therefore the new forms relate to what they have broken from, if only through negation.

But it is more complicated when we are trying to cross cultures. If I don't know anything conceptual or concrete about the Monkey Mask, and what it means for the artist and people to whom it belongs, it is unlikely that I will derive relevant meaning by interrogating it from my own cultural perspective.

Back to the Recipient

Reception approaches like those of the German sociologist Hans-Robert Jauss (1922–1997) also prioritize the experience of the reader or recipient, continuing to draw the emphasis away from the actual text or art object. With these approaches, the historical conditions and strategies that recipients use to read or analyze a work are foregrounded (Wolff, 1989:112). From this perspective, the recipient's dispositions and modes of reading are part of a broader historical situation and set of assumptions about form and context. The source of meaning is not given by the work. In the image by Albrecht Dürer (1471–1528) above, there is no saint sitting toward the back of a room. There is instead a graphic depiction of a man one-quarter of a way from the bottom of a flat plane. We understand this placement to mean that he is behind the depictions of animals and the table because of the representational codes that we have learned. To use the example of one-point perspective once again, two lines converging at a specific point somewhere around the middle of flat surface do not mean that the point represents the most distant point in the horizon. It means this to us because our cultural background disposes us to interpret certain types of compositional devices as representations of spatial distance (Elkins, 1994). It is the recipient, whose mode of apprehending the work is shaped by historically specific habits and assumptions, who provides meaning to the work. What the reception theorist analyzes is the way that an audience harnesses its culturally specific decoding strategies to receive a work and makes sense of it.

Decoding the Signs

So far, we have been discussing the question of meaning in works of art by looking for generalized correspondences between social systems and stylistic properties of works of art, or between society and forms of reception and perception. In the 1960s, literary and art critics were frustrated by the "fuzzy" and unscientific nature of existing interpretive strategies. They looked to linguistics to try and develop a more systematic method, and a toolkit of complicated terminology, for analyzing and describing literature and other cultural texts. They were especially influenced by the French linguist Ferdinand de Saussure (1857–1913). Saussure's linguistic theory was the starting point for a new approach to **semiotics**—the study of **signs** that people use to communicate with each other. Signs refer to the symbolic means through which meaning is communicated. A stop sign indicates that you should stop. A ring on the left ring finger (in the United States) means that you are married. When I type the letters R-E-D, I'm indicating a color to you with which we are all familiar. Saussure referred to the actual symbol used to communicate meaning as the "signifier" and the mental image that the symbol is supposed to communicate the "signified" (the actual thing to which the sign refers is the "referent"). Together these make up the sign. According to Saussure, the relationship between the signifier and the signified is arbitrary (see Storey, 2003: 115). We could just as easily use the letters P-I-D-A to indicate the color red, as long as that combination of letters was not already being used for some other purpose. This becomes clear when we think that so many different languages exist, each with their own word for "red." And different cultures have different signs indicating that a person is married. All that matters is that everyone agrees or understands the conventions of the given language or sign system. In addition, Saussure points out, signs make sense to people only in relation to one another, not as individual entities. Red is only meaningful to the extent that it is not green, or yellow. In musical language, for example, a D note is only meaningful in the context of the entire system of musical notation that we use in Western music. Even the signified—the sound that we think of when we read the note D—only makes sense in relation to the other notes (F flat, D sharp, and so on) that it is *not*. Meaning is created through chains of signifiers, which refer to one another and to the system as a whole. Some types of signifying systems, for example poetry and music, are especially self-conscious (if you can think of a symbolic system as having a "self" but that is another story). These systems foreground the formal qualities of the signs and their relationships within the system, leaving the symbolic, or referential, part of the sign in the background. Poets will often choose combinations of words because of the formal patterns of alliteration they create, or the number of syllables they contain (as in a Haiku) (see Eagleton, 1983: 85), or just because they

Photo 10.15 **Alice au pays des merveilles, John Tenniel, 1865.**

like the way that they sound together (like in the English writer Lewis Carroll's famous nonsense poem, Jabberwocky).

> Twas brillig, and the slithy togs
> Did gyre and gimble in the wabe:
> All mimsy were the borogoves,
> And the mome raths outgrabe.
>
> Jabberwocky Lewis Carroll (from *Through the Looking-Glass and What Alice Found There*, 1872)

Another insight of Saussure, and one which has been further explored by structural anthropologists, is that languages, or signifying systems, not only describe or reflect the way that we view reality, but they also shape the way we view reality. Where a naïve listener might not be able to distinguish between a Tchaikovsky symphony and the background music of a Western, someone who is trained in the specialized language of music theory and music history can easily identify one from the other. Semioticians analyze the specific patterns and logic by which the elements of a signifying system work together to communicate meaning to receivers. Within specific signifying systems (written English, Western oil painting, etc.) the various dimensions of the system (color, sound, tone, perspective of narrator, gesture, etc.) can be systematically categorized

Photo 10.16 **Lina Romay, pin-up, Yank: The Army Weekly, May 18, 1945.**

in terms of their relationship to the other elements of the system and in terms of the symbolic, "denotative," or referential component of the signs (this is not a concern of Saussure, however, (see Eagleton, 1982: 84)).

Some semioticians have combined a semiotic approach with aspects of Marxism, others with audience studies and more sociologically inclined analytical strategies. Roland Barthes (see Chapter Nine) for example, combines a Marxist style of ideology critique, phenomenology and psychoanalysis with a semiotic approach in his analysis of various signifying systems, including those of fashion, architecture, advertising, sports and photography (1972). Barthes does not deny that the relationship between signifier and signified is usually arbitrary (he does admit that photography, where the image is tied materially to what it signifies is a different case). This relationship, as we have seen, is established through convention and culture. When signs and a particular signification masquerade as "natural" or inevitable they become ideological, or, in his words, they enter the realm of "myth." Large breasts, or breasts in general, in our culture, have long signified, femininity, eroticism, and sexual availability. There is no natural relationship between breasts and these qualities. The connection between the two is arbitrary. But, images of women with large, exposed breasts have appeared so frequently in films, art, advertisements, and other cultural artifacts in a context that connotes a relationship between breasts and sexuality or breasts and sexual availability that this relationship seems natural. That particular social processes and attitudes about women, their sexuality, and their status as consumable objects (see Chapter Five) are guiding this pairing of signifier and signified are obscured by this naturalization. The primary level of signification is where the signifier—the word "breast"—and my mental image of breasts has morphed into a secondary level of signification. Here, the sign (the word plus the mental image) actually connotes a new signified, which is sexual availability. Secondary significations are key elements in the production of ideology (or mythology, in his terms).

In Barthes' view, realist literature (and one could probably expand this view to realism in other media like film) is also ideological. It claims to describe reality "as it really is." The language and literary or visual devices used in realism pretend to have some natural correspondence to reality. In fact, literary, or cinematic language no more corresponds with reality than do the letters C-A-T naturally call forth the image of a cat in your head. The relationship between the two is entirely cultural. Since symbolist or expressionist forms of art don't pretend to describe reality but instead create arbitrary relationships of signification, they are not ideological.

Semioticians have developed powerful strategies and terminology for analyzing the code within the text, image, or other cultural object through which ideology is transmitted symbolically. This code can be understood both in terms of individual units of signification and in terms of compositional, rhetorical or narrative strategies.

Back to the Recipient…Again!

Barthes is mostly concerned with how dominant idologies are transmitted through the codes, referent systems, or myths that make up our symbolic communicative systems and can by applied to anything from cars to paintings. Like Marxist theory, this type of analysis is susceptible to charges of reductionism. It assumes a one way and absolute transmission of ideological messages and minimizes the role played by active recipients as they make sense of the work. The British cultural studies theorist Stuart Hall (1932–), has taken the semiotic approach in a slightly different direction, incorporating the processes by which audiences read or "decode" cultural objects. He points out that audiences consume and decode culture in different ways. Their relationship to the material they are consuming is active rather than passive (Hall, 1980). Relying on the Italian Marxist theorist Antonio Gramsci (1891–1937) and others, he points out that ideology is complex and that dominant cultural forms and norms encounter resistance from subaltern (dominated) groups. Audiences may interact or interpret cultural objects in ways that go against the object's ideological "message."

Further Reflections

Most sociologists who study art come to the field with an interest or even passion for the arts that predates their study of sociology. Many, myself included, were actually practicing painters, musicians, dancers, or poets before they entered the less glamorous field of academia. The sociological perspective rounds out the "internalist" (the perspective that studies art works in relation to one another) relationship to the arts that many of us ultimately found to be limited. It helps us connect the things we love to society more broadly. Yet, in adopting the cold eye of science we might find the art works that held so much pleasure and meaning for us have become a bit paler and less meaningful. We may even have managed to drain these social objects of the very stuff that made us excited about studying sociology in the first place. The works of art have become lost in the forest of institutions, social processes, structural relationships, and variables that make up the more "legitimate" subject matter of sociology. The analytic strategies I have presented here (and there are many more approaches to analyzing works of art that I have not had time to introduce) are indeed difficult to reconcile with the main currents of sociology or other social sciences. And I'm not suggesting that such reconciliation is possible or even desirable. But I do think that there is still much work to be done to integrate art into a sociological study of art worlds. I hope that the discussion in this chapter, combined with what I have presented in the preceding chapters, has provoked you to make interesting connections between the art works—and cultural objects that are less often defined as "art"—and the society in which you live. Perhaps you will find bridges between art and sociology that haven't been discovered yet!

Questions Discussion

1. Why might it be more difficult to define the meaning of a contemporary work of art than one from an older, traditional society?
2. Simmel believes that people try and make order out of the social world through aesthetic forms like symmetry. What formal characteristics do contemporary art or cultural objects share? How might these formal characteristics help order our perception of contemporary society?
3. Why, according to Parsons, are works of art from complex modern societies more complex and abstract than art from simpler societies?
4. What, according to Marxism, is ideology? Analyze a form of art and culture that you consume from the perspective of ideology. How does this art reflect dominant ideology?
5. What do Marxist theorists like Adorno or Williams mean when they say that society does not appear directly in art, but is mediated through form? Give an example.
6. Compare Lukács and Adorno's positions on modern art.
7. What are the problems associated with cross-cultural analysis? Analyze a work of art or culture that is not from your culture. What problems come up? Do any of the theorists in the hermeneutic tradition help you with this? Explain.
8. Describe a work of art or cultural object that you think displays the characteristics of "secondary signification" or "myth." Explain how this happens.

BIBLIOGRAPHY

Adorno, Theodor W. 1955. *Prisms*, (trans.). Weber, Samuel and Weber, Shierry. London: Neville Spearman, 1967; Cambridge, MA.: MIT Press, 1981. (GS 10.1).

Adorno, Theodor W. 1973. *Philosophy of Modern Music*. New York: Seabury Press.

Adorno, Theodor W. 1978. "On the Fetish Character in Music and the Regression of Listening." In Arato, Andrew and Gebhardt, Eike. (eds.). *The Essential Frankfurt School Reader*. New York: Continuum Publishing. pp: 270–299.

Adorno, Theodor W., Benjamin, Walter, Bloch, Ernest, Brecht, Bertolt and Lukács, Georg. 1980. *Aesthetics and Politics: The Key Texts of the Classic Debate Within German Marxism*. With an Afterword by Jameson, Fredric. London/New York : Verso.

Adorno, Theodor W. 1989. "Perennial Fashion-Jazz." (trans.) Rabinbach, Anson, in *Critical Theory and Society: A Reader*. (ed.). Bronner, Stephen and Kellner, Douglas MacKay. London: Routledge. p: 212.

Adorno, Theodor W, Adorno, Gretel and Tiedemann, Rolf. 1997. *Aesthetic Theory*. Minneapolis, MN: University of Minnesota Press.

Alberti, Johanna. 1994. "The Turn of the Tide: Sexuality and Politics, 1928–31." *Women's History Review* 3 (2): 169–190.

Alexander, Jennifer. 1999. "The Impact of Devolution on Nonprofits." *Nonprofit Management and Leadership* 10 (1): 57–70.

Alexander, Victoria Dean. 1990. *From Philanthropy to Funding: The Effects of Corporate and Public Support on Art Museums*. Stanford, CA: Stanford University Press, *Poetics* 24 (2): 87–129.

Alexander, Victoria Dean. 2003. *Sociology of the Arts: Exploring Fine and Popular Forms*. Malden, MA: Blackwell.

Almeida, Bira. 1986. *Capoeira, a Brazilian Art Form: History, Philosophy, and Practice*. Berkeley, CA: North Atlantic Books.

Amaral, Leila. 2011. "The Festive Character of Cyber Art." *Technoetic Arts* 8 (3): 255–265.

Amin, Samir. 1977. *Imperialism and Unequal Development*. New York: Monthly Review Press.

Anderson, Benedict R. O'G. 1991. *Imagined Communities: Reflections on the Origin and Spread of Nationalism*. New York: Verso.

Androutsopoulos, Jannis and Scholz, Arno. 2003. "Spaghetti Funk: Appropriations of Hip-Hop Culture and Rap Music in Europe." *Popular Music and Society* 26 (4): 463–479.

Appadurai, Arjun. 1986. "Theory in Anthropology: Center and Periphery." *Comparative Studies in Society and History* 28 (2): 356–361.

Appadurai, Arjun. 1996. *Modernity at Large: Cultural Dimensions of Globalization*. Minneapolis, MN: University of Minnesota Press.

Arato, Andrew and Gebhardt, Eike. (eds.). *The Essential Frankfurt School Reader*. New York: Continuum Publishing.

Archer Straw, Petrine. 2000. *Negrophilia: Avant-Garde Paris and Black Culture in the 1920s*. New York: Thames & Hudson.

Arnold, Matthew. 1993. *Culture and Anarchy and Other Writings*. Collini, Stefan (ed.). New York: Cambridge University Press.

Aronowitz, Stanley. 1992. *The Politics of Identity: Class, Culture, Social Movements.* New York: Routledge.
Ashcroft, Bill, Griffiths, Gareth and Tiffin, Helen. 1989. *The Empire Writes Back: Theory and Practice in Post-Colonial Literatures.* London: Routledge.
Ashcroft, Bill, Griffiths, Gareth and Tiffin, Helen. 1995. *The Post-Colonial Studies Reader.* London: New York: Routledge.
Ashcroft, Bill, Griffiths, Gareth and Tiffin, Helen. 2006. *The Post-Colonial Studies Reader.* London: Routledge.
Ashton, Dore. 1973. *The New School: A Cultural Reckoning.* New York: Viking Press.
Aubrey, Jennifer Stevens. 2006. "Effects of Sexually Objectifying Media on Self-Objectification and Body Surveillance in Undergraduates: Results of a Two-Year Panel Study." *Journal of Communication* 56 (2): 366–386.
Auslander, Philip. 2006. "The Performativity of Performance Documentation." *Paj-Baltimore-PAJ: A Journal of Performance and Art* 28 (3): 1–10.
Austin, John L., Urmson, J. O. and Sbisà, Marina. 1975. *How to Do Things With Words.* Cambridge, MA: Harvard University Press.
Bagdikian, Ben H. 2002. *The Media Monopoly.* Boston, MA: Beacon Press.
Bailey, Peter. 1998. *Popular Culture and Performance in the Victorian City.* NY: Cambridge University Press.
Banks, Patricia A. 2010. "Black Cultural Advancement: Racial Identity and Participation in the Arts Among the Black Middle Class." *Ethnic and Racial Studies* 33 (2): 272–289.
Baraka, Amiri. 1963. *Blues People: Negro Music in White America.* New York: W. Morrow.
Barber, Benjamin. 2000. *Jihad Vs. McWorld.* Bloomington: Indiana University Press.
Barboza, David. 2009. "Artist Defies Web. Censors in a Rebuke of China." *New York Times (1923-Current File),* Mar 20, 2009, A6.
Barr, Donald A. 2008. *Health Disparities in the United States: Social Class, Race, Ethnicity, and Health.* Baltimore, MD: Johns Hopkins University Press.
Barthes, Roland. 1972. Lavers, Annette (trans.). *Mythologies.* New York: Hill and Wang.
Barnouw, Erik. 1975. *Tube of Plenty: The Evolution of American Television.* New York: Oxford University Press.
Baudrillard, Jean. 1983. *Simulations.* New York: Semiotext(e), Inc.
Bauman, Zygmunt. 2008. *Does Ethics Have a Chance in a World of Consumers?* Cambridge, MA: Harvard University Press.
Baudelaire, Charles. 2006. Waldrop, Keith (trans.). *The Flowers of Evil.* Middletown, CT: Wesleyan University Press.
Baxandall, Michael. 1988. *Painting and Experience in Fifteenth Century Italy: A Primer in the Social History of Pictorial Style.* New York: Oxford University Press.
Beaver, Travis D. 2012. "'By the Skaters, for the Skaters': The DIY Ethos of the Roller Derby Revival." *Journal of Sport and Social Issues* 36 (1): 25–49.
Beck, Ulrich. 2006. *The Cosmopolitan Vision.* Malden, MA: Polity Press.
Beck, Ulrich and Ritter, Mark. 1996. *Risk Society: Towards a New Modernity.* Thousand Oaks, CA: Sage.
Becker, Howard Saul. 1963. *Outsiders; Studies in the Sociology of Deviance.* Glencoe, IL: Free Press.
Becker, Howard Saul. 1974. "Art as Collective Action." *American Sociological Review* 39 (6): 767–776.
Becker, Howard Saul. 1982. *Art Worlds.* Berkeley: University of California Press.
Becker, Howard Saul, Faulkner, Robert R., Kirshenblatt-Gimblett, Barbara. 2006. *Art from Start to Finish: Jazz, Painting, Writing, and Other Improvisations.* Chicago, IL: University of Chicago Press.
Bell, Linda A. 1983. *Visions of Women: Being a Fascinating Anthology with Analysis of Philosophers' Views of Women from Ancient to Modern Times.* Clifton, NJ: Humana Press.
Belle, Jennifer. 2010. *The Seven Year Bitch.* New York: Riverhead Books.
Benhabib, Seyla 2002. *The Claims of Culture: Equality and Diversity in the Global Era.* Princeton, NJ: Princeton University Press.

Benjamin, Walter 1986. Arendt, Hannah. (ed.). *Illuminations.* New York: Schocken Books.
Benjamin, Walter, Eiland, Howard and Jennings, Michael William. 2006. *Walter Benjamin: Selected Writings, Vol. 3: 1935–1938.* Cambridge, MA: Belknap.
Bennett, Andy, Shank, Barry and Toynbee, Jason. 2006. *The Popular Music Studies Reader.* New York: Routledge.
Bennett, Tony, Grossberg, Lawrence and Morris, Meaghan. 2005. *New Keywords: A Revised Vocabulary of Culture and Society.* Malden, MA: Blackwell Publishing.
Bennett, Tony, Savage, Mike, Silva, Elizabeth, Warde, Alan, Gayo-Cal, Modesto and Wright, David. 2008. *Culture, Class, Distinction.* New York: Routledge.
Bennett, W. Lance. "Branded Political Communication: Lifestyle Politics, Logo Campaigns, and the Rise of Global Citizenship." In Micheletti, Michele, Føllesdal, Andreas and Stolle, Dietlind(eds.). 2004. *Politics, Products, and Markets: Exploring Political Consumerism Past and Present.* New Brunswick, NJ: Transaction Publishers, 101–125.
Berger, John. 1972. *Ways of Seeing.* London: BBC/Penguin Books.
Berger, Jonah. 2013. *Contagious: Why Things Catch On.* New York: Simon & Schuster.
Berger, Peter L. and Luckmann, Thomas. 1966. *The Social Construction of Reality: A Treatise in the Sociology of Knowledge.* Garden City, New York: Anchor Books.
Bernstein, Richard. 1994. *Dictatorship of Virtue: Multiculturalism, and the Battle for America's Future.* New York: A.A. Knopf.
Best, Steven and Kellner, Douglas. 1997. *The Postmodern Turn.* New York: Guilford Press.
Bielby, Denise D. 2009. "Gender Inequality in Culture Industries: Women and Men Writers in Film and Television." *Sociologie du Travail* 51 (2): 237–252.
Bielby, Denise D. and Bielby, William T. 1996. "Women and Men in Film Gender Inequality Among Writers in a Culture Industry." *Gender & Society* 10 (3): 248–270.
Bielby, Denise D. and Harrington, C. Lee. 2005. "Opening America?: The Telenovela-Ization of US Soap Operas." *Television and New Media* 6 (4): 383–399.
Blair, Karen J. (2006). Binkiewicz, Donna M. *Federalizing the Muse: United States Art Policy and the National Endowment for the Arts,* 1965–1980. Chapel Hill: University of North Carolina Press.
Blanchard, Pascal. 2008. *Human Zoos: Science and Spectacle in the Age of Colonial Empires.* Liverpool: Liverpool University Press.
Blassingame, John W. 1979. *The Slave Community: Plantation Life in the Antebellum South.* New York: Oxford University Press.
Bloom, Allan David. 1987. *The Closing of the American Mind: How Higher Education has Failed Democracy and Impoverished the Souls of Today's Students.* New York: Simon and Schuster.
Blumer, Herbert. 1969. *Symbolic Interactionism: Perspective and Method.* Englewood Cliffs, NJ: Prentice-Hall.
Boime, Albert. 2008. *Art in an Age of Civil Struggle, 1848–1871.* Chicago: University of Chicago Press.
Boltanski, Luc and Chiapello, Eve. 2005. *The New Spirit of Capitalism.* New York: Verso.
Bordo, Susan. 1993. *Unbearable Weight: Feminism, Western Culture, and the Body.* Berkeley: University of California Press.
Bordo, Susan. 1999. *The Male Body: A New Look at Men in Public and in Private.* New York: Farrar, Straus, and Giroux.
Bourdieu, Pierre. 1984. Nice, Richard (trans.). *Distinction: A Social Critique of the Judgement of Taste.* London: Routledge and Kegan Paul.
Bourdieu, Pierre 1993. Johnson, Randal (trans.). *The Field of Cultural Production: Essays on Art and Literature.* New York: Columbia University Press.
Bourdieu, Pierre 1977. Nice, Richard (trans.). *Outline of a Theory of Practice.* Cambridge: Cambridge University Press. pp: 82–83.
Bowles, Samuel and Gintis, Herbert. 2002. "Schooling in Capitalist America Revisited." *Sociology of Education* 75(1): 1–18.
Braverman, Harry. 1975. *Labor and Monopoly Capital: The Degradation of Work in the Twentieth Century.* New York: Monthly Review Press.

Brodkin, Karen. 1998. *How Jews Became White Folks and What That Says About Race in America.* New Brunswick, NJ: Rutgers University Press.
Brotton, Jerry. 2006. *The Renaissance: A Very Short Introduction.* Oxford, Oxford University Press.
Bull, Stephen. 2010. *Photography.* New York: Routledge.
Bunten, Alexis Celeste. 2008. "Sharing Culture or Selling Out? Developing the Commodified Persona in the Heritage Industry." *American Ethnologist* 35 (3): 380–395.
Burt, Ronald S. 2001. "Bandwidth and Echo: Trust, Information, and Gossip in Social Networks." In Rauch, James E. and Casella, Alessandra (eds.). *Networks and Markets.* New York: Russell Sage Foundation.
Buskirk, Martha. 2005. *The Contingent Object of Contemporary Art.* Cambridge, MA: MIT Press.
Butler, Judith. 1990. *Gender Trouble: Feminism and the Subversion of Identity.* New York: Routledge.
Byassee, William S. 1995. "Jurisdiction of Cyberspace: Applying Real World Precedent to the Virtual Community." *Wake Forest Law Review* 30: 197–219.
Cahill, Kevin and Johannessen, Lene. 2007. *Considering Class: Essays on the Discourse of the American Dream.* Berlin: Deutsch Nationalbibliothek.
Calhoun, Craig J. 2002. "The Class Consciousness of Frequent Travelers: Toward a Critique of Actually Existing Cosmopolitanism." *The South Atlantic Quarterly* 101 (4): 869–897.
Calhoun, Craig J. 2007. *Sociology in America: A History.* Chicago: University of Chicago Press.
Caves, Richard E. 2000. *Creative Industries: Contracts Between Art and Commerce.* Cambridge, MA: Harvard University Press.
Cazeaux, Clive. 2000. *The Continental Aesthetics Reader.* New York: Routledge.
Chambliss, William J. 1973. "The Saints and the Roughnecks." *Society* 11 (1): 24–31.
Chepp, Valerie. 2012. "Art as Public Knowledge and Everyday Politics the Case of African American Spoken Word." *Humanity & Society* 36 (3): 220–250.
Clark, Kenneth. 1956. *The Nude: A Study in Ideal Form.* New York: Pantheon Books.
Clarke, Peter. 2009. *Keynes: The Rise, Fall, and Return of the 20th Century's Most Influential Economist.* New York: Bloomsbury Press.
Clark, Timothy J. 1984. *The Painting of Modern Life.* Princeton, NJ: Princeton University Press.
Cohn, Theodore H. 2008. *Global Political Economy: Theory and Practice.* Harlow, UK: Addison-Wesley.
Connell, John and Gibson, Chris. 2003. *Sound Tracks: Popular Music Identity and Place.* New York: Routledge.
Connell, John and Chris, Gibson. 2004. "World Music: Deterritorializing Place and Identity." *Progress in Human Geography* 28 (3): 342–361.
Conor, Liz. 2004. *The Spectacular Modern Woman: Feminine Visibility in the 1920s.* Bloomington: Indiana University Press.
Coombe, Rosemary J. 1998. *The Cultural Life of Intellectual Properties: Authorship, Appropriation, and the Law.* Durham, NC: Duke University Press.
Coombes, Annie E. 1988. "Museums and the Formation of National and Cultural Identities." *Oxford Art Journal* 11 (2): 57–68.
Coontz, Stephanie. 1992. *The Way We Never Were: American Families and the Nostalgia Trap.* New York: Basic Books.
Coontz, Stephanie. 2005. *Marriage, a History: From Obedience to Intimacy Or How Love Conquered Marriage.* New York: Viking.
Corliss, Julia Candace. 1998. *Crossing Borders With Literature of Diversity.* Norwood, MA: Christopher-Gordon Publishers.
Cott, Nancy F. 1987. *The Grounding of Modern Feminism.* New Haven: Yale University Press.
Cowan, Ruth Schwartz. 1983. *More Work for Mother: The Ironies of Household Technology From the Open Hearth to the Microwave.* New York: Basic Books.
Crane, Diana. 1987. *The Transformation of the Avant-Garde: The New York Art World, 1940–1985.* Chicago, IL: University of Chicago Press.
Crane, Diana. 1989. "Reward Systems in Avant-Garde Art: Social Networks and Stylistic Change." In: Foster, Arnold W., & Blau, Judith R. (1989). *Art and Society: Readings in the Sociology of Arts.* Albany, NY: State University of New York press.

Crenshaw, Kimberle Williams. 1993. "Beyond Racism and Misogyny: Black Feminism and 2 Live Crew." In Matsuda, Mari J., Lawrence, Charles R. III, Delgado, Richard and Crenshaw, Kimberle Williams. *Words that Wound: Critical Race Theory, Assaultive Speech, and the First Amendment.* Boulder, CO: Westview Press. pp: 111–132.

Croteau, David and Hoynes, William. 2005. *The Business of Media: Corporate Media and the Public Interest.* London: Pine Forge Press.

Currier, Jennifer. 2008. "Art and Power in the New China: An Exploration of Beijing's 798 District and its Implications for Contemporary Urbanism." *Town Planning Review* 79 (2): 237–265.

Dahlberg, Lincoln. 2007. "The Internet, Deliberative Democracy, and Power: Radicalizing the Public Sphere." *International Journal of Media and Cultural Politics* 3 (1): 47–64.

Davis, Kingsley and Moore, Wilbert E. 1945. "Some Principles of Stratification". *American Sociological Review* 10 (2): 242–249.

De Lauretis, Teresa. 1984. "Desire in Narrative." *Alice Doesn't: Feminism, Semiotics, Cinema* pp: 103–157.

Deepwell, Katy. 1998. *Women Artists and Modernism.* Manchester: Manchester University Press.

DeNora, Tia. 1995. *Beethoven and the Construction of Genius: Musical Politics in Vienna, 1792–1803.* Berkeley: University of California Press.

DeRosa, David F. 2001. *In Defense of Free Capital Markets: The Case Against a New International Financial Architecture.* Princeton, NJ: Bloomberg Press.

Derrida, Jacques. 1976. *Of Grammatology.* Baltimore, MD: Johns Hopkins University Press.

Deutsche, Rosalyn and Ryan, Cara Gendel. 1984. "The Fine Art of Gentrification." *October* 31 (Winter): 91–111.

Devine, Fiona. 2008. "Class Reproduction and Social Reproduction in the USA." In Weis, Lois. (ed.) *The Way Class Works: Readings on School, Family, and the Economy.* New York: Routledge. pp. 100–116.

DiMaggio, Paul. 1991. "Cultural Entrepreneurship in Nineteenth-Century Boston." *Rethinking Popular Culture Contemporary Perspectives in Cultural Studies.* Berkeley: University of California Press. pp: 374–397.

DiMaggio, Paul and Fernández-Kelly, M. P. 2010. *Art in the Lives of Immigrant Communities in the United States.* New Brunswick, NJ: Rutgers University Press.

DiMaggio, Paul and Stenberg, Kristen. 1985. "Why do some Theatres Innovate More than Others? An Empirical Analysis." *Poetics* 14 (1): 107–122.

Dowd, Timothy J., Liddle, Kathleen and Nelson, Jenna. 2004. "Music Festivals as Scenes: Examples From Serious Music, Womyn's Music, and Skatepunk." *Music Scenes: Local, Translocal, and Virtual.* 149–167.

Downey, Liam and Brian Hawkins. 2008. "Race, Income, and Environmental Inequality in the United States." *Sociological Perspectives: SP: Official Publication of the Pacific Sociological Association* 51 (4): 759.

Drakes, Sean. 2008. "Artistic expression: perspectives on collecting African American art." Black Enterprise. (September 1). Retrieved at: http://www.thefreelibrary.com/Artistic%20expression:%20perspectives%20on%20collecting%20AfricanAmerican%20art.-a0187406435 (accessed June 22, 2013).

DuBois, William Edward Burghardt. 1961. *The Souls of Black Folk: Essays and Sketches.* Greenwich, CT: Fawcett Publications.

DuBois, William Edward Burghart. 1903. "The Talented Tenth." In Washington, Booker T. et al. *The Negro Problem: A Series of Articles by Representative American Negroes of Today.* New York: James Pott and Co.

Dubin, Steven C. 1992. *Arresting Images: Impolitic Art and Uncivil Actions.* New York: Routledge.

Dubin, Steven C. 1999. *Displays of power: Memory and Amnesia in the American Museum.* New York: NYU Press.

Dubin, Steven C. 2006. *Transforming Museums: Mounting Queen Victoria in a Democratic South Africa.* New York: Palgrave Macmillan.

DuBois, Ellen Carol. 1978. *Feminism and Suffrage: The Emergence of an Independent Women's Movement in America, 1848–1869.* Ithaca NY: Cornell University Press.

Dumlao, Maria, Kaufmann, Elaine, Mysliwiec, Danielle and Polashenski, Anne. 2007. "Brainstormers and Gender Inequity in the Art World." *Women's Studies Quarterly* 35 (3/4): 144–149.

Durkheim, Emile. 1995. *The Normal and the Pathological. Deviance:* In: Herman, Nancy J. (ed.). (1995) *Deviance: A Symbolic Interactionist Approach.* Lanham, MD: General Hall.

Durkheim, Emile. 1984. *The Division of Labor in Society.* New York: Free Press.

Dworkin, Andrea. 1981. *Pornography: Men Possessing Women.* New York: Perigee Books.

Eagleton, Terry. 1983. *Literary Theory: An Introduction.* Minneapolis: University of Minnesota Press.

Eder, Josef Maria. 1978. *History of Photography.* New York: Dover Publications.

Ehrenreich, Barbara and Hochschild, Arlie Russell. (eds.). 2003. *Global Woman: Nannies, Maids, and Sex Workers in the New Economy.* New York: Metropolitan Books.

Elias, Norbert. 1993. *Mozart: Portrait of a Genius.* Berkeley: University of California Press.

Elkins, James. 1994. *The Poetics of Perspective.* Ithaca, NY: Cornell University Press.

Engels, Friedrich. 1993. McLellan, David (ed.). *The Condition of the Working Class in England.* New York: Oxford University Press.

Epstein, Cynthia Fuchs, Seron, Carroll, Oglensky, Bonnie and Sauté, Robert. 1999. *The Part-Time Paradox: Time Norms, Professional Lives, Family, and Gender.* New York: Routledge.

Erickson, Bonnie H. 1996. "Culture, Class, and Connections." *American Journal of Sociology* 102 (1): 217–251.

Erikson, Robert and John H. Goldthorpe. 1985. "Are American Rates of Social Mobility Exceptionally High? New Evidence on an Old Issue." *European Sociological Review* 1 (1): 1–22.

Escobar, Arturo. 2000. "Beyond the Search for a Paradigm? Post-Development and Beyond." *Development* 43 (4): 11–14.

Esping-Andersen, Gøsta. 1990. *The Three Worlds of Welfare Capitalism.* Princeton, NJ: Princeton University Press.

Ewen, Stuart. 1976. *Captains of Consciousness: Advertising and the Social Roots of the Consumer Culture.* New York: McGraw-Hill.

Fabricant, Solomon. 1972. "The 'Recession' of 1969–1970." *Economic Research: Retrospect and Prospect Vol 1: The Business Cycle Today*, 89–136: National Bureau of Economic Research.

Faludi, Susan. 1991. *Backlash: The Undeclared War Against American Women.* New York: Crown.

Faulkner, Robert R. 1983. *Music on Demand: Composers and Careers in the Hollywood Film Industry.* New Brunswick, NJ: Transaction Books.

Feenberg, Andrew and Freedman, Jim. 2001. *When Poetry Ruled the Streets: The French May Events of 1968.* Albany: State University of New York Press.

Fine, Gary Alan. 2004. *Everyday Genius: Self-Taught Art and the Culture of Authenticity.* Chicago, IL: University of Chicago Press.

Flescher, Sharon. 1985. "More on a Name: Manet's 'Olympia' and the Defi ant Heroine in Mid-Nineteenth-Century France." *Art Journal* 45 (1): 27–35.

Flexner, Eleanor. 1975. *Century of Struggle: The Woman's Rights Movement in the United States.* Cambridge, MA: Belknap Press of Harvard University Press.

Florida, Richard L. 2003. *The Rise of the Creative Class: And How it's Transforming Work, Leisure, Community and Everyday Life.* New York: Basic Books.

Florida, Richard L. 2005. *Cities and the Creative Class.* New York: Routledge.

Foucault, Michel. 1970. *The Order of Things: An Archaeology of the Human Sciences.* New York: Pantheon Books.

Fraad, Harriet, Resnick, Stephen A. and Wolff, Richard D. 1994. *Bringing it all Back Home: Class, Gender, and Power in the Modern Household.* London: Pluto Press.

Frank, Andre Gunder and Gills, Barry K. 1993. *The World System: Five Hundred Years Or Five Thousand?* New York: Routledge.

Franklin, Benjamin. 1848 [1774]. *The Way to Wealth: As Clearly Shown in the Preface of an Old Pensylvania [sic] Almanack, Intitled Poor Richard Improved*. New York: New York Association for Improving the Condition of the Poor.
Frascina, Francis. 1985. *Pollock and After: The Critical Debate*. New York: Harper & Row.
Freedman, Estelle B. 2002. *No Turning Back: The History of Feminism and the Future of Women*. New York: Ballantine Books.
Freeman, Michelle. 1999. "First Amendment Protection for the Arts After NEA v. Finley." *Brandeis Law Journal*. 38: 405.
Friedman, Milton and Ebenstein, Alan O. 2012. *The Indispensable Milton Friedman: Essays on Politics and Economics*. Washington, DC: Regnery Publishing.
Frye, Marilyn. 1983. *The Politics of Reality: Essays in Feminist Theory*. Crossing Press Feminist pp: 17–40.
Gadamer, Hans-Georg. 1977. *Philosophical Hermeneutics*. Berkeley: University of California Press.
Gaines, Jane. 1991. *Contested Culture: The Image, the Voice, and the Law*. Chapel Hill: University of North Carolina Press.
Gans, Herbert Julius. 1979. "Symbolic Ethnicity: The Future of Ethnic Groups and Cultures in America." *Ethnic and Racial Studies* 2 (1): 1–20.
Gans, Herbert Julius. 1999. *Popular Culture and High Culture: An Analysis and Evaluation of Taste*. New York: Basic Books.
Garfinkel, Harold. 1967. *Studies in Ethnomethodology*. Englewood Cliffs, NJ: Prentice-Hall.
Gellner, Ernest. 1997. *Nationalism*. Washington Square: New York University Press.
Giddens, Anthony. 1976. *New Rules of Sociological Method: A Positive Critique of Interpretative Sociologies*. New York: Basic Books.
Giddens, Anthony. 1979. *Central Problems in Social Theory: Action, Structure, and Contradiction in Social Analysis*. Berkeley: University of California Press.
Giddens, Anthony. 1984. *The Constitution of Society: Outline of the Theory of Structuration*. Berkeley: University of California Press.
Giddens, Anthony. 1986. *The Constitution of Society: Outline of the Theory of Structuration*. Berkeley, CA: University of California Press.
Gilroy, Paul. 1993. *The Black Atlantic: Modernity and Double Consciousness*. Cambridge, MA: Harvard University Press.
Gitlin, Todd. 1980. *The Whole World is Watching: Mass Media in the Making & Unmaking of the New Left*. Berkeley: University of California Press.
Giulianotti, Richard and Robertson, Roland. 2006. "Glocalization, Globalization and Migration: The Case of Scottish Football Supporters in North America." *International Sociology* 21 (2): 171–198.
Gleadell Colin. 2011. http://www.telegraph.co.uk/culture/art/artsales/8135161/New-York-sales-Andy-Warhol-leads-recovery.html.
Glyn, Andrew. 2006. *Capitalism Unleashed: Finance Globalization and Welfare*. New York: Oxford University Press.
Goffman, Erving. 1959. *The Presentation of Self in Everyday Life*. Garden City, NY: Doubleday.
Goldberg, RoseLee. 1998. *Performance: Live Art Since 1960*. New York: Harry N. Abrams Publishers.
Goldin, Claudia and Cecilia Rouse. 2000. "Orchestrating Impartiality: The Impact Of 'Blind' Auditions On Female Musicians," *American Economic Review* 90 (4): 715–741.
Goldsmith, Pat Rubio. 2009. "Schools or Neighborhoods or Both? Race and Ethnic Segregation and Educational Attainment." *Social Forces* 87 (4): 1913–1941.
Goldwater, Robert John. 1986. *Primitivism in Modern Art*. Cambridge, MA: Belknap Press.
Graña, César. 1964. *Bohemian Versus Bourgeois: French Society and the French Man of Letters in the Nineteenth Century*. New York: Basic Books.
Grantmakers in the Arts (Organization). 2000. *Grantmakers in the Arts Reader*. Seattle, WA: Grantmakers in the Arts.
Greenberg, Clement. 1939. "Avant-Garde and Kitsch." *Partisan Review* 6 (5): 34–49.

Griswold, Wendy. 2012. *Cultures and Societies in a Changing World*. Thousand Oaks: SAGE Publications.
Grooms, Red, Stein, Judith E. Ashbery, John, Cutler, Janet K. and Pennsylvania Academy of the Fine Arts. 1985. *Red Grooms, a Retrospective, 1956–1984: Essays by Judith E. Stein, John Ashbery, and Janet K. Cutler*. Philadelphia: Pennsylvania Academy of the Fine Arts.
Habermas, Jurgen. 1989. *The Structural Transformation of the Public Sphere: An Inquiry into a Category of Bourgeois Society*. Cambridge, MA: MIT Press.
Hackworth, Jason. 2002. "Postrecession Gentrification in New York City." *Urban Affairs Review* 37 (6): 815–843.
Hall, Stuart. 1980. *Culture, Media, Language: Working Papers in Cultural Studies, 1972–79*. Birmingham: Centre for Contemporary Cultural Studies, University of Birmingham.
Halle, David. 1993. *Inside Culture: Art and Class in the American Home*. Chicago: University of Chicago Press.
Hamel, Pierre. (ed.) 2001. *Globalization and Social Movements*. Houndsmill, UK: Palgrave Macmillan.
Harrison, Nate. (n.d.). "The Pictures Generation, the Copyright Act of 1976, and the Reassertion of Authorship in Postmodernity." art&education Retrieved at: http://www.artandeducation.net/paper/the-pictures-generation-the-copyright-act-of-1976-and-the-reassertion-of-authorship-in-postmodernity/.
Harvey, David. 1990. *The Condition of Postmodernity: An Enquiry into the Origins of Cultural Change*. Cambridge, MA: Blackwell.
Harvey, David. 2003. *The New Imperialism*. New York: Oxford University Press.
Harvey, David. 2005. *A Brief History of Neoliberalism*. New York: Oxford University Press.
Hauser, Arnold. 1992. *The Social History of Art 2*. London: Routledge.
Heidegger, Martin. 1977. *The Question Concerning Technology, and Other Essays*. New York: Harper & Row.
Heinrich, Nathalie. 1997. *The Glory of Van Gogh: An Anthropology of Admiration*. Princeton, NJ: Princeton University Press.
Held, David. 2005. "Principles of the Cosmopolitan Order." In: Brock, Gillian and Brighouse, Harry, (eds.). *The Political Philosophy of Cosmopolitanism*. Cambridge: Cambridge University Press. pp: 10–27.
Herskovits, Melville J. 1958. *The Myth of the Negro Past*. Boston, MA: Beacon Press.
Hight, Eleanor M. and Sampson, Gary D. (eds.). 2002. *Colonialist Photography: Imag(in)ing Race and Place*. London: Routledge.
Hobsbawm, Eric J. 1987. *The Age of Empire, 1875–1914*. New York: Pantheon Books.
Hobsbawm, Eric J. and Ranger, Terence O. (eds.). 1983. *The Invention of Tradition*. Cambridge; New York: Cambridge University Press.
Holmes, Brian. 2007. *Unleashing the Collective Phantoms*. Autonomedia, Nueva York.
Hooks, Bell. 1992. *Black Looks: Race and Representation*. Boston, MA: South End Press.
Horkheimer, Maxa and Adorno, Theodor W. 2001. *Dialectic of Enlightenment*. New York: Continuum.
Howard, Philip N. and Hussain, Muzammil M. 2013. *Democracy's Fourth Wave?: Digital Media and the Arab Spring*. Oxford: Oxford University Press.
Huntington, Samuel P. 1996. *The Clash of Civilizations and the Remaking of World Order*. New York: Simon & Schuster.
Huyssen, Andreas. 1986. *After the Great Divide: Modernism, Mass Culture, Postmodernism*. Bloomington, IN: Indiana University Press.
Ignatiev, Noel. 1995. *How the Irish Became White*. New York: Routledge.
Indiana, Gary. 2010. *Andy Warhol and the Can that Sold the World*. New York: Basic Books.
Inglis, David and Hughson, John. 2002. *The Sociology of Art*. Basingstoke: Palgrave.
Irigaray, Luce. 1985. *This Sex Which Is Not One*. Ithaca, NY: Cornell University Press.
Iyengar, Sunil, Bradshaw, Tom and Nichols, Bonnie. 2009. National Endowment for the Arts, Research Division. *2008 Survey of Public Participation in the Arts*. National Endowment for the Arts.

Jackson, Julian. 2011. *May 68: Rethinking France's Last Revolution.* Houndmills, Basingstoke: Palgrave Macmillan.

Jaggar, Alison M. and Bordo, Susan. 1989. *Gender/Body/Knowledge: Feminist Reconstructions of Being and Knowing.* New Brunswick, NJ: Rutgers University Press.

Jameson, Fredric. 1991. *Postmodernism, or, the Cultural Logic of Late Capitalism.* Durham, NC: Duke University Press.

Jarvin, Linda and Subotnik, Rena F. 2010. "Wisdom from Conservatory Faculty: Insights on Success in Classical Music Performance." *Roeper Review* 32 (2): 78–87.

Jessup, Lynda, 2001. *Antimodernism and Artistic Experience: Policing the Boundaries of Modernity.* Toronto: University of Toronto Press.

Jones, Amelia. (ed.) 2003. *The Feminism and Visual Culture Reader.* London; New York: Routledge.

Jones, Caroline A. 1996. *Machine in the Studio: Constructing the Postwar American Artist.* Chicago: University of Chicago Press.

Joyce, James, 1946. *Ulysses.* New York: Random House.

Kadushin, Charles. 2012. *Understanding Social Networks: Theories, Concepts, and Findings.* New York: Oxford University Press.

Kaikati, Andrew and Kaikati, Jack. 2004. "Stealth Marketing: How to Reach Consumers Surreptitiously." California Management Review. Available at SSRN: http://ssrn.com/abstract=1394975.

Kant, Immanuel and Guyer, Paul, 2000. *Critique of the Power of Judgment.* New York: Cambridge University Press.

Kaprow, Allan 1993. Kelley, Jeff (ed.). *Essays on the Blurring of Art and Life.* Berkeley: University of California Press.

Karen C.C. Dalton. 2010. Bindman, David, Gates, Henry Louis (eds.). *The Image of the Black in Western Art.* Cambridge, MA/Houston, TX: Belknap Press of Harvard University Press. In collaboration with the W. E. B. Du Bois Institute for African and African American Research; Menil Collection.

Karp, Ivan, Lavine and Steven D. (eds.) 1991. *Exhibiting Cultures: The Poetics and Politics of Museum Display.* Washington: Smithsonian Institution Press.

Karttunen, Sari. 1998. "How to Identify Artists? Defining the Population for 'Status-of-the-Artist' Studies." *Poetics* 26 (1): 1–19.

Kearney, Mary Celeste. (ed.). 2012. *The Gender and Media Reader,* New York: Routledge.

Keller, Daphne. 2008. "The Musician as Thief: Digital Culture and Copyright Law." In Miller, Paul D. (ed.). *Sound Unbound: Sampling Digital Music and Culture.* Cambridge, MA: MIT Press. pp: 135–150.

Kelley, Norman. (ed.) 2002. *R&B, Rhythm and Business: The Political Economy of Black Music.* New York: Akashic.

Kenneally, James J. 1973. "Women and Trade Unions 1870–1920: The Quandary of the Reformer." *Labor History* 14 (1): 42–55.

Kimmelman, Michael. 2008. "Outrage at Cartoons Still Tests the Danes." *New York Times (1923-Current File),* March 20, 2008.

Kingston, Paul W. 2000. *The Classless Society.* Stanford, CA: Stanford University Press.

Knight, Brenda. 1996. *Women of the Beat Generation: The Writers, Artists, and Muses at the Heart of a Revolution.* Berkeley, CA: Conari Press.

Knoke, David. 2013. "Understanding Social Networks: Theories, Concepts, and Findings." *Contemporary Sociology: A Journal of Reviews* 42 (2): 249–251.

Kofsky, Frank. 1970. *Black Nationalism and the Revolution in Music.* New York: Pathfinder Press.

Kofsky, Frank, 1998. *Black Music, White Business: Illuminating the History and Political Economy of Jazz.* New York: Pathfinder Press.

Kohler, Karl and von Sichart, Emma. 1963. *A History of Costume.* New York: Dover Publications.

Koestenbaum, Wayne. 2001. *Andy Warhol.* New York: Viking.

Kowalski, Robin M. (ed.). 2001. *Behaving Badly: Aversive Behaviors in Interpersonal Relationships.* Washington, DC: American Psychological Association.

Lamont, Michèle. 1992. *Money, Morals, and Manners: The Culture of the French and American Upper-Middle Class*. Chicago: University of Chicago Press.

Lamont, Michèle and Bail, Christopher. 2008. *Bridging Boundaries: The Equalization Strategies of Stigmatized Ethno-Racial Groups Compared*. CES Working Papers no. 154, 2008.

Lamont, Michèle and Fournier, Marcel. 1992. *Cultivating Differences: Symbolic Boundaries and the Making of Inequality*. Chicago: University of Chicago Press.

Lamont, Michèle and Lareau, Annette. 1988. "Cultural Capital: Allusions, Gaps and Glissandos in Recent Theoretical Developments." *Sociological Theory* 6 (2): 153–168.

Lamont, Michèle and Molnár, Virág. 2002. "The Study of Boundaries Across the Social Sciences". *Annual Review of Sociology* 28: 167–95.

Lareau, Annette and Weininger, Elliot B. 2003. "Cultural Capital in Educational Research: A Critical Assessment". *Theory and society* 32(5-6), 567–606.

Lareau, Annette. 2011. *Unequal Childhoods: Class, Race, and Family Life*. Berkeley: University of California Press.

Lareau, Annette and Weininger, Elliot B. In: Lareau, Annette and Conley, Dalton. 2008. *Social Class: How Does it Work?* New York: Russell Sage Foundation.

Lemann, Nicholas. 1991. *The Promised Land: The Great Black Migration and How it Changed America*. New York: A.A. Knopf.

Lenin, Vladimir Ilich. 1943. *State and Revolution*. New York: International Publishers.

Lessig, Lawrence. 2004. *Free Culture: How Big Media Uses Technology and the Law to Lock Down Culture and Control Creativity*. New York: Penguin Press.

Leuthold, Steven. 2011. *Cross-Cultural Issues in Art: Frames for Understanding*. New York: Routledge.

Levine, Lawrence W. 1977. *Black Culture and Black Consciousness: Afro-American Folk Thought from Slavery to Freedom*. New York: Oxford University Press.

Levine, Rhonda F. 1998. *Social Class and Stratification: Classic Statements and Theoretical Debates*. Lanham, MD: Rowman & Littlefield Publishers.

Lewis, Jon. 2000. *Hollywood v. Hard Core: How the Struggle Over Censorship Saved the Modern Film Industry*. New York: NYU Press.

Lievrouw, Leah A. 2011. *Alternative and Activist New Media*. Malden, MA: Polity.

Lim, Youngmi. 2009. "Reinventing Korean Roots and Zainichi Routes." In Ryang, Sonia and Lie, John (eds). *Diaspora Without Homeland: Being Korean in Japan*. Berkeley: University of California Press.

Lin, Nan, Cook, Karen S. and Burt, Ronald S. (eds.) 2001. *Social Capital: Theory and Research*. New Brunswick, NJ: Transaction Publishers.

Lipset, Seymour Martin and Marks, Gary. 2001. *It Didn't Happen Here: Why Socialism Failed in the United States*. New York: W.W. Norton & Co.

Lipsitz, George. 1990. *Time Passages: Collective Memory and American Popular Culture*. Minneapolis: University of Minnesota Press.

Lipsitz, George. 1994. *Rainbow at Midnight: Labor and Culture in the 1940s*. Urbana: University of Illinois Press.

Lloyd, Genevieve. 1984. *The Man of Reason: "Male" and "Female" in Western Philosophy*. Minneapolis: University of Minnesota Press.

Lloyd, Richard D. 2006. *Neo-Bohemia: Art and Commerce in the Postindustrial City*. New York: Routledge.

Locke, Alain. 1997. *The New Negro*. New York: Simon & Schuster.

Lopes, Paul Douglas. 2002. *The Rise of a Jazz Art World*. New York: Cambridge University Press.

Lorber, Judith. 1994. *Paradoxes of Gender*. New Haven: Yale University Press.

Lott, Eric. 1993. *Love and Theft: Blackface Minstrelsy and the American Working Class*. New York: Oxford University Press.

Lu, Wei-Ting. 2013. "Confucius or Mozart? Community Cultural Wealth and Upward Mobility Among Children of Chinese Immigrants." *Qualitative Sociology* 36 (3): 303–321.

McChesney and Robert Waterman. 1999. *Rich Media, Poor Democracy: Communication Politics in Dubious Times*. Urbana: University of Illinois Press.

Macdonald, Dwight. 1960. "Mass & Midcult." *Partisan Review* (Spring).
McGee, Micki. 2005. *Self-Help, Inc.: Makeover Culture in American Life*. New York: Oxford University Press.
MacLean, Nancy. 2009. *The American Women's Movement, 1945–2000: A Brief History with Documents*. Boston: Bedford/St. Martin's.
McLeod, Kembrew. 1999. "Authenticity Within Hip Hop and Other Cultures Threatened with Assimilation." *Journal of Communication* 49 (4): 134–150.
McLuhan, Marshall. 1962. *The Gutenberg Galaxy: The Making of Typographic Man*. Toronto: University of Toronto Press.
McLuhan, Marshall and Fiore, Quentin, 1967. *The Medium is the Message*. New York: Random House.
Mahar, William J. 1999. *Behind the Burnt Cork Mask: Early Blackface Minstrelsy and Antebellum American Popular Culture*. Urbana: University of Illinois Press.
Mahsun, C. A. R. 1989. *Pop Art: The Critical Dialogue*. Ann Arbor: UMI Research Press.
Marcus, George E. and Myers, Fred R. 1995. *The Traffic in Culture: Refiguring Art and Anthropology*. Berkeley: University of California Press.
Marcus, Steven. 2008. *The Other Victorians: A Study of Sexuality and Pornography in Mid-Nineteenth-Century England*. New York: Transaction Publishers.
Marcuse, Herbert. 1964. *One-Dimensional Man*. Boston: Beacon Press.
Marcuse, Herbert, 1978. *The Aesthetic Dimension: Toward a Critique of Marxist Aesthetics*. Boston: Beacon Press.
Marcuse, Herbert, 2007. *Art and Liberation*. London: Routledge.
Marcuse, Peter. 2002. "Urban Form and Globalization After September 11th: The View from New York." *International Journal of Urban and Regional Research* 26 (3): 596–606.
Marx, Karl, 1947. *Critique of the Gotha Program*. Moscow: Foreign Languages Pub. House.
Marx, Karl. (1935). Aveling, Eleanor Marx (trans.). *Value, Price, and Profit*. New York: International Publishers.
Marx, Karl. 1859. http://www.marxists.org/archive/marx/works/1859/critique-pol-economy/preface.htm
Marx, Karl and Engels, Friedrich. 1964. *The Communist Manifesto*. New York: Monthly Review Press.
Marx, Karl and Engels, Friedrich. 1968. *Karl Marx and Frederick Engels; Selected Works in One Volume*. New York: International Publishers.
Marx, Karl 1977. Fowkes, Ben. (trans.). *Capital. V.1: A Critique of Political Economy*. New York: Penguin.
Mason, Michael, 1994. *The Making of Victorian Sexual Attitudes*. New York: Oxford University Press.
Mathews, Nancy Mowll. 1998. *Mary Cassatt: A Life*. New Haven: Yale University Press.
Matisse, Henri and Flam, Jack D. 1995. *Matisse on Art*. New York: Phaidon.
Mele, Christopher. 1996. "Globalization, Culture, and Neighborhood Change: Reinventing the Lower East Side of New York." *Urban Affairs Review* 32 (1): 3–22.
Menger, Pierre-Michel. 1999. "Artistic Labor Markets and Careers." *Annual Review of Sociology* 25: 541–574.
Meskimmon, Marsha. 2011. *Contemporary Art and the Cosmopolitan Imagination*. New York: Routledge.
Mill, John Stuart. 1933. *On Liberty: Representative Government; The Subjection of Women*. London: Oxford University Press.
Mills, C. Wright. 1951. *White Collar: the American Middle Classes*. New York: Oxford University Press.
Mills, C. Wright. 1959. "The Promise." In: Mills, C. Wright. (ed.). *The Sociological Imagination*. New York: Oxford University Press.
Mills, Maree. 2009. "Pou Rewa: The Liquid Post, Maori Go Digital?" *Third Text* 23 (3): 241–250.
Mizruchi, Ephraim Harold. 1987. *Regulating Society: Beguines, Bohemians, and Other Marginals; with a New Preface*. Chicago: University of Chicago Press.
Moore, Ryan, "Digital Reproducibility and the Culture Industry: Popular Music and the Adorno-Benjamin Debate," *Fast Capitalism*, Vol. 9.1 (2012). http://www.uta.edu/huma/agger/fastcapitalism/9_1/moore9_1.html

Morning, Ann Juanita, 2011. *The Nature of Race: How Scientists Think and Teach about Human Difference.* Berkeley: University of California Press.
Moscardo, Gianna M. and Philip L. Pearce. 1986. "Historic Theme Parks: An Australian Experience in Authenticity." *Annals of Tourism Research* 13 (3): 467–479.
Moses, Wilson J. 2001. "Rod Bush. We are Not What We Seem: Black Nationalism and Class Struggle in the American Century." *The American Historical Review* 106 (1): 201–202.
Moulin, Raymonde. 1978. "La genèse de la rareté artistique." *Ethnologie française.* 8(2/3): 241–258.
Moulin, Raymonde. 1987. *The French Art Market: A Sociological Perspective.* New Brunswick, NJ: Rutgers University Press.
Mukerji, Chandra. 1997. *Territorial Ambitions and the Gardens of Versailles.* New York: Cambridge University Press.
Mulvey, Laura. 1975. "Visual Pleasure and Narrative Cinema." *Screen* 16 (3): 6–18.
Museum of Primitive Art. 1961. *Traditional Art of the African Nations.* New York: Distributed by University Publishers.
Nagourney, Adam. 2008. "Obama." *New York Times (1923-Current File),* November 5, 2008, A1.
Navas, Eduardo. 2012. *Remix Theory: The Aesthetics of Sampling.* Wien: Springer.
Nietzsche, Friedrich Wilhelm, Kaufmann, Walter Arnold and Hollingdale, R. J. (trans.) 1968. *The Will to Power.* New York: Vintage Books.
Nietzsche, Friedrich Wilhelm and Handwerk, Gary. 2013. *Human, All Too Human, II: And Unpublished Fragments from the Period of "Human, All Too Human II" (Spring 1878-Fall 1879).* Stanford, CA: Stanford University Press.
NEA. 2009. *2008 Survey of Public Participation in the Arts.* Washington, DC: National Endowment for the Arts.
Nochlin, Linda. 1971. "Why Have There Been No Great Women Artists?" In Jones, Amelia. (ed.). *The Feminism and Visual Culture Reader.* New York: Routledge. pp: 229–233.
Nochlin, Linda. 1988. *Women, Art, and Power and Other Essays.* New York: Harper & Row.
Obama, Barack. 2004. *Dreams from My Father: A Story of Race and Inheritance.* New York: Three Rivers Press.
Oberholzer-Gee, Felix and Strumpf, Koleman. 2007. "The Effect of File Sharing on Record Sales: An Empirical Analysis." *Journal of Political Economy* 115 (1): 1–42.
Oliver, Mary Beth, Sargent, Stephanie Lee and Weaver, James, 1998. "The Impact of Sex and Gender Role Self-Perception on Affective Reactions to Different Types of Film." *Sex Roles* 38 (1/2): 45–62.
O'Mara, John T. 1964. "Obscenity: Roth Goes to the Movies." *Buffalo Law Review.* 14: 512.
O'Rourke, Kevin H. and Williamson, Jeffrey G. 1999. *Globalization and History: The Evolution of a Nineteenth-Century Atlantic Economy.* Cambridge, MA: MIT.
Ostrower, Francie. 1997. *Why the Wealthy Give: The Culture of Elite Philanthropy.* Princeton, NJ: Princeton University Press.
Ostrower, Francie. 2004. *Attitudes and Practices Concerning Effective Philanthropy: Survey Report.* Washington, DC: Urban Institute Press.
Painter, Nell Irvin. 2007. *Creating Black Americans: African-American History and its Meanings, 1619 to the Present.* New York: Oxford University Press.
Pak, Hyong-yu. 2013. *Heritage Tourism.* New York: Routledge.
Panofsky, Erwin. 1972. *Renaissance and Renascences in Western Art.* New York: Harper & Row.
Paolini, Albert J., Elliott, Anthony and Moran, Anthony. 1999. *Navigating Modernity: Postcolonialism, Identity, and International Relations.* Boulder, CO: L. Rienner Publishers.
Park, Kyeyoung. 1997. *The Korean American Dream: Immigrants and Small Business in New York City.* Ithaca, NY: Cornell University Press.
Parker, Rozsika. 1984. *The Subversive Stitch: Embroidery and the Making of the Feminine.* London: Women's Press.
Parsons, Talcott. 1968. *The Structure of Social Action: A Study in Social Theory with Special Reference to a Group of Recent European Writers.* New York: Free Press.

Parsons, Talcott. 1991. *The Social System.* London: Routledge.
Pascoe, Cheri J. 2012. *Dude, You're a Fag: Masculinity and Sexuality in High School.* Berkeley, CA: University of California Press.
Penner, James. 2011. *Pinks, Pansies, and Punks: The Rhetoric of Masculinity in American Literary Culture.* Bloomington, Indiana University Press.
Peterson, Richard A. 1982. "Five Constraints on the Production of Culture: Law, Technology, Market, Organizational Structure and Occupational Careers." *The Journal of Popular Culture* 16 (2): 143–153.
Peterson, Richard A. 1992. "Understanding Audience Segmentation: From Elite and Mass to Omnivore and Univore." *Poetics* 21 (4): 243–258.
Peterson, Richard A. 1997. *Creating Country Music: Fabricating Authenticity*. Chicago: University of Chicago Press.
Peterson, Richard A. and Anand, Narasinhan. 2004. "The Production of Culture Perspective." *Annual Review of Sociology*: 30: 311–334.
Peterson, Richard A. and Kern, Roger M. 1996. "Changing Highbrow Taste: From Snob to Omnivore." *American Sociological Review* 61(5): 900–907.
Pinder, Kymberly N. (ed.). 2002. *Racing Art History: Critical Readings in Race and Art History.* New York: Routledge.
Pine, B. Joseph and Gilmore, James H. 2011. *The Experience Economy.* Boston: Harvard Business Review Press.
Plattner, Stuart. 1998. "A most Ingenious Paradox: The Market for Contemporary Fine Art." *American Anthropologist* 100 (2): 482–493.
Poovey, Mary. 1985. *Scenes of an Indelicate Character: The Medical Treatment of Victorian Women.* Milwaukee, WI: Center for Twentieth Century Studies, University of Wisconsin–Milwaukee.
Post, Robert. (ed.) 1998. *Censorship and Silencing: Practices of Cultural Regulation.* Los Angeles: Getty Research Institute for the History of Art and the Humanities.
Powdermaker, Hortense. 1950. *Hollywood, the Dream Factory: An Anthropologist Looks at the Movie-Makers.* Boston: Little, Brown.
Quemin, Alain. 2006. "Globalization and Mixing in the Visual Arts: An Empirical Survey of 'High Culture' and Globalization." *International Sociology* 21 (4): 522–550.
Reed, Christopher, 2011. *Art and Homosexuality: A History of Ideas.* New York: Oxford University Press.
Reynolds, David S. 2011. *Mightier than the Sword: Uncle Tom's Cabin and the Battle for America.* New York: W. W. Norton & Co.
Ritzer, George. 2004. *The McDonaldization of Society.* Thousand Oaks, CA: Pine Forge Press.
Roberts, Dorothy E. 2011. *Fatal Invention: How Science, Politics, and Big Business Re-Create Race in the Twenty-First Century.* New York: New Press.
Robertson, Geoffrey. 2010. "The trial of Lady Chatterley's Lover." *Guardian* (October 22). Retrieved at: http://www.guardian.co.uk/books/2010/oct/22/dh-lawrence-lady-chatterley-trial.
Rodenbeck, Judith F. 2011. *Radical Prototypes: Allan Kaprow and the Invention of Happenings.* Cambridge, MA: MIT Press.
Roediger, David R. 1991. *The Wages of Whiteness: Race and the Making of the American Working Class.* New York: Verso.
Roediger, David R. 2008. *How Race Survived US History: From Settlement and Slavery to the Obama Phenomenon.* New York: Verso.
Rogala, Miroslaw. 2011. "The Virtual and the Vivid: Reframing the Issues in Interactive Arts." *Technoetic Arts* 8 (3): 299–309.
Romanowski, William D. and Denisoff, R. Serge. 1987. "Money for Nothin' and the Charts for Free: Rock and the Movies." *The Journal of Popular Culture* 21 (3): 63–78.
Rose, Tricia. 1994. *Black Noise: Rap Music and Black Culture in Contemporary America.* Hanover, NH: University Press of New England.
Rosenblum, Naomi. 1994. *A History of Women Photographers.* New York: Abbeville Press.

Rothenberg, Julia. 2012a. "Selling Art to the World in Chelsea." *Visual Studies* 27 (3): 277–294.
Rothenberg, Julia. 2012b. "Art after 9/11: Critical Moments in Lean Times". *Cultural Sociology*, 6 (2): 177–200.
Rothenberg, Julia and Fine, Gary Alan. 2008. "Art Worlds and their Ethnographers." *Ethnologie française* 38 (1): 31–37.
Rubenfeld, Florence. 1997. *Clement Greenberg: A Life*. New York: Scribner.
Rucker, Walter C. 2006. *The River Flows On: Black Resistance, Culture, and Identity Formation in Early America*. Baton Rouge: Louisiana State University Press.
Russell, Catherine. 1999. *Experimental Ethnography: The Work of Film in the Age of Video*. Durham NC: Duke University Press.
Saez, Emmanuel and Recession, G. 2013. Striking it Richer: The Evolution of Top Incomes in the United States (Updated with 2011 estimates). *University of California-Berkley working Paper*, 1–8.
Said, Edward W. 1978. *Orientalism*. New York: Pantheon Books.
Saltz, Jerry. 2007. "Seeing Dollar Signs Is the Art Market Making Us Stupid? Or Are We Making It Stupid?" *Village Voice* (January 16). Retrieved from: http://www.villagevoice.com/2007-01-16/art/seeing-dollar-signs/.
Sandler, Martin W. 2002. *Against the Odds: Women Pioneers in the First Hundred Years of Photography*. New York: Rizzoli.
Sassen, Saskia. 1991. *The Global City: New York, London, Tokyo*. Princeton, NJ: Princeton University Press.
Sassoon, Donald. 1996. *One Hundred Years of Socialism: The West European Left in the Twentieth Century*. New York: New Press.
Savran, David. 1998. *Taking it Like a Man: White Masculinity, Masochism, and Contemporary American Culture*. Princeton, NJ: Princeton University Press.
Sayer, Henry M. 1989. *The Object of Performance: The American Avant-Garde since 1970*. Chicago: University of Chicago Press.
Schmutz, Vaughn and Faupel, Alison. 2010. "Gender and Cultural Consecration in Popular Music". *Social Forces* 89 (2): 685–707.
Schneeman, Carolee and Max Hutchinson Gallery (New York, NY.), 1982. *Carolee Schneeman*. New Paltz, NY: Document text, in association with Max Hutchinson Gallery, New York City.
Schopenhauer, Arthur. 1969. *The World as Will and Representation* Vol. 1. New York: Dover Publications.
Schrecker, Ellen. 1998. *Many are the Crimes: McCarthyism in America*. Boston: Little, Brown.
Schuler, Catherine. 2013. "Reinventing the Show Trial: Putin and Pussy Riot." *TDR/The Drama Review* 57 (1): 7–17.
Scott, Allen J. (2010), "Cultural Economy and the Creative Field of the City." Geografiska Annaler: Series B, Human Geography, 92 (2): 115–130.
Sedgwick, Eve Kosofsky. 1993. "Queer Performativity: Henry James's the Art of the Novel." *GLQ: A Journal of Lesbian and Gay Studies* 1 (1): 1–16.
Senie, Harriet, 2002. *The Tilted Arc Controversy: Dangerous Precedent?* Minneapolis: University of Minnesota Press.
Sennett, Richard. 1998. *The Corrosion of Character: The Personal Consequences of Work in the New Capitalism*. New York: Norton.
Sewell Jr. William H. 1992. "A Theory of Structure: Duality, Agency, and Transformation." *American Journal of Sociology* 98(1): 1–29.
Shammas, Carole. 1993. "A New Look at Long-Term Trends in Wealth Inequality in the United States." *American Historical Review* 98 (2): 412–431.
Sholette, Gregory. 1998. *News from Nowhere: Activist Art and After: A Report from New York City*. Third Text 13(1): 45–62.
Skeggs, Beverley. 1997. *Formations of Class and Gender: Becoming Respectable*. Thousand Oaks, CA: SAGE.

Smith, Adam and Skinner, Andrew S. (ed.) 1999. *The Wealth of Nations Books I-III*. Harmondsworth: Penguin.
Smith, Neil. 1996. *The New Urban Frontier: Gentrification and the Revanchist City*. New York: Routledge.
Smith, Philip. 1998. *The New American Cultural Sociology*. New York: Cambridge University Press.
Smith, Roberta. 1990. "Review/Art; 3 Museums Collaborate To Sum Up a Decade." *New York Times* (May 25). Retrieved at: http://www.nytimes.com/1990/05/25/arts/review-art-3-museums-collaborate-to-sum-up-a-decade.html.
Smith, Sidonie and Watson, Julia. 2005. *Interfaces: Women, Autobiography, Image, Performance*. Ann Arbor: University of Michigan Press.
Smith, Thomas M. 2003. "The Effect of NEA Grants on the Contributions to Nonprofit Dance Companies." *The Journal of Arts Management, Law, and Society* 33 (2): 98–113.
Solnit, Rebecca. 2003. *River of Shadows: Eadweard Muybridge and the Technological Wild West*. New YorK: Viking.
Stallabrass, Julian. 2004. *Art Incorporated: The Story of Contemporary Art*. New York: Oxford University Press.
Stansell, Christine. 2011. *Feminist Promise: 1792 to the Present*. New York: Random House.
Stein, Judith. 2010. *Pivotal Decade: How the United States Traded Factories for Finance in the Seventies*. New Haven, CT: Yale University Press.
Stein, Rebecca Luna. 1998. "National Itineraries, Itinerant Nations: Israeli Tourism and Palestinian Cultural Production." *Social Text* 56: 91–124.
Steinem, Gloria. 1977. *Pornography—Not Sex But the Obscene Use of Power*. Ms (August 1977), 44.
Steinberg, Steven. 2001. *The Ethnic Myth: Race, Ethnicity, and Class in America*. Boston: Beacon Press.
Sterling, Christopher H. and Kittross, John M. 2001. *Stay Tuned: A History of American Broadcasting*. Mahwah, NJ: Lawrence Erlbaum Associates.
Stiglitz, Joseph E. 2006. *Making Globalization Work*. New York: W.W. Norton & Co.
Stimson, Blake and Gregory Sholette. 2007. *Collectivism After Modernism: The Art of Social Imagination After 1945*. Minnesota: University of Minnesota Press.
Storey, John. 2003. *Inventing Popular Culture: From Folklore to Globalization*. Malden, MA: Blackwell.
Storey, John. 1996. *Cultural Studies and the Study of Popular Culture: Theories and Methods*. Edinburgh: Edinburgh University Press.
Strausbaugh, John. 2006. *Black Like You: Blackface, Whiteface, Insult and Imitation in American Popular Culture*. New York: Jeremy P. Tarcher/Penguin.
Szántó, András. 2003. "Hot and Cool: Some Contrasts between the Visual Art Worlds of New York and Los Angeles." in Halle, David (ed.). *New York & Los Angeles: Politics, Society, and Culture: A Comparative View*. Chicago: University of Chicago Press.
Tanner, Jeremy. (ed.). 2003. *The Sociology of Art: A Reader*. New York: Routledge.
Taylor, Billy and Reed, Teresa L. 2013. *The Jazz Life of Dr. Billy*. Bloomington: Indiana University Press.
Thompson, Edward P. 1980. *The Making of the English Working Class*. V. Gollancz.
Tocqueville, Alexis de 2003. Goldhammer, Arthur. (trans.). *Democracy in America*. New York: Library of America.
Toepler, Stefan, Annette, Zimmer, Crane, Diana, Kawashima, Nobuko and Kawasaki, Kenichi. 2002. "'Subsidizing the Arts'." in Crane, Diana, Nobuko Kawashima, and Kenichi Kawasaki, (eds.). *Global Culture: Media, Arts, Policy, and Globalization*. New York: Routledge.
Toll, Robert C. 1974. *Blacking Up*. New York: Oxford University Press.
Turner, Jonathan H. 1997. *The Institutional Order: Economy, Kinship, Religion, Polity, Law, and Education in Evolutionary and Comparative Perspective*. New York: Longman.
Tyler, Tom R. 2002. "Is the Internet Changing Social Life? It Seems the More Things Change, the More they Stay the Same." *Journal of Social Issues* 58 (1): 195–205.

Tzara, Tristan. 1992. "Dada Manifesto 1918." (trans.). Ralph Manheim, *Dada Painters and Poets* in Motherwell, Robert. (ed.). 1951. *The Dada Painters and Poets; An Anthology.* New York: Wittenborn, Schultz.

Vaidhyanathan, Siva. 2001. *Copyrights and Copywrong: The Rise of Intellectual Property and How it Threatens Creativity.* New York: New York University Press.

Valls, Andrew. 2005. *Race and Racism in Modern Philosophy.* Ithaca, NY: Cornell University Press.

Van Deburg, William L. 1992. *New Day in Babylon: The Black Power Movement and American Culture, 1965–1975.* Chicago: University of Chicago Press.

van Wyck, Gary. (ed.). 2013. *Shangaa: Art of Tanzania.* Bayside, New York: QCC Art Gallery, City University of New York and Portland Museum of Art.

Vasari, Giorgio. 1965. *Lives of the Artists.* Harmondsworth, New York: Penguin Books.

Vasari, Giorgio. (n.d.). *Lives of the Artists (selections).* Retrieved at: www.fordham.edu/halsall/basis/vasari/vasari-lives.html.

Veith, Gene Edward. 1995. "The Velvet Prison and the Closed Academy." *Society* 32 (4): 47–52.

Veblen, Thorstein. 1934. *The Theory of the Leisure Class: An Economic Study of Institutions.* New York: Modern Library.

Velthuis, Olav. 2005. *Talking Prices: Symbolic Meanings of Prices on the Market for Contemporary Art.* Princeton, NJ: Princeton University Press.

Velthuis, Olav. 2008. "Accounting for Taste: The Economics of Art." *Artforum* 46 (8): 304–309.

Vine, Richard. 2008. *New China – New Art.* Munchen: Prestel.

Volti, Rudi. 1995. *Society and Technological Change.* New York: St. Martin's Press.

Wagner-Pacifici, Robin and Schwartz, Barry. 1991. "The Vietnam Veterans Memorial: Commemorating a Difficult Past." *American Journal of Sociology*: 97(2): 376–420.

Warhol, Andy, 1975. *The Philosophy of Andy Warhol: From A to B and Back Again.* New York: Harcourt Brace Jovanovich.

Warhol, Andy. and Hackett, Pat. 1980. *POPism: The Warhol '60s.* New York: Harcourt Brace Jovanovich.

Warner, W. Lloyd, Meeker, Marchia and Eells, Kenneth. 1949. *Social Class in America; A Manual of Procedure for the Measurement of Social Status.* Oxford, England: Science Research Associates.

Weber, Max, 1998. Parsons, Talcott. (trans.). *The Protestant Ethic and the Spirit of Capitalism.* Los Angeles: Roxbury.

Weber, Max, 1968. *Economy and Society: An Outline of Interpretive Sociology.* New York: Bedminster Press.

Weber, Max. 2005. "Remarks on Technology and Culture." *Theory, Culture & Society* 22 (4): 23–38.

Weber, Max, Gerth, Hans Heinrich and Mills, C. Wright. (eds.). 1946. *From Max Weber: Essays in Sociology.* New York: Oxford University Press.

Welch, Vincent Jr. and Kim, Yonghyun. 2010. "Race/Ethnicity and Arts Participation: Findings from the Survey of Public Participation in the Arts." Washington, DC: National Endowment for the Arts.

Wells, Tom. 1994. *The War Within: America's Battle Over Vietnam.* Berkeley: University of California Press.

West, Candace and Don H. Zimmerman. 1987. "Doing Gender." *Gender & Society* 1 (2): 125–151.

Wheaton, Belinda. 2000. "'New Lads'? Masculinities and the 'New Sport' Participant." *Men and Masculinities* 2 (4): 434–456.

White, Harrison C. and White, Cynthia A. 1993. *Canvases and Careers: Institutional Change in the French Painting World: With a New Foreword and a New Afterword.* Chicago: University of Chicago Press.

Williams, David R. 1999. "Race, Socioeconomic Status, and Health the Added Effects of Racism and Discrimination." *Annals of the New York Academy of Sciences* 896 (1): 173–188.

Williams, Raymond. 1958. *Culture and Society, 1780–1950.* New York: Columbia University Press.

Williams, Raymond. 1982. *The Sociology of Culture.* New York: Schocken Books.
Willis, Paul E. 1977. *Learning to Labor: How Working Class Kids Get Working Class Jobs.* New York: Columbia University Press.
Wilson, William Julius. 1978. *The Declining Significance of Race: Blacks and Changing American Institutions.* Chicago: University of Chicago Press.
Wolfe, Tom. 1968. *The Pump House Gang.* New York: Farrar, Straus & Giroux.
Wolff, Janet. 1989. *The Social Production of Art.* New York: New York University Press.
Wollstonecraft, Mary. American Imprint Collection (Library of Congress). 1792. *A Vindication of the Rights of Woman: With Strictures on Moral and Political Subjects.* Philadelphia, PA: Printed by William Gibbons.
Woodmansee, Martha. 1994. *The Author, Art, and the Market: Rereading the History of Aesthetics.* New York: Columbia University Press.
Wu, Chin-Tao. 2002. *Privatising Culture: Corporate Art Intervention since the 1980s.* London; New York: Verso.
Yúdice, George. 2003. *The Expediency of Culture: Uses of Culture in the Global Era.* Durham, NC: Duke University Press.
Zolberg, Vera L. 1990. *Constructing a Sociology of the Arts.* New York: Cambridge University Press.
Zolberg, Vera L. and Cherbo, Joni Maya. 1997. *Outsider Art: Contesting Boundaries in Contemporary Culture.* New York: Cambridge University Press.
Zukin, Sharon. 1982. *Loft Living: Culture and Capital in Urban Change.* Baltimore, MD: Johns Hopkins University Press.
Zweig, Michael. 2000. *The Working Class Majority: America's Best Kept Secret.* Ithaca, NY: ILR Press.

GLOSSARY/INDEX

Page numbers in *italic* type refer to pictures.

Abramovicc, Marina and Ulay: *Imponderabilia Performance* 54–5, *54*
Abstract Expressionism a school of American art that flourished in the late 1940s and 1950s. Headquartered in New York City its leading lights included Jackson Pollack, Willem de Kooning, Helen Frankenthaler, Lee Krasner, and Mark Rothko. In painting, abstract expressionism was marked by attention to surface brushstrokes and huge canvasses. It was the first American school of art to attain international recognition 48–9, 93, 144, 207–8, *208*, 213; state funding 148–9
abstraction 71, 148
access to the arts: social structures affecting 9
Achebe, Chinua 175
ACT UP 153, 158
Adorno, Theodor 31–3, 60, 158–9, 221, 235, 236, 238–40
aesthetic disposition Pierre Bourdieu's term (1984, *Distinction*) for the ability to make decisions about taste that are informed by a cultural orientation acquired not by study but by lifestyle 77
aesthetic drive 227–8
aesthetics the branch of philosophy that addresses questions of beauty, art, and perception 13; aesthetic disposition 76–9; aesthetic distance 77–8; discipline of, generally 13–14; factors influencing 24–5; and group identity 8–9; Kantian 23–5, 76, 96, 200; social science compared 2
African Americans: Afro-centric identity 124–5; anti-war movement 130; Black Nationalism 120, 123; Black Panthers 122–3, *123;* Black Power movement 122–4, *123*, 125; caste-based stratification 66; Civil Rights movement 122; as collectors 124–5, 129, 223; election of Obama 105–6, 132; Harlem Renaissance 119–20; jazz 89, 120–2; legacy of slavery 107, 114–17, 119; middle class 124–5, 130; Nation of Islam 123–4; New Negro Movement 120, 122; racial stereotyping 117–18; spoken poetry 124, 144; symbolic ethnicity 125; *see also* race and the arts
agency the ability or intention to push through one's own interests or agenda 59; generally 59; individual 9
agitation propaganda/agitprop especially performance with an explicitly political message 157
Ai Weiwei 134–7, 142, 144, 149, 194; *Sichuan Earthquake Photos* 135, *135; Study of Perspective — Tiananmen* 134
AIDS crisis 153, 158
alienated/alienation for Marx a condition that results from capitalist relations of production in which workers are unable to realize their full human potential. Alienation results from a worker's inability to control her labor process and retain her fruits of labor. As a result workers more greatly resemble a machine than a creative autonomous individual 63
Anand, N. 50
Anderson, Benedict 29
anthropological holism 225–30
Antin, Eleanor 102; theatre of the self 99
Appadurai, Arjun 177
Appiah, Anthony 178
Aristotle 13
Armstrong, Louis *121*, 123
Arnold, Matthew 30, 31, 33
art dealers 142–3, 183, 210
art for art's sake a movement that began in 19th-century France that asserted that the

value of art was to be found solely in its aesthetic power and should serve no didactic or moral purpose 24, 46–7, 205–6
art history: cultural categorization 17–20; origins 14
art market: art as commodity/investment 42, 161–2; boom in 161–2, 208, 210–11; capitalism 40–2, 141–2, 160, 192, 194; globalization 179–80; influence of 192, 194
art world: globalization 174–85; use of term 3–4
Arte Povera 241
artists: artistic freedom 26–7, 148, 203, 205; bohemian persona 203; in collectivist societies 195–6; and consumers 216–17; de-marginalization 207, 210; genius, concept of 195, 199–201; great, as figment of gender 95–7; institutionalization 206–13; Marx 202; median income 213; media representations 189–90; notion of individualism 194–7, 199–200; social construction of 12, 190–206; social status 12, 26–7, 196, 205, 206–13; sociologists view of 190–1; success as constraint on development 162; theory of reputations 194, 195
Asante, Okyrema 175
aspiration, signaling 73
aura the distance that viewers feel from works of art and the sense of awe and un-approachability that classical works of art are meant to inspire 182
auratic art 182–3
autonomous free-standing and independent. Here a term for art that was believed to be free from any social influences 158
autonomy of art 24–5, 45–6, 148, 158–9, 199–200, 204, 205–6
avant-garde: de-politicization 207; government hostility to 148, 153–5; social critique 160, 239

Baez, Joan *19*, 20
Baker, Josephine 89, *90*
Balzac, Honoré de 233, 234
Banks, Patricia 125, 223
Baraka, Amiri 122, 123; *Blues People* 122
Barber, Benjamin 179
Baroque period 198
Barthes, Roland 215; "The Death of the Author" 215–16
Basie, Count 121
Baudelaire, Charles 27, 46, *46*, 86; "To the Reader" 46

Baudrillard, Jean 213
Bauman, Zygmund 186
Bearden, Romare 120; *The Train 120*
Beat movement 93
Beats the post-war generation of American writers who challenged norms in fiction, poetry, sexuality, and lifestyle. Allen Ginsburg, Jack Kerouac, and William S. Burroughs began their bohemian adventures in New York City but moved to San Francisco where the Beat generation served as a precursor to the hippie counterculture 93
beauty: as goal 45–6; Kantian aesthetics 23–5, 96
Beauvoir, Simone de: *The Second Sex* 100, 101
bebop 48
Becker, Howard 3–4, 12, 56, 95, 190–1, 193–5
Beckett, Samuel 234, 238–9
Beethoven, Ludwig van 96, 194, 238
Belle, Jennifer 58
Bellini, Giovanni 196
Benjamin, Walter 168, 182–3, 184, 216–17
Berger, John 97, 232–3
Berliner, Geoffrey *6, 7*
Berman, Nina 156
Best, Steve 213
Black Panthers 123, *123*
Black Power an African American political movement of the late 1960s and early 1970s that advocated for self-determination for people of the African diaspora. It self-consciously identified itself as an alternative to the liberalism of the civil rights movement 122–4, *123*, 125, 155
Bloom, Harold 31
blue-chip artists those artists whose works consistently sell for a high value 142
bohemia a cultural community whose members choose lifestyles in contrast to social and political norms. Bohemians often renounced materialism and experimented with alternative sexualities and forms of consciousness 27; concept of 27, 203
Bono, Chastity 103
Bookchin, Natalie *186*, 187
Bordo, Susan 99
Boroughs, William S. 93
Bourdieu, Pierre 203, 204, 205, 207; criticisms of 79; cultural capital theory 74–9, 80, 205–6; *Distinction* 75; habitus and aesthetic disposition 76–9

bourgeoisie the social class that in full-fledged capitalist societies owns the means of production; it arose in the Middle Ages out of a group of merchants whose political and economic interests were frequently in opposition to the feudal order 20; capitalism 20, 24, 41, 64; gender stereotypes 103; individualism as bourgeois value 148, 199–201; Marxist theory 64, 66, 231; self-identity 26
Bowie, David 103
breaching experiment 53–5
Brecht, Bertolt 156, 157; *Verfremdungseffekt* 55
Buonarroti, Michelangelo 197, 198–9, *198*; *David* 242, 243
bureaucratization: and rationalization 43–5
Butler, Judith 101–2

Cameron, Julia Margaret *172*
canon the body of knowledge considered important by scholars and taught in schools 94
Capitai, Alfredo: Film poster for *Gilda* 32
capitalism a social and economic system in which capital assets are owned privately, markets are the dominant method of economic distribution, and labor is sold for money. In capitalism the prime motive for owners of capital is the accumulation of greater amounts of capital 40; art market 42, 141–2, 162, 192, 194; bourgeoisie 20, 24, 26, 41, 64, 65; consumer capitalism 186; cultural ideologies 42–3; effect 11, 25; Engels 41; globalization 64, 166–8, 176; and individualism 137, 148, 238; instrumental rationality 44–7; invisible hand of the free market 138–9; market-based distribution 25–7, 34, 141–2; Marxist theory 40–3, 64, 232–3; means of production 40–1; mechanics of 137; mode of production 41; overproduction 141–2; popularism 10; proletariat 41, 63–4; Protestant ethic and 44; relations of production 41–2; social critique 159; surplus value 63; Weber 40, 43–7; *see also* consumption
capoeira 114, *114*
Caravaggio 198; *The Musicians* 199
Carlyle, Thomas 85–6
Carmichael, Stokely 122
Carroll, Lewis: "Jabberwocky" 245
Cassatt, Mary 87–8; *The Child's Bath* 88
caste-based stratification systems hierarchical social divisions based on fixed (ascribed) categories such as race, religion at birth, or inherited social order 66
categorization: European tradition 17–18; fine art 4, 5, 17–18; popular culture 5, 18; "primitive" art 17–18, 129; social construction 17–20
Catholic Church: bureaucratization 44–5; as patron 21, 25–6
censorship 10, 136, 149–51, 162–3, 180; obscenity laws 150–1
Césaire, Aimé 119; *Notebook of a Return to the Native Land* 118
Chagall, Marc 149
Chang, Jeff 132
Chaplin, Charlie: *Modern Times* 173, *203*
Charmet, Marc: *La Goulue 28*
Chicago, Judy 95; *Dinner Party* 95
China: Ai Weiwei 134–7, 142, 144, 149; Cultural Revolution 146–8, *147;* state arts funding 151
Choen, John: *At the Cedar Bar 143*
Civil Rights movement 122
civilization: and culture 30–2; and materialism 30
Clang, John: *Being There 164*, 165
class consciousness the set of beliefs an individual or group has about its economic position in society. Marxist theorists frequently distinguish between the consciousness of a class "in itself" (an understanding of one's position in the economic hierarchy) and "for itself" (the knowledge that a particular class has interests and the ability to act on those interests opposed to another class or classes) 65
class structure: artists' position in 65; black middle class 124–5, 129; Bourdieu's theory 74–9, 80; bourgeoisie *see* **bourgeoisie**; caste-based 66–7; class-consciousness 65–72; class as social relationship 63–4; collective and antagonistic nature 64–5; and consumer culture 69–71; continuing significance 80–1; cultural capital theory 74–9; economic influences 63, 64, 81; and education 62–3, *61*, 72–3, 75–6; European society 66–7; expectations of mobility 83–4; and globalization 64; habitus and aesthetic disposition 76–9; high culture reinforcing 62–81, 129–30; and individualism 65, 66; and interior decoration 71–2; market position 72; Marxist theory 64–7, 72, 73, 84, 231; mass culture 65; professional/intellectual class 64; proletariat 41, 63–4;

and race 116; regulation of consumption 67–9; role of the arts 29–31, 62–81; role of popular culture 65–6; signaling aspiration 73; social critique 160; and social inequality 8–9, 62; status groups 68, 72–4; symbols of 75–6, 78–9; and taste 75; U.S. society 67–72, 79, 80, 116, 124–5; Weber's theory 72–4; "working-class majority" 64
Claudel, Camille 87–8
Cobain, Kurt 206
Cockcroft, Eva 148
Cohen, Steven A. 161
Cold War the period from 1947 to 1991 in which the United States and its allies experienced political and military antagonism with the Soviet Union and its allies. While the two blocs vied for global influence they avoided outright military conflict, most likely because they both possessed the nuclear capability to destroy each other. The Cold War ended with the dissolution of the Soviet Union in 1991 138; Abstract Expressionism 148–9; McCarthyism 149–50
collective consciousness refers to a process by which individuals identify with social groups of which they are members. First coined by Émile Durkheim in the *Division of Labor in Society* (1893), it refers to the of which they are members values, beliefs, and ideas shared by a social group. In traditional societies, widespread similarity creates mechanical solidarity and shared. In modern societies the interdependencies of the division of labor create a form of organic solidarity, which replaces similarity as the driving force for collective consciousness 47–8
collective process, arts as 3–4, 12, 190–1, 194
collectivist societies 195
collectors 210; African American 124–5, 129, 223; art dealer gallery system 142–3; influence 3, 34, 70; investors as 161–2
colonialism a system by which a nation-state or empire establishes political and economic control over another geographic region for the purposes of exploiting the colonized region's resources 107; and European identity 106, 108–11; slavery 114
Columbus, Christopher 166, *166*
commercialization 30
commodification the tendency to reduce social phenomenon to entities tradable or measurable by money 157

commodities for Marx a commodity is a good or service that contains human labor and is sold in a market. A more vernacular definition emphasizes standardized, mass production 43
commodity, art as 42
communications technology *see* technologies, new
constraint social or material conditions or structures that restrict or determine outcomes 60
consumer capitalism a form of capitalism that is thought to be more driven by the marketing and consumption of products than the actual production of products 186
consumption: and class structure 67–71; conspicuous 68–70; consumer capitalism 186; consumer culture 32, 69–70; and individualism 185–6; influence 3; and mass culture 65, 80
contingency accident; an event that may occur but is not necessarily anticipated; alternative 60
copyright legislation 201, 216, 217–20
cosmopolitanism 179–80, 183
counterculture 158
craft objects 224
craftsmen 12
Crane, Barbara 207
Crane, Diana 39–40
creative economy an economy or sector thereof that produces cultural goods and services or is geared to innovation 10
creative workers those who hold primary positions in the creative economy 10
creativity: modern notion of 195–6; Parsons' theory 48; social significance 12; status accorded to 12
creole a language with origins in a hybrid of more than one language. Creole languages are spoken in Haiti, Jamaica, and elsewhere. Creole often emerges as a result of colonization 109
creole cultures 109
critics: influence 3; role 4; stereotyping by 96–7
Cubism 113, 238
cultural capital the valuable cultural knowledge, sensitivities, and resources an individual possesses 75; Bourdieu's theory 74–9, 80, 205–6; and economic capital 75–6, 78; symbolic importance 75–6, 78–9

cultural convergence a growing cultural unity around the world. When diverse world cultures begin to merge into a shared common culture 175–9

cultural gatekeepers 192; gender stereotyping by 96–7; influence 4, 18, 19, 96; Internet bypassing 183

cultural hierarchies: museums reinforcing 128–30

cultural imperialism the practice of promoting or forcing the cultural practices of a dominant culture on dominated regions. Some critics believe that the United States enforces its interests around the globe by promoting consumerism and Western commercial culture 175–6, 178

cultural omnivores a term popularized by sociologist Richard Peterson (Peterson and Kern 1996 pp. 900–907) are individuals who consume cultural products across a range of genres cultural omnivores may consumer murder mysteries, murder mysteries and French cuisine, high and low forms of art, opera and bluegrass music, Shaker furniture and African pottery. Sociologist Shamus Khan (2012. "The New Elitists." July 7 *New York Times*, http://www.nytimes.com/2012/07/08/opinion/sunday/the-new-elitists.html?pagewanted=all) sees cultural omnivores enforcing a new version of elite exclusion through their ability to apply resources to an ever more diverse sampling of culture 34, 181

cultural universal 19

culture is a contested term but at a minimum it is a system of meanings, rituals, and traditions that are shared by a community 227

culture industry term coined by Theodor Adorno and Max Horkheimer in *Dialectics of Enlightenment* (1944). The culture industry is the metaphorical factory that produces all manner of commercial, popular culture, which tends to replace the more intellectually and aesthetically challenging forms of high culture 31–2

Dada 10, 157, 158, 159, 182
Daguerre, Louis Jacques 171
Danto, Arthur 209
Daumier, Honoré: *This year again ... Venus* 204
David, Jacques-Louis: *Death of Marat* 26, *26*

Davis, Miles: *Kind of Blue* 1–2, *1*
Debord, Guy 157–8

deconstruction a method of analysis that derives from the work of the French philosopher Jacques Derrida (1976). Deconstructionism emphasizes that texts have no stable reference point. Instead it attempts to undermine hierarchies by dissolving binary oppositions such as true/false, knowledge/ignorance, or freedom/oppression 100

Degas, Edgar: *Dance Class at the Opéra* 174
Delaroche, Paul 171
democracy: and the arts 31, 85; and communications technology 181–5; media control 181–2
DeNora, Tia 96
Deren, Maya 113
Descartes, René 197
deterritorialization 165

deterritorialized weakening of ties between culture, economic production, politics and place 165

deviant subcultures 56–9
digital divide 170
DiMaggio, Paul 129

discourses "organized and organizing bodies of knowledge, with rules and regulations that govern particular….ways of thinking and acting" (Storey, 2006: 101) 100

disposition *see* habitus

distribution: art dealer gallery system 142–3; impact of the Internet 11–12; localized networks 143–4; market-based 25–7, 34, 141–2; nonprofit systems 144–5

division of labor describes how work is divided grossly into occupations and finely into specific tasks. The concept was first elaborated by Scottish moral philosopher and political economist Adam Smith (1776) to explain how the organization of work by more specialized tasks could effect efficiencies in production. French sociologist Emile Durkheim described how the occupational division of society brought about interdependencies and shared norms. German social critic Karl Marx pointed out how the division of labor removed workers from the mental and manual aspects of work and alienated them from its creative processes 48

Dix, Otto 155–6; *Card Players* 155
Dodge, Mabel 89

dominant ideology the ideology of a ruling class, "In most class societies a pervasive set of beliefs that broadly serves the interests of the dominant class. This dominant ideology is then adopted by subordinate classes which are thereby prevented from formulating any effective opposition." (Abercrombie and Turner, 1978: 149–50) 43

Douglas, Emory *123*

dramaturgical analysis derives its intellectual energy from the idea that "life is a play." Its earliest progenitor was Ervin Goffman whose *Presentation of Self in Everyday Life* (1959) developed metaphors such as front-stage and back-stage to describe how symbolic interactionism analyzes the different roles that actors (individuals and groups) play in social situations 55–6

Du Bois, W.E.B. 120, 125

Dubin, Steve 126, 154

Duchamp, Marcel: *Fountain 52*, 54; *Nude Descending a Staircase 174*

Dürer, Albrecht: *St. Jerome in His Study 237*, 244

Durkheim, Emile 39, 47–8

Dylan, Bob *19*, 20

Eagleton, Terry 241

Eastman, George 171

economic and cultural capital 75, 79

economic development: arts aiding 10–11, 145, 161, 211; experience economy 11; tourism industry 11, 145, 161

economic institutions, influence 9, 10

economic power, Bourdieu's theory 79

economic systems 137–41; access to means of production 64, 72; and the arts generally 9, 10, 135–7; and class structure 63, 64, 81; distribution and patronage *see* distribution; distribution of resources 9, 139, 141; free market 138–9, 141–2, 148, 205; globalization/deterritorialization 165; laissez faire 140; market-based distribution 10, 141–2, 205; mixed economies 138; multinational conglomerates 176; neoliberalism 140–1, 161, 186; social critique 160; socialism 137–8; state arts funding 136, 141, 145–9, 161, 205, 207; welfare state 138–9; *see also* **capitalism**

education: access to 62–3, *62*, 95, 116; and arts attendance 8, 72–3; canon 97; feminist movement 95, 97; government funding 161; habitus and aesthetic disposition 76–7; institutional nature 9–10; non-Western arts and culture 108–9; and social class 62–3, *62*, 76–7; status groups 72–4; teaching high culture 30–1; U.S. slaves 116; women 87, 95

Egmont, Justus Van: *Louis XIII 67*, *67*

Ehrhart, S.D.: *The letter of the law 42*

Eisenstein, Sergei 182, *182*; *October* 183

elite culture: aesthetic preferences reinforcing 24, 76–9; elitism 30–3; habitus and aesthetic disposition 76–9; nonprofit institutions 144–5; *see also* high culture

Eliot, George 89

Ellington, Duke 121

empirical based on observation, experience, or experiment 39

empirical investigation 39, 49

Engels, Friedrich 41, 85, 165–6

Enlightenment or Age of Reason was an intellectual movement from approximately 1650 to 1800, which challenged faith and tradition with reason, particularly the scientific method 22, 202; aesthetic philosophy 14, 23–5, 28–9; autonomy of art 199–200; bourgeoisie 20, 24, 26, 199; gender stereotypes 97; generally 20–2, 111; Kantian aesthetics 23–5, 96, 200; postmodern theory 214; racial stereotypes 106; rationalism 29, 111–12, 215; universalism 215

Enlightenment rationalism the idea made popular during the Enlightenment that all knowledge could be gained through the use of reason. Enlightenment rationalism explicitly rejected tradition and theology as sources of knowledge 28–9

equalization strategies 117–18

essential/essentialism the concept that for any social group there is a set of characteristics that define its function and identity. Gender essentialism presents characteristics that are fixed and distinguish men from women 99

ethnocentrism viewing one's own culture as normal and natural. Judging other cultures from the perspective of one's own culture 122, 129

ethnography the holistic study of a social group through close observation. Ethnographies typically involve immersion in the subject and are based on data collected through direct observation, in-depth interviews, and historical research. Ethnographers may use statistical

data but usually to support qualitatively acquired insights 53
ethnomethodology 52–5
European tradition: class structure 67–8; Western canon 31
exploitation/exploited the condition in which workers are not paid the full value of their labor (*see* **surplus value**) 63
expression 234; as goal 45–6; Parsons' theory 48
Expressionism 113, 148

Faupel, Alison 96
feminist movement 10, 31, 117; access to education 95; de Beauvoir 100, 101; educational canon 97; feminists and inclusion 94–5; first-wave 85, 94; Freud's theories 97–8; great artist as figment of gender 95–7; inclusion model 85, 97; objectification of women 97–9; particularistic strategies 117–18; second-wave 84, 94–100; women's traditional crafts 95; *see also* gender and the arts
feminists advocates for the equality of the sexes. Feminist theory combines a critique of male dominance with intellectually grounded strategies to overcome it 31
Fichte, Johann Gottlieb 201
film 173, 181–2; artists depicted in 189–90; objectification of women 98
fine arts *see* high culture
First-Wave feminism first organized social movement for women's equality began in the late-19th century in the United Kingdom and United States and was concerned primarily with securing voting and other legal rights for women 85, 94
folk art and culture: categorization as 5; idealized view of 28–30; and nationalism 29–30; social perception of folk artists 12; as socially recognized label 5; and urbanization 28–30
formalism an approach to art and art criticism that emphasizes the technical aspects of a piece of art. In painting, for example, formalism would focus on shape, color, texture and composition. As a theory of artistic creation it tends to see a piece of art as understandable solely by its components divorced from social context 24
Foucault, Michel 5; *History of Sexuality* 100–101
Fox Talbot, William Henry 170–1

France: class structure 79; Negrophilia 118–19
Franklin, Benjamin 44, *45*
freedom of expression 10, 136, 149–51; and market systems of support 205; obscenity laws 150–1; sexual 153
Freud, Sigmund 97–8
Friedan, Betty 93–4; *Feminine Mystique* 94
Friedman, Milton 140
Frohnmayer, John 154–5
functionalism, structural 47–8
Fyff, Will 65

Gadamer, Hans Georg 241–2
Gainsborough, Thomas: *Mr and Mrs Andrews* 232–3, *233*
Galindo, Regina José: *Quien puede borrar las huellas?* 91, *91*
gallery system 142–3; globalization 180
Gandhi, Mahatma 158
Gans, Herbert 33–4, 70, 125
Garfinkel, Harold 53–4
Garvey, Marcus 120
gatekeepers authorities or influential individuals responsible for determining who gets access to art institution resources. These may be museum directors or curators, editors, movie executives, critics, or academics 4
Gauguin, Paul 112; *Man with an Adze 112*
Gell, Alfred 225
gender and the arts: access to education 87, 95; African American women 89, *90;* cultural gatekeepers 96–7; deconstruction 100; emerging fields 88; Enlightenment philosophy 97; gender norms and expectations 84, 85, 92–3, 95–6, 101–2, 103, 106; gender as social construction 100, 101; gender-blind view 84; generally 82–4; great artist as figment of gender 95–7; jazz 89; objectification of women 97–9, 183; patriarchal structures 85–6, 92, 95; popular culture 87, 92–3, 103; pornography 98; post-structuralism 100; postmodernism 100–1; postwar society 92–3; present day 103–4; queer theory 100, 102–3; separation of spheres 85–92; sexual discourses 101; Victorian family structure 85–7; visual arts 90–1; women writers 89; women's traditional crafts 95; *see also* feminist movement
genius, concept of 195, 199–201
Giacometti, Alberto: *Woman of Venice VII* 242
Giddens, Anthony 59

Gide, André 89
Ginsburg, Alan 93
Giotto di Bondone 196
Giuliani, Rudolph 174
globalization 164–8, 173; art market 162; arts and culture 174–85; capitalist system 64, 166–8, 176; communications technology 164–5, 170, 183; cultural aspects 165; cultural clashes 178; cultural convergence 175–9; economic dimensions 165; global cities 179–80; impact of 11–12; and inequality 140, 167, 179–80; media control 176; multiculturalism 162; multinational conglomerates 176; social impact 185–6; urban cosmopolitanism 179–80; U.S. commercial culture 176–7
glocalization 177
Goethe, Johann Wolfgang von 200, 201
Goffman, Erving 55–6
Goldman, Emma 89
government involvement *see* politics and the arts
Gramsci, Antonio 247
Gran Fury 158
Grateful Dead 159
Great Depression 138–9, 156, *156*; Work Projects Administration 62–3, *62*, *139*
Griffin, Kenneth 161
Grimm, Jacob and Wilhelm 29
Griswold, Wendy: cultural diamond 50–1, *50*, *52*
Grooms, Red 160
group identity 8–9, 24
Guggenheim, Peggy 192, 210

Habermas, Jürgen 24, 181
habitus "matrix of perceptions, appreciations and actions" (citations) that allow individuals to feel at ease with high culture and to demonstrate this ease 76; and aesthetic disposition 76–9
Haggedorn, Jessica 131
Hall, Stuart 247
Halle, David 71, 223
Hammons, David: "Injustice Case" 124
Hanks, Eric 124
happenings movement 160
Harlem Renaissance cultural movement that took place in the 1920's in Harlem, New York. Many African American scholars and artists of this movement addressed the unique position of African Americans in U.S. society 119–20

Hartney, Eleanor 179
Harvey, David 170
Hauser, Arnold 195, 196
Heartfield, John 183
Hegel, Georg W.F. 106
Heidegger, Martin 241
Helms, Jesse 154
Hendrix, Jimi 159
Herder, Johann Gottfried von 28–9, 30
heritage industry 178
hermeneutics the study of the interpretation of texts and artistic objects 240–3
high culture: Abstract Expressionists 207; adoption of populist style 70, 80–1; categorization as 4, 5, 17–20, 195–6; and civilization 29–31; and class structure 62–81, 129–30; invention 27–31; and market forces 34; and mass culture 33–4, 80–1; purpose 224, 235; as socially recognized label 5; value attributed to 27–8; Western canon 31; *see also* elite culture
hip-hop 144
historians, influence 3
Hitler, Adolf 149
Holiday, Billie 89
Holzer, Jenny 183
Horkheimer, Max 31–2
Hottentot Venus 127–8, *127*
Hughes, Langston 120; "The Negro Speaks of Rivers" 119
Hugo, Victor: *Les Misérables* 79
Huntington, Samuel 175
Husserl, Edmund 240
Huyssens, Andreas 25
hybridized a form of culture that results from the intersection or cross fertilization of two or more cultures 165
hyperdemocracy the barbaric rule of the masses or mob rule 31
hypersocial objects, artworks as 224

iconography a branch of art history that identifies and interprets the meaning of the content of images 224
identity: arts and self-identity 26–7; shaping and expressing 117; and social structures 8
ideology a set of conscious and unconscious ideas that represent the attitudes, aspirations, and values of social groups 43; dominant 43
imagination: Kantian aesthetics 23; sociological 3

imperialism the economic and cultural domination of the peoples and resources of one geographical territory by another 108–10; cultural 175–6, 178; enduring effect 110; and European identity 107, 108–11; museum collections 127; White supremacy ideology 122
Impressionism 27, 46
income: correlation with arts attendance 8, 10; structural inequality 9
individual action: agency 9; and social structures 7–9
individualism: and artistic expression 194–7, 199–200, 228–9, 238; Barthes "Death of the Author" 215–16; as bourgeois value 148, 199–200; capitalist system 137, 148, 238; and class structure 65, 66, 148; and consumerism 185–6; individualist societies 195–6, 228–9; Parsons' theoretical framework 48; structural-functionalism 48; Western societies 65, 66, 178, 195
Industrial Revolution: birth of modern art 203–5; gender roles 85; middle class growth 170, 203; new technologies 168, 170, 171; social fragmentation 66
inequality: and class structure 63; and globalization 140, 167, 179–80; structural 7–9
institutional structures: distribution of resources 9, 141; economic 9, 10; influence 9–11; reinforcement of social structures 9
instrumental rationality a logical and behavioral orientation that employs value-free reasoning as a "mean[s] for attainment of the actors' own rationally pursued and calculated ends" (Weber, 1968: 24) 44–7
Internet: impact of 11–12, 162, 169–70, 183–5; *see also* technologies, new
interpretive paradigm views social phenomena with the assumption that reality is constructed by subjective perceptions. It primarily uses qualitative methods to "get inside" the subject to uncover how people create meaning and interpret events 52–9
investment, art as 161
invisible hand the mechanism, according to the political economist Adam Smith, by which markets regulate themselves if economic competition is allowed to freely develop 138

Jakobson, Roman 55

Jamal, Amaney 74
James, Henry 102
Jameson, Fredric 213, 239
Jauss, Hans-Robert 243
jazz 1–2, 33, 93; bebop 48; female performers 89, 93; race and culture 121–2
Jefferson Airplane 159
Johnston, Frances Benjamin: *Gertrude Käsebier 88*
Jones, LeRoi 122
Joplin, Janis 159
Joyce, James 234–5
justice system, institutional nature 9

Kafka, Franz 234
Kahlo, Frida 90–1; *Self-portrait with Thorn Necklace and Hummingbird 91*
Kant, Immanuel (1724–1804) a German Enlightenment philosopher who put the human subject at the center of philosophical inquiries 25, 96, 106, 199, 200; concept of genius 200; *Critique of Judgment* 23–5, 77
Kaprow, Allan 159
Käsebier, Gertrude 88, *88*
Kellner, Douglas 213
Kelly, Mary: *Post-Partum Document* 99
Kerouac, Jack: *Dharma Bums* 93
Keynes, John Maynard 138, 140
Kids Are Alright, The 117
King, Martin Luther 122, 158
Kipling, Rudyard: "The White Man's Burden" 108, 110–11
Kirstenblatt-Gimlett, Barbara 125–6
Koons, Jeff: *String of Puppies* 218
Kosloz, Max 148
Kounellis, Jannis *221*, 222, 225, 230, 240–1
Krasner, Lee 93, 190
Kruger, Barbara 99, 183

Lady Gaga 103
Ladysmith Black Mambazo 175
Lamont, Michèle 117
Lange, Dorothea 156, *156*
Lautréamont, Comte de 159
Lawrence, D.H.: *Lady Chatterley's Lover* 150
Lawrence, Jacob 120
Leavis, F.R. 30–1, 33
Lee, Spike 117; *Do the Right Thing* 107, *108*
Leonardo da Vinci 196, 197, *198*
Levine, Sherrie 218
Liberalism 215
Lichtenstein, Roy: *Masterpiece 191*
Lim, Youngmi 180

Lin, Maya: *Vietnam Veterans Memorial Wall* 152, *152*
Lipsitz, George 65
Literature: classification as 4; impact of globalization 175; modernist 234–5; Negritude 119; social conception of the author 201; women 89
Locke, Alain 119–20
Locke, John 140
Loeb, Daniel 162
Louis XIII, King of France 67–8, *67*
Lukács, Georg 148, 234

Madonna 103, 184
Mahler, Gustav 33
Malevich, Kazmir: *The Knife Grinder 237*
Manet, Eduard 27, 45, 46–7, 86, 204–5; *Olympia* 37–8, *37*, 40, 46–7; *Portrait of Baudelaire 46*
Mann, Thomas 234
Mannerism 198
Mao Zedong 147
Maplethorpe, Robert 154, *154*
Marcuse, Herbert 32, 158, 235
market: globalization 12, 165–8; stealth-marketing 58
market economy *see* **capitalism**
Márquez, Gabriel García 175
Martins Manjibula Jackson Helmet Mask *223*, 224, 225, 243
Marx, Karl 8, 20, 40–1, 157, 202, 215; access to means of production 64, 72; analysis of capitalism 40–3, 232, 233; call for gender equality 85; collective and antagonistic nature of class 65–7; "Critique of Political Economy" 43; culture in Marxist theory 43, 230–2; "Estranged Labor" 63; on globalization 165–6, 170, 175; market position concept 64, 72; materialism in Marxist theory 231–2; socialist system 139; theories of class 64–7, 72, 73, 84
mass culture usually refers to products of the culture industry and is frequently defined in opposition to high culture. Critic Dwight MacDonald disparagingly characterized it as "manufactured wholesale for the market ... solely and directly for mass consumption, like chewing gum." [MacDonald, Dwight. 1957]. Less negative definitions stress its wide acceptance among the populace. 27; categorization as 5, 18; and class structure 66; as commodity 33; and consumption 66, 80; as controlling tool 31–2; high art compared 33; hyperdemocracy 31; interaction with high culture 33–4, 80–1; Internet as vehicle 169; invention 27–31; new technologies 31, 169
material culture the components of culture that take material form, such as clothing, artifacts, and tools 225
materialism: civilization leading to 30; Marxist theory 231–2
materialist adhering to the Marxist position that social phenomenon and history can be explained by socio-economic forces 231
Matisse, Henri 2, 149
McCarthyism refers to the practices that took place during the Cold-War in the United States when many citizens were persecuted for communist or anti-government activities by the U.S. Government based on scant evidence. The republican senator Joseph McCarthy (1908–1957) was a leading figure in this persecution 149–50
McDarrah, Fred W.: *Party at the Sculls* 71
McLuhan, Marshall 168
meaning and interpretation 221–48; aesthetic and social forms 227–30; anthropological holism 225–30; art historical approach 224; craft objects 224; fine arts 224; hermeneutics 240–3; iconography 224, 225; internalist approaches 247–8; Marxist approaches 230–40; mediation 235–40; phenomenology 240; reception approaches 243; reflection theory 232–5, 238; semiotics 244–7
means of production physical, non-human, aspects of the productive process such as machinery, raw materials, land, and infrastructure. The means of production are a subset of the mode of production (*see* **mode of production**) 41
mechanical reproduction, impact of 181–3, 216–17
media, control of 176, 180–1
mediation how social material gets actively transformed in the art process 235–40
middle-brow culture culture that falls between the rarified world of the fine arts and mass produced commercial output. Middle-brow culture was famously derided by the critic Dwight MacDonald in his article "Masscult and Midcult" (1961) for watering down high culture. The British novelist Virginia Woolf (1942) mocked its

adherents for consuming what they are told is good 79
Mill, Maree 177
Mills, C.W. 3
Minnelli, Vincente: *Lust for Life* 189
minstrel shows *115*, 116–17
mode of production a central concept in Marx's analysis of economic and social life. It includes everything necessary for the production of life, including the *forces of production* (labor, machinery, technology, and raw materials), and the *relations of production* (the social relations and institutions that regulate how the forces of production are employed) 41
Modern Masters generally refers to artists of the 20th century and later who are acknowledged as especially important and whose work commands very high prices 142
modernism a cultural movement that challenged traditional aesthetic standards and stressed innovation. Beginning in the last decades of the 19th century and lasting until the 1960s, it rejected realism and the Enlightenment's confidence in the power of reason 24, 120, 208, 214; government hostility to 148; influence of non-Western art 109, 111–13, 112, 113, 118–19, 129; market economy 25–7; mediation theory 238; modernist values 27; Nazi censorship 149
Morisot, Berthe 87
Moritz, Karl Philipp 199–200, 201
Morton, Jelly Roll 120
Mozart, Wolfgang Amadeus 238
Mukerji, Chandra 230
multiculturalism 130–2, 162
museum displays: cultural categories 17–19; cultural hierarchies 128–30; ethnographic 125–8, 129; impact of globalization 174–5, 179–80; imperialist collections 127; influence 3, 125–6; middle-brow culture 79; multiculturalism 130–2; people/human remains 126–8, *127*; racial and cultural hierarchies 128–30; staged authenticity 128
music: avant-garde 2; control of music recording industry 176; cultural categories 19; female performers 89, 93, 94, 96, 97; impact of globalization 175; Internet, impact of 183; jazz 1–2, 33, 93, 120–2; minstrel shows *115*, 116–17; modernist 238; music academies 9–10; rationalization 44–5; remix culture 219; rock and roll 65; social structures 8
Muybridge, Eadweard James 171–3, *171*

nationalism: arts used for 146–9, 162; folk art and culture 29–30
Negritude is an artistic, literary and ideological movement developed by French speaking Black intellectuals in Paris in the 1930's. These thinkers advocated developing a shared Black identity and opposed French colonial racism 119
Negrophilia 118–19
Neshat, Shiren 177–8, 179, 180
Neue Sachlichkeit 156
Newton, Huey 122
Ngourney, Adam 105
Niépce, Nicéphore 171
Nietzsche, Friedrich Wilhelm 202
Nochlin, Linda: "why have there been no great women artists" 95
Nolde, Emile 149
non-Western arts and culture: education about 108–9; imperialism's enduring effect 110; influence on modernism 109, 111–13, *112, 113*, 118–19, 129; Orientalism 111, *111*; primitive, categorization as 17–18

Obama, Barack 105–6, *105*, 132, 184
oeuvres the body of work of an individual artist 224
Ofili, Christopher 180; *The Virgin Mary* 174–5, 178–9
O'Keefe, Georgia 90–1
Old Masters European artists who lived before the 20th century who are considered to be especially important. Their work commands very high prices 142
Ono, Yoko 184
Orientalism term made famous by the literary scholar Edward Said (1978), that refers to stereotyped depiction of Asian, middle-eastern, and African peoples in European art and culture 111, *111*
originality 214, 215–16; mechanical reproduction 216–17
Orr-Cahill Christina 154
Ortega y Gassett, José 31
Ostrower, Francine 79
overproduction, reasons for 141–2

Parsons, Talcott 48–9, 229–30
participant observation a research methodology in which the researcher takes part in the phenomenon which she is studying 53
particularistic strategies 117–18
patriarchal controlled by men 85
patriarchal structures 85–6, 92, 95
patronage: Church 21, 25–6; and control 203; market economy 25–7, 141–2; Renaissance 196–7; state arts funding 26–7, 136, 141, 145–9, 161, 207
Paul, Ru 103
peer groups, influence 57–9
performance: as social critique 157; social production of self 55–6
Peterson, Richard 34, 49, 70
phenomenology branch of philosophy devoted to the structures of consciousness and subjective experience 240
photography: impact of 181–2; invention and market for 170–2; as social critique 156; women photographers 88, *88*
Picasso, Pablo 129, 149, 173, 217; Cubism 113, *113*; *Standing Nude* 113
Piñero, Miguel 131
Piscator, Erwin 157
Plato 13
poetry, spoken 124, 144
politics and the arts: artistic autonomy 148, 158–9; censorship 10, 136, 149–51, 162–3, 180; Cold War 148–9; controversial projects 151–5; freedom of expression 148; generally 134–7, 161–3; hostility to the avant-garde 148, 153–5; influence of political institutions 9, 10; McCarthyism 149–50; nationalism 146–9, 162; obscenity laws 150–1; propaganda *147*, 148–9; social critique 10, *19*, 20, 134–7, 155–60, 184; state funding 136, 141, 145–9, 161, 207; *see also* **capitalism**; economic systems
Pollock, Jackson 93, 190, 192, 207–8, *208*, 213
Pop art 70, 183, 208–11
Pop artists creators of works of visual art that typically employ commercial art methods to portray objects and events of everyday life especially in popular culture. Andy Warhol, Roy Lichtenstein, and Peter Max were creators of pop art in the 1960s and 1970s 69
popular culture popular culture has several meanings, which are not necessarily mutually exclusive. One meaning is that which is not high culture; another is the education and culturedness of the working class; some definitions emphasize the commercial production of culture for mass audiences; and other definitions focus on the authentic culture of the people 27; adoption by high culture 70, 80–1; categorization as 5, 18; criticism of 30–1; defenders of 33–4; and the fine arts 4, 25; gender stereotypes 92–3, 103; Internet as vehicle 169; invention 27–31; Kantian aesthetics 25; objectification of women 98–9; rising status 80; role in class-consciousness 66–7; as socially recognized label 5; women's access to 87
popularism and capitalism 10
pornography 98
positivist an orientation toward the study of things that can be experienced through sensory perception and especially that can be measured or counted 13
positivist inquiry 13
postcolonial theorists advocates for the intellectual movement that investigates and responds to the legacy of colonialism and imperialism. Postcolonial theorists are concerned with the politics of knowledge and critique schools of thought about and arguments for the superiority of Western culture 31
postcolonial theory 31
post-industrial a stage in the development of capitalism in which the service sector, and especially information services, eclipses the manufacturing sector. By the late-20th century, with the exception of resource extracting countries such as Saudi Arabia, every high income country is post-industrial 10
postmodernism is a movement of critique that questions the certainties that grew out of the Enlightenment's reliance on the scientific method and the possibility of achieving definitive knowledge. As a movement of the arts it deliberately creates a pastiche of different styles and schools of art 100, 213–17, 239; gender and the arts 100–1; remix culture 217–20
post-structuralism 100
Powdermaker, Hortense 51–2
power, institutional structure 9
Pretty Woman 76, *76*, 77

primitive art: categorization as 17–18, 129; *see also* non-Western arts and culture
Prince 103
Prince, Richard 218–19
production of culture is an approach to studying the arts that maintains that "the symbolic elements of culture are shaped by the systems within which they are created, distributed, evaluated, taught, and preserved" (Peterson and Anand, 2004). Culture of production typically focuses on structural, organizational, institutional, and economic factors external to the creation of art objects 49, 201
proletariat in Marxist theory one of the two major classes that comprise capitalist society. Opposed to the bourgeoisie, who own the means of production, proletarians own no productive property and as a result have no choice but to sell their labor on the job market for wages 41, 63–64
propaganda: agitation (agit prop) 157; use of arts for *147*, 148–9
protest art 10, *19*, 20, 134–7, 155; communications technology 184
public sphere the literal and figurative space where people come together to form the "public," a space in which persons could organize and debate separate from state authorities. The free flowing exchange of ideas that occurred in the public sphere set the stage for a culture of political and social participation that eventually led to the flowering of lively debates about the arts and served as a model for ideas about democracy 24
publicists, influence 3
Pughe, John: *How John May Dodge the Exclusion Act 118*
Pussy Riot 184

qualitative methods are usually contrasted with quantitative methods and tend to emphasize observation across a range of characteristics rather than those that can only be represented numerically. Major qualitative methods include participant observation, in-depth interviewing, textual analysis, and historical comparisons. Data uncovered by qualitative methods can be treated quantitatively by categorizing and counting 53

quantitative data information that can be counted or represented numerically 39, 49
queer theory 100, 102–3

race and the arts: in the Americas 105–7, 113–17; Black Power movement 122–4, *123*, 125, 155; education 108–9; Enlightenment philosophy 106; equalization strategies 117–18; ethnocentrism 129; Harlem Renaissance 119–20; jazz 89, 120–2; legacy of slavery 107, 114–17, 119; minstrel shows *115*, 116–17; multiculturalism 130–2; museum displays 125–32; Negrophilia 118–19; objectification 97–8; race and opportunity 8; race as social construction 107–8; racial stereotypes 106, 116–17, 132; representations of non-Western people 110–11; symbolic ethnicity 125; *see also* African Americans
Radcliff, Carter 207
ranking systems, generally 3–4
Rapa Nui people: *Male Figure 112*
rationalism: in art and music 44–7; and bureaucratization 43–5; Enlightenment 29, 111–12, 215; instrumental 44–7; Marx and Weber 40–7
rationalization is a process most thoroughly analyzed by the German intellectual Max Weber in which tradition, charisma, and values are replaced by means-ends rationality, the choice of suitable means to achieve an end 40
Reagan, Ronald 140, 153–4, 161
realism 148, 234, 247
reflection theory 232–5, 238
relations of production Marx's concept of the social relations and institutions that regulate how the forces of production are employed. Private property and wage labor are relations of production 41
Rembrandt van Rijn: *The Anatomy Lesson...* 20–1, *21*, 25
remix culture 217–20
Renaissance: Church patronage 21–2, 25; concept of genius 195; patronage 196–7; use of perspective 238
Renoir, Pierre Auguste: *Madame Georges Charpentier and Her Children* 86
Rilke, Rainier Maria: "Letters to a Young Poet" 200
Ringold, Faith: "Flag for the Moon, Die Nigger" 124
Ritzer, George 176

Rivera, Diego 90
Roach, Max 225
rock and roll 66
roles socially expected behaviors tied to occupation or status 8
Romantic movement 14, 200, 202, 204
Roosevelt, Franklin D. 138–9
Rosie the Riveter 92
Rubens, Peter Paul: *St. Thomas* 229, *229*
Rugendas, Johann Moritz: *Capoeira or the Dance of War 114*
Rumford, Christopher Crupper: *Love and beauty 127*
Rushdie, Salman 175; *The Satanic Verses* 149
Ruskin, John 85
Russian formalism 55
Russian formalist adherent of a school of literary criticism active in the late days of Tsarist Russia and the early years of the Soviet Union, approximately 1910 to 1930. Russian formalists explored the role of literary language and devices and how they differed from the everyday vernacular. Despite the eclectic political leanings of its practitioners, the often difficult and highly abstract arguments of Russian formalists attracted the ire of Soviet dictator Joseph Stalin, who attacked formalists for their elitism 55

Said, Edward 111
Salgado, Sebastião 156
Sanger, Margaret 89
Saussure, Ferdinand de 244–6
Savage, Augusta 120
scenes shared behaviors similar to subcultures, in which the participant's identity is closely tied to a shared, display, creation, practice, or consumption of a particular type of culture 58
Schad, Christian 89
Schelling, Friedrich Wilhelm 200
Schlegel, Friedrich 200
Schlovski, Viktor 55
Schmutz, Vaughn 96
Schnabel, Julian 211–12, 213, 214
Schneeman, Carolee 100, 103
Schoenberg, Arnold 238, 239
Schopenhauer, Arthur 200
Scull, Robert and Ethel 70, *71*, 210
Seale, Bobby 122
Second-Wave Feminist 84
Sedgwick, Eve Kosofsky 102

semiotics the study of signs that people use to communicate with each other 244–7
Sennett, Richard 185
Serra, Richard: *Tilted Arc* 151–2, *151*
Serranno, Andres 154
sexual politics and expression 153: queer theory 100, 102–3
Shaw, George Bernard: *Pygmalion* 77
Sherman, Cindy 56, 103, 183, 194; *Metro Pictures* 66; *Untitled Film Still #6 102, 103*
signs refer to the symbolic means through which meaning is communicated 244
Simkus, Albert 70
Simmel, Georg 227–9
Simon, Paul: "Graceland" 175
Situationist International 157–8
Smith, Adam 140
Smith, Bessie 89
Smith, Roberta 131
Smith, Roger: *Street Musicians in Harlem 67*
Smithson, Robert: *Spiral Jetty* 160
social activity, art as 4
social change: analysis 38–9; art reflecting 38
social class refers to the axis of inequality that has to do primarily with the division of economic resources 62; *see* class structure
social constructionism is a sociological approach to knowledge that explains the origin and evolution of phenomena are contingent on social and historical processes. It rejects the idea that social phenomena are inevitable. Early pioneers of social constructionism Peter Berger and Thomas Luckmann wrote in *The Social Construction of Reality* (1966) that the taken-for-grantedness of everyday life was the result of social interactions, and those interactions resulted in social perceptions of reality 53
social critique: arts used for 10, *19*, 20, 134–7, 155–60; direct 155–8; indirect 158–60; and postmodernism 239
social inequality refers to the unequal distribution of social resources including wealth, power, status, health, education, leisure time, and housing within a society 62
social institutions are relatively stable and ongoing social arrangements through which the needs of society are managed (Turner, 1997) 9
social networks the ties between social actors (usually individuals or organizations) that make up social structures. Social

network analysis focuses on the characteristics of relationships between social actors rather than the characteristics of those individuals or groups 57; influence of 58–9

social reproduction generally the replication of patterns of structures and activities from one generation to the next. Frequently, social reproduction refers to the transmission of patterns of inequality across generations 59

social solidarity the ties that bind individuals to social groups or societies 47–8

social structure stable patterned social relations or institutions 59; aesthetic expression of 227–30; capitalism *see* **capitalism**; class *see* class structure; collective consciousness 47–8; collectivist 195; group identity 8–9, 24; identity and 8–9; and individual actions 7–9; individualist 195–6; influence of race 8; influence on taste 8–9; institutional structures 9–11; mass culture used to control 31–2; meaning 7–9; social solidarity 47–8; structural-functionalism 47–8; structural inequality 7–9

socialism an economic system based on the public ownership of the means of production and the allocation of resources according to need 137–8

Socialist Realism a style of realist art that was developed and promoted in the Soviet Union and later in other socialist countries. Socialist realism glorifies the working class and depicts historical and political subjects that are in line with the aims of socialist regimes 147, *147*

sociological perspectives: agency 59; on the arts 3–5; breaching experiment 53–5; capitalism 40–3; close-up 5–7, 40, 52–9, 60; constraint 60; contingency 60; dramaturgical analysis 55–6; empirical, data-driven 39, 49; ethnomethodology 52–5; generally 5–7, 38–40, 224; Griswold's cultural diamond 50–1, *50*, 52; instrumental rationality 44; interpretive paradigm 52–9; macro 5–7, 38–48, 60; medium-range 5–7, 47, 48–52, 59–60; Parsons' theoretical framework 48; participant observation 52; production of culture approach 49, 201; qualitative methods 52; rationalization and bureaucracy 44–7; structural-functionalism 47–8; structure and agency 59–60; subcultures and deviance 56–9

Spekter, Otto: *Rapunzel* 29
Spinoza, Baruch 197
spiritual experiences 2
staged authenticity 128
standardization 30, 32, 34
status: art and culture signaling 73; class and 68, 72–4; global, maintaining 179–80; groups 72–4; Weber on class and 72–4
stealth-marketing 58
Stein, Gertrude 89, 90
Steinbeck, John: *The Grapes of Wrath* 156
Stewart, Potter 150
Stieglitz, Alfred 91
Stowe, Harriet Beecher: *Uncle Tom's Cabin 115*, 116
Stravinsky, Igor: *Le Sacre du Printemps* 1

structural-functionalism an approach to sociological theory that assumes social formations are complex systems whose parts work together to form an integrated whole. Structural functionalism tends to assume that the specific parts of any social formation, or society, exist because they fulfill a need 47–8

structured inequality the social inequalities that result from the unequal access that different groups have to power to everyday institutional arrangements. Structured inequality can result from differential access to housing healthcare, or political resources 8

sublime, Kantian aesthetics 96

surplus value the value of an item, or commodity, above and beyond what it costs to produce that commodity 63

Surrealism 53, 113, 158, 159, 234
symbolic capital 205–6

symbolic ethnicity a term coined by sociologist Herbert Gans (1979) that signifies the enactment of a nostalgic longing of second- and third-generation offspring of European immigrants for an imagined ethnicity 125

symbolic interactionism a sociological theory that explains how individuals use symbols in their communication with one another. The term was coined by sociologist Herbert Blumer (1969) but the concepts came from two turn-of-the-20th-century figures, philosopher George Herbert Mead and sociologist-economist Charles Horton

Cooley, whose work emphasized that people respond to other people and things according to the meaning they have assigned to them 53
Symbolic Interactionists 191
symbolist movement 27
symbols, cultural: auratic art 181–2; class symbols 75–6, 78–9; indicators of wealth 161–2; social function 229–30; symbolic ethnicity 125
Szanto, Andras 211

tango 84
Tarantino, Quentin: *Django Unchained* 216, 241
taste cultures a concept that explains the broad affinity that groups have for similar types of culture – classical music, museum going, martial arts films, soap operas, country music and so forth – was developed by sociologist Herbert Gans (1974) as an alternative to Adorno and Horkheimer's critique of mass culture. Taste cultures lack the hierarchical value judgments that mass culture critics attribute to culture, but class, race, and gender influence their content 33–4
taste: Bourdieu's theory 75, 80; factors influencing 24–5; habitus and aesthetic disposition 76–9; influence of social structures 8–9; Kantian aesthetics 24–5, 77, 96; middle-brow 79
Taylor, Frederick Winslow 173
technologies, new: access to audiences 180, 183–4; control of 176, 180–1; and democracy 180–5; digital divide 170; and globalization 164–5, 170, 173, 176; impact of 11–12, 162, 164–5, 168–70; market for 170–1; and mass culture 31, 169; negative consequences 184–5; protest art 184; as a tool 186–7
Tenniel, John *245*
Thatcher, Margaret 140, 161
theatre as social critique 157
theory of reputations 194, 195
Thompson, E.P. 65
Titian: *Venus of Urbino* 37–8, *38*, 40
Tobin, M.F.: *The first sight of the new world...* 166

Toklas, Alice 89
Toulouse-Lautrec, Henri de 27, 86; *The Sofa* 87
tourism industry: arts contributing to 11, 145, 161, 211; cultural tourism 178
transformative experiences 2
Trockadero Ballet 82–3, *82*, 84, 102

urban cosmopolitanism 179–80
urban policy, influence 10–11

Van Gogh, Vincent 113, 194, 206
Vasari, Giorgio 198–9
Velthuis, Olaf 161
Verfremdungseffekt 55
Vidal, Gore: "Sex is Politics" 100
Vietnam War: anti-war movement 130, 159; Memorial 152, *152*
visual arts: feminist works 99–100; Harlem Renaissance 120; objectification of women 98, 183; Orientalism 111, *111;* women artists 90–1, *90*, *91*, 93, 117
Vollmer Adams, Joan 93

Walker, Kara: *Untitled 116*, 117
Waller, Fats 120
Warhol, Andy 70, 80–1, 180, 183, 208–11, *209*, 213
Warner, W. Lloyd: *What Social Class Is In America* 80
Weber, Max 39, 40; on class and status 72–4; rationalization 43–7; *The Protestant Ethic and the Spirit of Capitalism* 44
Webern, Anton 238
Western canon a body of Western literature and art that scholars consider to be the best examples of culture. They at times hold out the Western canon as a metric against which cultural artifacts can be considered art. Advocates for the existence of a Western canon have met opposition from feminists, postcolonial theorists, and others critical of the lionization of high art 31

X, Malcolm 123

Custom Materials
DELIVER A MORE REWARDING EDUCATIONAL EXPERIENCE.

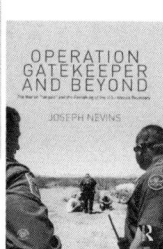

University Readers — Custom Publishing Evolved.

Routledge — Taylor & Francis Group

The Social Issues Collection

This unique collection features 250 readings plus 45 recently added readings for undergraduate teaching in sociology and other social science courses. The social issues collection includes selections from Joe Nevins, Sheldon Elkand-Olson, Val Jenness, Sarah Fenstermaker, Nikki Jones, France Winddance Twine, Scott McNall, Ananya Roy, Joel Best, Michael Apple, and more.

1 Go to the website at routledge.customgateway.com

2 Choose from almost 300 readings from Routledge & other publishers

3 Create your complete custom anthology

Learn more:
routledge.customgateway.com | 800.200.3908 x 501 | info@cognella.com

University Readers is an imprint of Cognella, Inc. ©1997-2013

Taylor & Francis

eBooks
FOR LIBRARIES

ORDER YOUR FREE 30 DAY INSTITUTIONAL TRIAL TODAY!

Over 22,000 eBook titles in the Humanities, Social Sciences, STM and Law from some of the world's leading imprints.

Choose from a range of subject packages or create your own!

Benefits for you
- Free MARC records
- COUNTER-compliant usage statistics
- Flexible purchase and pricing options

Benefits for your user
- Off-site, anytime access via Athens or referring URL
- Print or copy pages or chapters
- Full content search
- Bookmark, highlight and annotate text
- Access to thousands of pages of quality research at the click of a button

For more information, pricing enquiries or to order a free trial, contact your local online sales team.

UK and Rest of World: online.sales@tandf.co.uk
US, Canada and Latin America:
e-reference@taylorandfrancis.com

www.ebooksubscriptions.com

ALPSP Award for BEST eBOOK PUBLISHER 2009 Finalist

Taylor & Francis eBooks
Taylor & Francis Group

A flexible and dynamic resource for teaching, learning and research.